Conquests and Historical
Identities in California

Mission Indian Federation Convention, October 9, 1924. Courtesy Donald Doram.

...vention, October 9, 1924.
... Grounds
...rside, California.

Conquests and Historical Identities in California, 1769–1936

Lisbeth Haas

UNIVERSITY OF CALIFORNIA PRESS

Berkeley / Los Angeles / London

University of California Press
Berkeley and Los Angeles, California

University of California Press, Ltd.
London, England

© 1995 by
The Regents of the University of California

First Paperback Printing 1996

Library of Congress Cataloging-in-Publication Data

Haas, Lisbeth.
    Conquests and historical identities in California, 1769–1936 /
Lisbeth Haas.
        p.   cm.
    Includes bibliographical references and index.
    ISBN 0-520-20704-1
        1. San Juan Capistrano (Calif.)—History.   2. Santa Ana
(Calif.)—History.   3. Mexican Americans—California—San Juan
Capistrano—Land tenure.   4. Indians of North America—
California—San Juan Capistrano—Land tenure.   5. Mexican
Americans—California—Santa Ana—Land tenure.   6. Indians of
North America—California—Santa Ana—Land tenure.   I. Title.
F869.S395H33   1995
979.4'96–dc20
[979.4'96]   94-44519
                                                          CIP

Printed in the United States of America
9 8 7 6 5 4 3 2 1

The paper used in this publication meets the minimum
requirements of American National Standard for Information
Sciences—Permanence of Paper for Printed Library Materials,
ANSI Z39.48-1984. ∞

*To my daughter, Sophia Zamudio-Haas,
and her four grandparents and great grandmother,
who have inspired us and carried us forward
with their love*

Contents

APPENDIXES

Illustrations and Tables

Maps

Figures

Tables

Acknowledgments

I am grateful, first of all, to those individuals who have shared stories about their lives with me. They include my very first informants, people who had been deeply engaged in urban struggles during the 1970s and early 1980s in Santa Ana, California, and whose consciousness of rights came out of their understanding and interpretations of the past; they focused my attention backward in time. I met women who, like Jovita Hernandez, awakened my appreciation for the central role of women in history and subsequently helped to shape my manner of inquiry and interpretation. I thank members of the Juaneño Council of San Juan Capistrano, especially Donald Doram, Evelyn Villegas, and David Belardes, who contributed material that enabled me to finish this book. I am also compelled to express my deep appreciation to those I met, indirectly, in archival documents. Their behavior and ideas defined crucial dimensions of the society in which they lived their lives. Their records informed my understanding of change and endeared them to me.

I am extremely appreciative of the rich body of historiography that historians in my field have produced over the past twenty-some years. My debt to them, and to my colleagues at the University of California, Santa Cruz, is great, and primarily expressed through citations and references to their work in the following pages. I want especially to thank my professors Albert Camarillo, Jeanne Chase, Mary Ryan, Jon Wiener, and Tomás Ybarra-Frausto, whose mentorship and ideas shaped my early work on this subject. I was fortunate to have developed fundamental parts of my intellectual life with Victor Zamudio, and will always be grateful to him for those years we shared. From our reading groups at UCSC I want particularly to recognize the astute and helpful commentary of David Anthony, Nancy Grey Osterud, Cynthia Polecritti, Lynn Westerkamp, and especially Dana Frank, who has been a close friend and critic. Their comments on versions of this manuscript enabled me to define this project more clearly. I thank Michael Schuster for his reading of chapter 4; our discussions of popular theater, and the very special relationship between our families, sustained me as I wrote the first chapters of this book. Ramón Gutiérrez and Sarah Deutsch read the entire manuscript; they provided excellent, detailed criticism that guided my revisions and challenged me to examine and refine my formulation of key concepts. Their own work influenced me substantially, and their comments definitively shaped the final version of this text. My colleagues who were fellows at the Minority Discourse Seminar at the University of California Humanities Research Institute provided an exceptional context to carry my thoughts into new projects after this book was finished. I especially thank Norma Alarcón and George Sánchez for the relentless intellectual engagement they brought to reading this and other work; they have inspired me to make yet further interventions into the copyedited text.

My research assistants contributed tremendous energy and intelligence at each stage of the writing of this book. José Orosco provided useful commentary and careful notes as we carried out research in the court archives during the summer of 1988. Over the next two years Cerina Herrera created a huge census data base and helped to analyze the output. Her care and insight were invaluable as I worked on the outline of this book, and as I wrote chapter 1. Toni Nelson-Herrera worked intensively on many aspects of the book as I wrote. Her keen insight and tireless effort and our endless conversations about the larger implications of each piece of the research made my writing more meaningful. Jesus Cisneros provided valuable assistance as I completed the final revisions of the manuscript.

I am very grateful to the University of California, Santa Cruz, for the Faculty Senate Research Grants that supported research assistance and travel as well as manuscript preparation. The Minority Internship Program at UCSC contributed money for research assistance through a valuable mentorship program. I thank the University of California MEXUS program and the UCSC Humanities Division for funding research in Mexico and California. A grant from the National Endowment for the Humanities enabled me to examine theater archives at the Benson Latin American Library, Mexican-American Collection, University of Texas, Austin. I am also grateful to UCSC for providing course relief so that I could finish this book. My teaching informed my writing, and I thank my students for their many questions and ideas, which in turn helped me to refine my own.

Zoe Sodja and Cheryl VanDerVeer at UCSC prepared the manuscript with patience and care. They always made it possible for me to finish promptly. Barbara Reitt was the first to edit the manuscript, and her excellent suggestions helped me to revise it. I have enjoyed the skillful editing of copy editor Anne Geissman Canright, who understood the book well. For their effective comments and support I heartily thank Anne, project editor Dore Brown, and general editor Lynne Withey of the University of California Press. Finally, I am very grateful to Chip Lord for his loving presence and careful reading as I completed the book, and to Sophia, for her thirteen years of intelligence, sensitivity, and imagination.

Introduction

"This Land Belongs to Me"

In 1889 a young woman, Modesta Avila, was brought to trial in Orange County Superior Court, accused of placing an obstruction on the tracks of the Santa Fe railroad, which had recently been laid some fifteen feet from the doorstep of her home in San Juan Capistrano, a former mission and Mexican pueblo. The obstruction was simply a heavy fence post laid across one rail and another one hammered into the ground between the tracks, with a paper stuck to it that read: "This land belongs to me. And if the railroad wants to run here, they will have to pay me ten thousand dollars."[1] Max Mendelson, merchant, postmaster, and express agent in San Juan, was waiting for the daily train when he discovered the obstruction. As he quickly dismantled it, Modesta Avila sat quietly watching from her door. Mendelson reported that he told her not to do that, as someone could get hurt; she responded, "If they pay me for my land, they can go by." Avila reported forcing the railroad to compensate her to individuals who represented the new economic order and legal authority established in the American era: a banker, bank teller, sheriff, and judge, all from Santa Ana, the American town that had been founded in 1869, some twenty miles to the north of San Juan. At the bank she inquired about the quickest method to receive the anticipated payment of ten thousand dollars. She then asked the sheriff whom she could hire to keep peace at a dance she was giving in Santa Ana to celebrate receiving the money. While holding this dance, she was arrested for disturbing the peace. At her arraignment, she also told the judge about her purported victory over the railroad. Avila paid dearly for her defiance. She was sentenced to three years in prison and subsequently died in San Quentin. At the time of her death she was in her mid-twenties.

Avila's story is significant to this book because it addresses the dynamics of power that shaped land policy. Modesta Avila was born in 1867, in the midst of the American conquest. During the decade of the 1860s, Californios lost the vast majority of their land to settlers from elsewhere; Avila was thus motivated to take action by her generation's experience of land loss. Her story is one among many stories of individuals I will tell because they vividly depict the processes and implications of the conquests of this region.[2]

In the following paragraphs, let me briefly introduce my subject, my terminology, and my orientation. I will also describe San Juan Capistrano and Santa Ana, where most of the events in this book took place. By *conquest* I mean the process that extends the political, economic, and social dominion of one empire, nation, or society over another one. Because conquest involves the systematic acquisition of land, it is intricately linked with policies of territorial expansion. During the conquests of North America by Spain and the United States, populations were submerged and reconfigured partly by being renamed. The populations from colonial Mexico that settled on the California frontier between 1769 and 1821 called themselves *gente de razón*, people who possessed reason. Indian peoples, in contrast, were assigned such names as *indios, neofitos* (neophytes), and *gente sin razón*, people without reason. Mission Indians were identified by the mission of their birth or baptism.

San Juan Capistrano was founded as a mission in Acâgchemem territory in 1776; by 1796, nearly one thousand Acâgchemem resided at the mission (see map 1). Between the late eighteenth century and 1812, the mission gained control of the entire Acâgchemem country, changing its cultural, economic, political, and spatial order. These peoples called themselves Acâgchemem through the early nineteenth century; by mid-century, however, they went by the name *gente* (people) and Juaneños, after the mission. Mission San Luis Rey was established in 1798 in Quechla, the territory of the Quechnajuichom, who became known as Luiseños. Sometime in the latter part of the nineteenth century, most Juaneños were forced to leave their villages; they relocated to Quechla. Some of these villages became reservations. Anthropologists have sub-

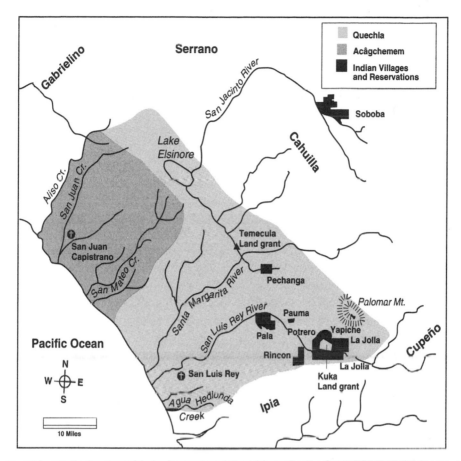

Map 1.   Reduction of Acâgchemem and Quechla territories from the preconquest period to the early twentieth century.

sequently studied both populations as a single cultural and linguistic group under the name Luiseño. The colonial experiences of mission Indians provided an element of shared historical identity when mission Indians federated and demanded recognition in the early twentieth century.[3]

Californios first articulated their own territorial identity during the early 1830s, in political debates between the California territorial legislature and the Mexican federal government over the emancipation of neophytes and secularization of the California missions. Californios used Spanish colonial ideas to define their territorial government's right to control the land of mission Indians. When emancipation and secularization were enacted in 1834, Californios gained control of the countryside. Most of the rural area along the California coast was granted in ranchos. Californios were also granted the extensive lands immediately around San Juan in 1841, when the mission was made into a pueblo. (See map 2 for the imprint of this process on the land around San Juan Capistrano.)

Californios defined their status against that of Indians, who were virtually dispossessed of the lands they claimed during the Mexican era (1821–1848). In the official documents written during this period, individual Indians were referenced with only a single, Spanish name; in census records, the many skills they possessed and tasks they performed were not recorded. Indians typically did not receive title to the rural village and town lands that a majority of former neophytes were allotted upon their emancipation from the missions—a fact that simplified matters for the U.S. government when it sought to claim Indian lands as public domain in the American period.

The 1848 Treaty of Guadalupe Hidalgo that ended the Mexican-American War (1846–1848) initiated the second territorial conquest. By the end of the 1860s, most of the ranchos depicted on map 2 were sold or lost, a divestment of property that affected large numbers of Californio heirs and Indian peoples alike. The legal partition of Rancho Santiago de Santa Ana in 1868 partially illustrates this process (map 3).

In 1870, Santa Ana was one of three American towns that had been established on this former rancho. By the time Orange County was founded in 1888, the Anglo-American farmers who had settled the town were the largest ethnic population in the area. The land politics that shaped the American conquest were similar to those that sustained capitalist agriculture elsewhere in the nation: land and natural resources became commodities, while people who had capital monopolized credit and transportation and established the conditions for an agricultural industry. In coastal Southern California and elsewhere in the Southwest, capitalist industrialization required that Indian populations be further deterritorialized, meanwhile supporting the interests of (usually self-defined "white") squatters and land speculators.

The core of this book is the problem of identity. I am concerned, that is, with the encounters that produced a sense of historical consciousness. Hence, although the book covers over 160 years—from 1769, the date of the Spanish conquest, to 1936, when regional strike waves in agriculture generated a new sense of collective interests on the part of the Mexican American population—it is not primarily organized according to a linear chronology. While the first two chapters do proceed along a historical time line from Spanish conquest through U.S. territorial conquest, with the consequent loss of land and spatial isolation of Californios and Indians, in the second half of the book the focus shifts to explore some of the more qualitative dimensions of this multiethnic history around the turn of the century (roughly 1880 to 1930): the persistence of Californio and Indian societies, the meanings these groups gave to the past, and the larger historical imagination that took hold during this process of social self-definition. Included in this analysis are the ideas about history, nation, and religion conveyed by Mexican regional culture. The book takes an extended look at the historical references and shared language of patriotic and religious history that shaped part of the meaning of Mexican-American identity in the twentieth century. As a sort of case study, the book also examines the construction of racial and national identities in the American town of Santa Ana.

In paying particular attention in this book to places (such as Indian communities, towns, barrios, and the imaginary ties that link specific places together) I am influenced by writers who view space as an active agent in social change. For Edward Soja, social meaning is derived largely through the organization of space. Soja laments that geography became a field primarily authorized to describe and set the stage for action. During the course of its development, he says, geography increasingly turned positivist and instrumentalist, attending ever less to "the formative spatiality of social life as a template of critical insight."[4] The favoring of time and devaluation of space in social theory and history is similarly problematic. The linear story—the story built around time—necessarily submerges and peripheralizes the geographical or spatial imagination.

Space, according to Soja, is an analytic category with a multiplicity of theoretical and methodological underpinnings. Soja, like Michel Foucault, finds relations of power and discipline inscribed into "the apparently innocent spatiality of social life."[5] Foucault, for example, notes how metaphors such as field, region, and territory can serve to designate particular forms of domination. Spatial metaphors, he argues, are "equally geographical and strategic" because geography grew up in the shadow of the military.[6] This emphasis on the spatial embeddedness of power relations has strongly informed my work. I thus ended up situating this history within a geographical framework that embraces

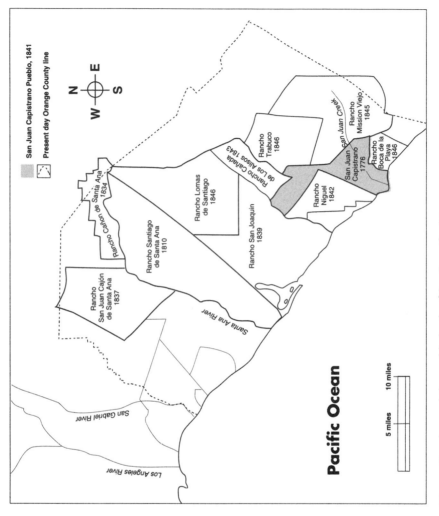

Map 2. Ranchos and the pueblo lands of San Juan Capistrano.

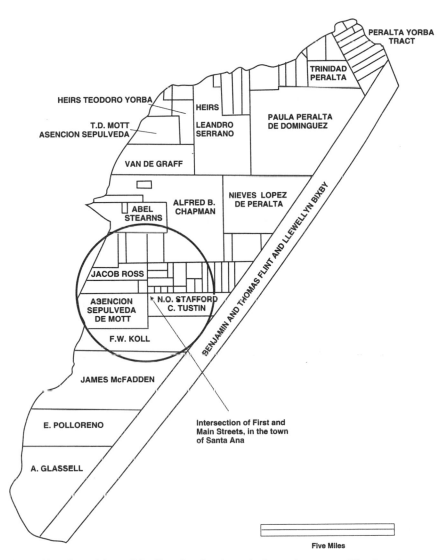

Map 3. Legal partition of the Rancho Santiago de Santa Ana, 1868. The American town of Santa Ana was established in 1869 and expanded to incorporate the land within the circle.

the Spanish colonial world, the culture of Greater Mexico, the U.S. Southwest as a region, and the Borderland.[7]

The Annales school of social historians incorporated spatial issues into their analyses of rural society and region, and their work represents another influence on my own.[8] In studying the social and economic connections between regions, they rethought historical time, questioning the importance of the "event" in history. Instead they examined the imaginary, the symbolic, and the history of beliefs and mental structures. They conceived of large questions and issues by examining themes not previously covered by historians, including the history of the face, *l'histoire du visage,* and the history of national memory, as in the series of books dedicated to monuments and other *lieux de mémoire* (places of memory).[9]

Spatial dimensions of change, such as territorial conquest and the formation of the barrios, were among the first things studied by Chicano historians. Albert Camarillo originated the term *barrioization* to describe "the formation of residentially and socially segregated Chicano barrios or neighborhoods."[10] The process Camarillo depicted involved social, economic, familial, urban, and demographic change. Many historians have studied the formation of the barrios as urban and social history; the barrios also figure large in the work of novelists, poets, and artists.[11]

During the 1970s the barrios garnered attention thanks to land-based grassroots politics, which drew in well over a generation of scholars and artists, including myself. This movement embraced multiple peasant- and migrant-led land takeovers in Mexico, especially in Tijuana and elsewhere in northern border states, and urban movements in U.S. cities. I became interested in the grassroots movement that arose in the city of Santa Ana in the early 1980s partly because of the stories barrio residents told to the press about their neighborhoods. The women and men who engaged in this neighborhood insurgency made the barrio part of their claim to power; its historical space gave them a sense of their right to demand representation in urban politics and funds for neighborhood improvement. Telling their stories to all who would listen, they encouraged people to see the barrio as descriptive terrain recording the social interrelationships that had developed over time. The stories I heard created a social meaning for the neighborhood, a meaning that was layered in the physical place.[12] I wanted to capture that sense of place and of collective history in my work.

In urban struggles, and in the scholarly literature cited above, the

politics of space is closely connected to the formation of collective identities that are grounded in particular interpretations of the past. In this
regard Stuart Hall's discussion of the relationship between identity and
history is instructive. He argues that cultural identities are not fixed in
a single or hidden history but are "subject to the continuous 'play' of
history, culture, and power. Far from being grounded in a mere 'recovery' of a past just waiting to be found, . . . identities are the names
we give to the different ways we are positioned by, and position ourselves within, the narratives of the past."[13] Joan Scott also writes against
unilinear accounts of experience, identity, and politics. She says,

> If identities change over time and are relative to different contexts, then
> we cannot use simple models of socialization that see gender as the
> more or less stable product of early childhood education in the family
> and the school. We must also eschew the compartmentalizing tendency
> of so much of social history that relegates sex and gender to the institu-
> tion of the family, associates class with the workplace and community,
> and locates war and constitutional issues exclusively in the domain of
> the "high politics" of governments and states.[14]

Identities are grounded in the particular relationships formed through
histories of race, gender, class, and place. One identity does not displace
another. Historical identities, especially, are generally structured in relationship to particular readings of geographic areas, such as are found
in the "imagined community" of the nation.[15]

Despite critical studies of the formation of nationalisms, many historians still work with a bipolar model of national culture. That approach has meant that Mexican immigrants are understood by scholars
as having just two options: to "become American" or "remain Mexican." George Sánchez criticizes such a static notion of ethnic identity.
In the United States, he argues, the invention of new "traditions" and
the abandonment or radical transformation of older customs are in fact
common. He also reminds us that in Mexico a similar invention of
traditions has worked to forge national unity. Mexican American ethnicity in Los Angeles, Sánchez says, developed from interactions between Mexicans and Mexican Americans as well as "through dialogue
and debate with the larger cultural world encountered in Los Angeles."[16]

The views of other scholars complement that of Sánchez. Paul Gilroy, for example, calls race "socially and politically constructed" and
charges that "elaborate ideological work is done to secure and maintain

the different forms of 'racialization' which have characterized capitalist development."[17] David Roediger, documenting the pervasiveness and centrality of racial identification for white Americans, examines "white" identity as it is assumed by a sector of the U.S. working class. Race, says Roediger, is constructed differently over time by people in the same social class, and differently at any given time by people of varying class positions.[18] In this book, I examine the way a white racial identity was given meaning in the American period not within a particular class, but as it was configured through urban and institutional structures.

Although ideas about "race" were present in the identities forged during all three periods that I cover, the meaning of color was never singularly interpreted, nor was color status ever entirely nonnegotiable. In the Spanish colonial and Mexican periods, the ascriptive status of the Spanish/*casta* population as *de razón* (having reason) allowed that group to downplay the significance of racial background and emphasize instead the simple distinction between Catholic settlers and *indios*. But that comparatively ample tolerance for color difference was not shared by the Anglo American population, which had generally accepted a set of ideas about "white" racial superiority just prior to the Mexican-American War of 1846. After 1900, difference in terms of skin color superseded all other distinctions, and it became harder for Californios to negotiate a favorable status. Thus, race identity became central to the construction of national identity, with "American" being equated with whiteness. The notion of white racial superiority reaffirmed the equation of "white" with "American" and "citizen," and that mindset came to define urban politics and to prevail in individual and collective statements of identity.

This book is a multiethnic history that examines the politics of space and the construction of identities. Chapter 1 looks at the Spanish conquest. Here I build on Ramón Gutiérrez's description of conquest and colonization as a process whereby missionaries sought to establish their authority over native peoples, an effort that in turn shaped important dimensions of society.[19] I also discuss the comparable process of emancipation and address the questions central to New World politics in nations where enslaved or coerced peoples were emancipated: What did freedom mean? Who owned the land? Who controlled labor?[20]

Chicano historians have described the capitalist transformation of the countryside in California, though in some accounts the American conquest plays the central role in this transformation, with little or no attention given to the general economic transition that was in fact occurring nationwide. Moreover, while historians have provided a needed analysis of the ethnic dimension of this transition, they have tended to define ethnic and national categories in static terms, as being constant over time.[21] An exception to this rule is David Montejano, whose work on the emergent meaning of "white" and "Mexican" in south Texas simultaneously explores the political economy of the transition to capitalist agriculture.[22] In chapters 2 and 3 of the present study I explore some of these ideas, focusing on the effects of territorial conquest and land politics on Indian peoples as well as on Californios. Like Ramón Gutiérrez, Sarah Deutsch, Deena Gonzalez, and others, moreover, I also address the gender politics of conquest.[23]

By providing a detailed view of the social world of San Juan Capistrano at the turn of the twentieth century, chapter 3 traces the history of change in San Juan's preindustrial, multiethnic (but primarily Californio and Indian) society. This town's history is similar to that of others in the Southwest, places where the regional Mexican and Indian populations remained demographically strong even as they lost economic and political power.[24]

Américo Paredes, in examining the role of history in south Texan culture, situates the Southwest within the larger cultural area of Greater Mexico.[25] I follow his lead in chapter 4, where I examine Spanish-language theater and cinema, modes of representation that form part of the content and expressive means of a regional culture that is Mexican, Mexican American, and highly influenced by Spanish peninsular culture and performance.[26] The historical imagination that shaped interpretations of the past in Californio society was informed by this vibrant regional culture.

The theater was one way of telling patriotic stories and shaping national identity; in chapter 5, we see how the ordering of institutional and social space served a similar function. Here I examine the history of the American town of Santa Ana and its barrios, to present a case study on urban politics and race relations in an early-twentieth-century southern California community populated by people of widely diverse backgrounds and allegiances.

This region has been shaped, in part, by the distinctive histories of Indian peoples, Spanish, Mexican, and American colonists, and transnational migrants, yet, as are other regional histories, its story is wholly American. Central to the story are the processes of conquest and immigration, by which the nation changed fundamentally as new populations merged to create a multiethnic society. During the years of industrialization particularly, ideas about what constituted America and the American changed so rapidly that native-born citizens and immigrants alike constantly confronted them as new. "The very things which strike the native born (Americans) as foreign seem to her (the new immigrant) as distinctly American," stated a member of the Immigrant Protection League in 1913.[27] Organizing the perception of "the American" was one of the central processes that defined American society during this period. Hence, the pivotal question asked in this book is not, How was a population "Americanized" or, at an earlier date, "Hispanicized"—that is, persuaded to adopt Spanish customs, dress, and speech? Rather, the core question is, How and why did ethnic and national identities acquire their particular meanings? They were forged, I argue, through the struggles between contending social groups over who had access to the land and to the rights of citizenship.

CHAPTER I

Indio and Juaneño,
De Razón and Californio

In 1775 on the site that would soon become Mission San Juan Capistrano, soldiers and a Spanish lieutenant constructed, raised, and venerated a large cross; then the missionary Father Lasuén prepared an altar and said the Catholic mass. By this ceremony the Spaniards declared formal possession of the land of the Acâgchemem for the Spanish crown. The site chosen for the mass, significantly, was one that symbolized the independence of the Acâgchemem from surrounding Indian peoples. It was here that they had named themselves, thus defining their autonomy from the Pubuiem, and that they had declared their territorial sovereignty from the Pubuiem's land, a territory to the north that was claimed by Mission San Gabriel in 1771 and further colonized in 1781 with the founding of El Pueblo de la Reina de Los Angeles.[1] The missionary's selection of this site illustrates a deliberate strategy used by the Spaniards in their conquest of the Americas, one that had served them well already for three centuries prior to the conquest of this area of California. By choosing such locally meaningful places for their own rituals of appropriation, the missionaries attempted to replace indigenous structures of authority, power, and memory with their own.[2] This process of superimposition was reflected in the mission's initial name of San Juan Capistrano de Quanís-savit, which acknowledged the Acâgchemem as a people who came from savit yet at the same time declared San Juan Capistrano their patron saint.[3]

This act of taking formal possession of the lands of the Acâgchemem initiated a process of colonization that would subsume a five-hundred-square-mile territory of roughly five thousand people in fifteen villages scattered from the sea to the mountains.[4] Conquest of these people necessarily involved their conversion to Catholicism. In accord with the Law of the Indies that regulated the American colonies, the mission held the territory of the converts in trust, to be returned to them once they had adopted Spanish social, cultural, linguistic, and economic behaviors.[5] Generally the converts resided within the mission compound, yet in San Juan Capistrano some converts (called *indio neofitos* [neophytes] or Juaneños, after the mission) remained with the unconverted, or gentile, Indians in the countryside, in villages that were claimed as "villages of this mission" less than a generation after the mission was founded. The coexistence of mission compound and native settlements, converted and unconverted villagers, and colonial cultural, political, and material practices and persistent indigenous practices and beliefs, defines the complex, multicultural and multilingual society of the mission period.

Violence toward the Acâgchemem and other indigenous peoples was a constant element of this society from the conquest forward. The missionaries came with soldiers, who used force to put down any overt resistance to their presence. Soldiers raped Indian women and committed other atrocities that created fear and reticence on the part of indigenous people who had initially welcomed them, and engendered multiple revolts against the missions and presidios.[6] Steady demographic decline of the Acâgchemem, the result in large measure of plagues (in any given year, one-tenth of the mission population might be wiped out), created painful scars of conquest, which survivors had to negotiate as they struggled to shape and explain their collective place within colonial society.

With the exception of a young man named Pablo Tac, mission Indians left no written trace of how they understood their position in the missions. Tac's manuscript identifies the most important features of conquest and mission life as he saw them. Pablo Tac was born at the Mission of San Luis Rey de Francia in 1822. San Luis Rey had been founded in 1798, twenty-two years after the founding of San Juan Capistrano, and encompassed the territory of the Quechnajuichom, immediately to the south of the Acâgchemem. The brief story of how Tac came to write his manuscript is instructive, for it explains quite a bit about how California mission Indians fit into the colonial order.

When Pablo Tac was eleven years old, a missionary from San Luis Rey chose to take him to Rome with another Luiseño youth, Agapito

Amamix. Once there, they began a four-year course in Latin, though Amamix died before completing it. Pablo Tac lived on to study rhetoric, humanities, and philosophy in Rome. Despite a severe case of smallpox he contracted as a teenager, Tac survived to the age of twenty. At his death he left for the chief custodian of the Vatican Library the manuscript and a grammar of his native language.[7] The presence of these two youths in Rome is reminiscent of the first appearance of Americans in the sixteenth-century Spanish court and the ensuing procession of New World goods that so revolutionized Europe. More than three centuries had passed, however, since those early military and religious conquests of indigenous empires and societies throughout the Americas. In nineteenth-century Rome, Tac and his fellow students from elsewhere in the Americas, Africa, and Asia represented distant peoples whose histories had long been marked by colonial domination.

The colonizing process described in Tac's manuscript reflects the complex history of conquest in all the Spanish Americas. In the sixteenth century, in the heart of the Spanish American empire in central Mexico, similar treatises were written by members of a native intelligentsia who were well versed in numerous autochthonous languages and who had learned Latin, Greek, and Spanish as well. Though they worked under the supervision and vigilance of Spaniards, their intention in recording their histories and the history of the conquest was to create records that embodied a knowledge of their pasts, since most records had been violently destroyed by the conquerors.[8] Pablo Tac's treatise is but a sketch in comparison with these works, which were informed by well-established indigenous traditions of graphic expression. Tac's society had not previously recorded its history pictographically. His is, moreover, the first literary text produced by a native of the Californias.

Although Pablo Tac's manuscript was titled *Conversión de los San Luiseños de la Alta California,* it is important not for its discussion of conversion, which, according to Tac, was something that simply followed once the missionary and Spanish soldiers were given permission to stay in the territory, but for Tac's descriptions of the land, people, and structure of mission society and for his use of language. Consider, for example, this passage:

> When the missionary arrived with a few people to our Country, our Chief and the others, seeing them from afar, were alarmed, but they didn't flee or take up arms to kill them, but rather sat and watched them. When they came near, the chief stood up (because he was seated with the others) and met them. They stopped, and the missionary began

to speak. The chief perhaps said in his language, "Hichsom iva haluon, puluchajam cham quinai" "*What are you looking for? Leave our country,*" but they did not understand him. They responded in Spanish. The chief began to use signs, and the Franciscan understood him, gave him presents, and in this manner befriended him. The chief returned to his people (so I believe) and, judging the whites favorably, allowed them to sleep here.

Pablo Tac addressed thanks to God for this happy day when his ancestors—"[we] called *Sosabitom*"—first saw the white people. He then goes on, in a brief paragraph, to discuss their subsequent "conversion":

> The Franciscan Father stayed in our Country; with the few people he brought he made a camp, and here he lived for many days, saying mass in the morning and afterward discussing with himself how he would baptize them, where he would put his House, the Church, and what he would do with five thousand souls (the number of Indians). How he would accomplish this and their sustenance. Having the chief for a friend, he wasn't afraid of anything. It was a great blessing that the Indians didn't kill the Spaniards when they arrived, and very admirable, because they never wanted other People to live with them, because until those days they were at war.[9]

In these passages Tac provides a clear statement about the territorial integrity of his "Country" (*Pays* in the Spanish original) and the autonomy of his "People" (*Gente*). He calls the villages in which the five thousand people lived "countries" (*payses,* lower cased). His terminology and his story of encounter suggest the exact way in which the land was divided and exclusively possessed by groups of villages, village nobility, and individual villagers and the relatively insular society that resulted.

The encounter that Tac describes took place in 1798, comparatively late in the history of the southern California missions, and he treats it rather matter-of-factly, noting no open resistance. At the same time, he neglects to mention similar encounters among neighboring groups— including the Acâgchemem, with whom Tac's people shared social, cultural, linguistic, and political ideas and organizations. Perhaps Tac's simplification of the story of encounter, and the absence in his account of any discussion of violent resistance or of the colonization of surrounding lands, reflects not only the ideas of an exemplary convert, but also the conscious determination by the village leaders that revolt, as experiences at other missions had shown, would be fruitless. The colonization of surrounding lands also explains why conversions at San Luis Rey took place at a relatively quick pace: over two hundred Indians of all ages were baptized in the first six months of San Luis Rey's existence, in contrast to twenty-four persons, mostly children, who were baptized in the first two years at San Juan Capistrano.

As Tac notes, the division of Quechla (his people's territory) into a "Country" and "countries," or villages, reflects a larger political division of land. The adjoining territories of the Quechla and the Acâg-chemem stretched from sea level to six thousand feet in the Sierra Santa Ana, and Quechla territory alone covered approximately one thousand square miles.[10] Each Acâgchemem and Quechnajuichom village possessed sites in every ecological zone from the ocean to the mountains, so that they had continual access to specific hunting, gathering, and fishing areas. Subsistence activities were generally conducted within a day's walk from the village. Foods included game, coastal marine animals, and freshwater fish; six species of acorns; various seeds, greens, and cactuses; and bulbs, roots, and tree fungi. Teas, tobacco, and datura were used for medicinal cures and sacred rituals, and some of these were also cultivated in private gardens. Among villagers, land was acknowledged to be the property of an individual, a family, the chief, or the group collectively. This property was inherited patrilineally, and it could be passed by the owner to anyone of his choosing. Trespassing onto individual property and taking its resources brought severe penalty, sometimes even death. Trespassing onto communal property by members of other villages or groups was cause for the warring that Tac discussed. War and marriage expanded Acâgchemem and Quechnajuichom territory.

This complex ordering of place sustained the social relations that defined power and knowledge. Because each sedentary and autonomous village was headed by certain ruling families, intermarriage between these families interlocked the various villages. Each village, moreover, was made up of persons who were patrilineally related.[11] Political authority and most forms of religious knowledge were embodied in the chief of the village and a general council, or *puplem*, composed only of men.[12] Knowledge of all historical, religious, and practical affairs related to food, war, medicine, and the production of goods was passed from these male elders to young men, usually to a son, son-in-law, or nephew who had demonstrated an ability to absorb this knowledge and power.[13] The position of chief was inherited by the first-born son or, if no heir existed, the chief's nearest male relative; a wife or daughter could act as chief if the male heir was not yet old enough to rule. An heir could be bypassed for the next in line if he was considered unworthy or lacking the appropriate qualities to rule.

In Tac's account we see how the mission undermined this political ordering of space and brought baptized and unconverted villagers alike under its control. Although Tac was born at the mission and was considered a model convert, his focus on work and authority reveals his sensitivity to this experience of subjugation. The missionaries, he states, relied on Spanish soldiers on horseback to maintain discipline and order. But to establish their influence deep in the Country they used native *alcaldes,* who acted as mediators between missionaries and Indian populations and as spokesmen for the Indians, and who wielded multiple kinds of authority that had been granted to them by the missionaries.[14] (As elsewhere in the New World, the symbol of these *alcaldes'* power was the cane.) The *alcaldes* at San Luis Rey, Tac explains, were appointed because they knew some Spanish and their behavior was considered appropriate. Often, however, *alcaldes* were appointed because they already held positions of authority or because, as Tac notes, they were able to move between cultural systems easily. Their main task, in Tac's eyes, was to judge, punish, and control other Indians. The chief (who appears in Tac's account as a single person, suggesting the disappearance of the preconquest system in which a chief headed each Luiseño village) dressed like a Spaniard to symbolize his noble place, but, Tac states, he no longer had the authority over his people that he had once had. Instead he and the *alcaldes* served to extend the authority of the missionary into the countryside.

Every afternoon the *alcaldes* would travel to the mission from their villages to report on that day's events and to receive orders for the next day. Passing through other villages on their way back to their own, they would broadcast these orders, calling out in their native language: "Tomorrow the harvest begins! Laborers should gather at the chicken yard." The following day a Spanish overseer and the *alcaldes* would go to the fields to supervise the day's work: as Tac put it, "The lazy would be hurried, and those guilty of slow work or leaving their task would be punished."[15]

Tac, a second-generation neophyte, was taken as a boy to Rome because of his exemplary knowledge, abilities, and Christian belief. Yet in his manuscript his strong sense of identity as Quechnajuis is clear. Tac wrote his account in Spanish and used Spanish words when he wanted to describe the colonized social identities and experiences of the

"Luiseños" and "Sanjuaneños" (the converted Indians of Mission San Juan Capistrano), names fully grounded in the mission experience. Tac emphasizes that only the Franciscans referred to the region as San Luis Rey; his people, by contrast, called the local territory (including the mission itself) Quechla, after the name of a stone found in their country. We, he states, "call ourselves Quechnajuichom in plural, Quechnajuis in singular, that means the inhabitants of quechla."[16]

Tac's treatise, in essence, defines the complex social identities that developed among California's mission Indian populations through conquest and colonization. As a Quechnajuis, he expresses obliquely through his own language some of the deeper understandings of his people and their historic place; as a Luiseño, he describes his world as having been shaped by two generations of mission life. And while Tac speaks favorably of a contact that "took us out of our miseries," he inscribes into history the memory of the demographic disaster that followed, stating that two thousand of his people died as a "result of a sickness that came to California." He also notes that many chose to leave "for the woods" rather than endure conquest.[17] Tac's approach to this story of conversion and his use of language denote a quiet resistance to the humiliations of conquest, particularly the renaming practices that threatened group history and identity. In his own way, he makes clear the vulnerabilities that he and other Quechnajuichom and Luiseños experienced as they negotiated their past and present as mission Indians. With these negotiations in mind, let us now return to the processes of conquest and colonization among the Acâgchemem.

Territorial Conquest

The 1775 erection of a cross and celebration of mass on an Acâgchemem religious site was followed shortly by the Spaniards' retreat to the presidio at San Diego as a result of an Indian revolt against the Mission San Diego. It was therefore not until one year later that the process of building a mission and converting the Acâgchemem population began. The vast majority of initial converts at San Juan Capistrano were children, a common pattern in most of the missions.[18] The children were likely brought by their parents to make alliances with the missionaries, who not only possessed new knowledge and goods but also presented the threat of force. The military was in fact crucial to the encounter between missionaries and potential converts, even though most soldiers and Spanish settlers did not live near either the missions or Indian villages. One confrontation between Father Serra, the president of the California missions and head of the colonization effort in California, and a number of armed Acâgchemem illustrates the relations of power that sustained this colonial encounter. Father Serra was approaching San Juan Capistrano from the north, having left Mission San Gabriel with livestock and neophytes who would help build the mission and serve as interpreters for the priests. The group had divided, and Father Serra was traveling in the company of one soldier and one neophyte. As they entered Acâgchemem territory, these three suddenly found themselves surrounded by a crowd of painted and well-armed Indians, some of whom put arrows to their bowstrings as though they intended to kill the Spanish intruders. The neophyte, however, shouted in their language that they should not hurt the missionary because many soldiers were coming behind who would kill them all. Accordingly, they desisted, aware of the serious threat that military retaliation represented.[19]

In December 1776, four children between the ages of two and seven were baptized at Mission San Juan Capistrano. The first of these was a boy named Hanajiban. Upon his baptism, the missionary changed his name to Juan Baptista after the biblical prophet who announced the coming of Jesus Christ and baptized the population in preparation for this event. This meaning-laden naming practice exemplified the missionaries' consistent use of ceremonial events to convey Christian mythology, history, and worldview. Meanwhile, the parents of Hanajiban remained unconverted to Christianity. The first adult was baptized in January 1777 and promptly renamed Juan Capistrano, after the mission's patron saint. Among the few other early adult converts, interestingly, were several spiritual leaders who went to the mission to gain access to the *ayelkwi* (a concept that means both knowledge and power) possessed by the missionary.[20]

Although only twenty-four persons were baptized in 1776 and 1777, these baptisms helped to establish alliances between the villages and the mission, which in turn fostered continuing conversions through 1783—still mostly of children, who constituted some two-thirds of the 428 baptisms that were performed at the mission. Indeed, by October 1778 many of the children being baptized at San Juan already had a relative, usually a brother or sister, living as a neophyte at the mission. Parents may have been influenced in their decision by having had favor conferred on them for the initial baptism. In any event, with the presence of more than one child from a single family, the mission was creating a nucleus of converts capable of attracting still more Acâgchemem.

During the first two years of the mission's existence, it was common for the *padrinos* and *padrinas*—godparents, whose role it was to look after the Christian education and general well-being of their godchildren—to be chosen from among the soldiers and their wives. In this manner formal ties of personal responsibility were established between the guards and their families, on the one hand, and the Juaneños, on the other, in relationships that otherwise tended to be unidirectional and exploitative of the Indian population. Reinforcing this bond was the fact that Juaneños commonly received one or more of their *padrinos'* names upon baptism.[21]

As the number of converts grew, however, the soldier-Juaneño tie through the godparent institution became less prevalent. Already in 1778, some *padrinos* of new converts were being selected from among the recently converted Juaneños or from among the Indians from Baja California and the Gabrileños (from Mission San Gabriel) who taught and interpreted at Mission San Juan Capistrano. The presence of these latter two groups created greater linguistic and ethnic diversity within the mission; it also allowed the history of conversion and colonial life to be viewed from perspectives other than those offered by Spanish *padrinos* and the missionary.[22] The importance of the Indian *padrino* cannot be overemphasized. Because these individuals were at liberty to interpret Christianity for their newly converted charges, syncretized belief systems and behavior were fostered from within the very institutions of mission life.

Although before 1783 Juaneños, both children and adults, represented a relatively small percentage of the Acâgchemem population, all that changed between 1790 and 1812, when the vast majority of remaining nonconverts were baptized. During this period, too, the mission economy was extended over the Indians' entire territory, completely reshaping the countryside. Between 1790 and 1804, for example, mission herds increased in size from 8,034 head to 26,814 head.[23] Recall that each preconquest Acâgchemem village had had access to specific hunting, collecting, and fishing areas, and that within these collectively owned areas villagers also possessed private property. Imagine the effect that mission use of certain areas for grazing and of others for horticulture would have on this land tenure system. I suspect that it was this imbalance in the related ordering of material, sacred, and political space, augmented by the fact that the rural population was slowly being consumed by European disease, that led to the steady rise in the number of converts, which in turn stimulated further economic expansion.

After 1793, the baptism of entire families became increasingly common. Their baptisms, and those of individuals from a single village or from diverse villages, were sometimes performed in the countryside instead of in the mission church.[24] This change in baptismal patterns—from largely children to whole families—suggests the depth of the missions' dominion over rural society. Already in 1791, a slight majority of the children baptized were considered "legitimate children"—that is, they were the babies of Juaneños who had married in a Christian ceremony. Others were children of Acâgchemem who were receiving religious instruction from Juaneño and other Indian catechists; and of course, some were the offspring of parents who still professed no interest in Christianity. A single generation later, however, by 1812, the majority of children baptized were born of Christian parents. During the intervening years massive conversions had taken place, sometimes in large groups. In 1793, for example, 228 Acâgchemem were baptized; in 1805, 329; and in 1812, 240 (see table 1).

These years of steady growth were accompanied by periods of severe plague, with measles, smallpox, and influenza causing massive numbers of deaths. In 1800 alone, 115 people died—approximately 10 percent of Juaneños living at the mission. In 1806 (just after the single largest number of conversions), 213 died, and in 1811, 130 (5 persons fewer than the number baptized that year)—approximately 16 percent of the Juaneño population died in 1806, and another 10 percent died in 1811. Despite the steadily rising number of deaths, prior to 1812 fewer Juaneños died than were baptized; thereafter, this trend reversed. Besides European diseases, moreover, syphilis had become a problem owing to rape and sexual liaisons between soldiers and Indian women. Apolinaria Lorenzano, a nurse at Mission San Diego, stated that although headaches and simple fevers were common, syphilis and *llagas,* syphilitic sores, were fairly widespread among married men and women who lived outside the mission compound.[25]

By 1812, at the height of the mission's prosperity, 3,340 persons had been baptized at the mission, and 1,361 Juaneños resided in the mission compound. From 1812 to 1834, baptisms were performed predominantly on the legitimate children of Juaneño parents, though occasionally unconverted Acâgchemem parents sought baptism for their children as well, and some Acâgchemem continued to request baptism as they ap-

Table 1. *Baptisms, Deaths, and Total Juaneño Population at Mission San Juan Capistrano, 1776–1847*

	No. Baptized	No. Died	Total Pop.		No. Baptized	No. Died	Total Pop.		No. Baptized	No. Died	Total Pop.
1776	4	—	—	1800	92	115	1,046	1824	51	54	1,060
1777	20	3	—	1801	75	61	1,022	1825	40	69	1,031
1778	120	4	—	1802	57	55	1,013	1826	49	38	1,043
1779	70	4	—	1803	106	85	1,025	1827	47	139	958
1780	54	11	—	1804	83	84	1,024	1828	41	51	947
1781	61	20	—	1805	329	32	1,250	1829	42	55	934
1782	50	25	—	1806	74	213	1,062	1830	40	47	926
1783	46	14	381	1807	103	58	1,109	1831	52	42	939
1784	122	18	429	1808	71	68	1,096	1832	34	62	900
1785	101	17	544	1809	59	52	1,094	1833	35	62	853
1786	62	24	544	1810	62	40	1,138	1834	28	39	861
1787	78	25	593	1811	125	130	1,209	1835	30	37	—
1788	100	36	660	1812	240	108	1,361	1836	21	25	—
1789	63	25	698	1813	27	68	1,249	1837	27	28	—
1790	78	68	737	1814	48	55	1,244	1838	25	27	—
1791	35	41	735	1815	54	78	1,198	1839	17	17	—
1792	88	31	850	1816	43	67	1,142	1840	15	15	—
1793	228	54	971	1817	51	74	1,138	1841	19	24	—
1794	66	55	978	1818	50	62	1,128	1842	28	13	—
1795	74	50	983	1819	41	58	1,078	1843	9	—	—
1796	93	84	994	1820	43	55	1,064	1844	13	—	—
1797	116	46	1,107	1821	57	65	1,050	1845	2	—	—
1798	65	64	1,109	1822	45	46	1,052	1846	11	8	—
1799	69	83	1,060	1823	42	38	1,062	1847	18	—	—

SOURCE: California Mission Statistics, Bancroft Collection, Bancroft Library, University of California, Berkeley, Folder 17.

proached death. San Juan Capistrano's ability to continue expanding, however, was limited by the size of Acâgchemem territory and population and, after 1812, by the high death rate of Juaneños. The Juaneño population living at the mission declined slowly from 1,361 in 1812 to 800 at the time of emancipation, in 1834; nevertheless, they continued to cultivate for their own subsistence, as well as producing a surplus of hides, tallow, and other goods throughout that period.

Building the mission involved claiming and transforming the territory of the Acâgchemem, in part through the imposition of new work processes and a new ordering of time and social space for Juaneños living within the mission compound and in rural villages that the missionaries claimed to be, by 1790, *rancherías de este misión* (villages belonging to this mission).[26] (Life and work both at the mission and in those villages were regulated by a framework that included spatial confinement, formal work schedules, and surveillance by the priest, who introduced new structures of authority and privilege.) Figure 1 depicts one part of the mission. Juaneño women often sat in lines along these arcades weaving textiles or preparing food. The tiles and adobe bricks were made by Indian artisans who similarly plastered and whitewashed the arches that sculpted the interior patio. The mission was built through colonial relations of work and coercion. Opening onto this patio were the rooms that fostered the perpetuation of this social world: dormitories for unmarried Indian youths, the eating commons for the more than 3,500 Juaneños who lived at this mission during its fifty-eight years, a jail for neophytes who awaited lashes and other forms of public humiliation, and the priest's quarters. Some of the doors off these arcades opened onto other courtyards that embraced workshops, storage rooms, and the church. The quarters for soldiers, their families, and married neophytes with very young children were built near this complex.[27]

Indians acquired positions of authority that promised them a relatively high standing within the limitations of neophyte existence—that is, they might receive more food, better clothing, and greater latitude to negotiate their families' well-being. As we saw in Pablo Tac's manuscript, Indian *alcaldes* both supervised and punished other neophytes. Other Indians who wielded some power included *padrinos*, catechists, interpreters, cantors, and midwives.

Indians held positions of authority in every type of job. In her oral memoirs, for example, Eulalia Pérez, the Spanish/mestiza *llavera* (matron of the keys) at San Gabriel Mission from 1821 to 1833, mentions "Luis el Jabonero," who was in charge of the soap room. She explains that for every type of production, an Indian who was acculturated to the Spanish way would learn the job from a Spaniard, then assume the task of overseeing production; these native teachers she defined as "[gente] ya de razón é instruido."[28] In this manner, Indian women and men were trained as artisans in the making of saddles, boots, and shoes; they worked as spinners of cotton and wool, dyers and weavers of cloth; they cut and sewed clothing; they made soap and adobe bricks; they worked as carpenters, chocolate makers, winemakers, and olive press workers; and they performed rural work in fields and orchards, on the

Fig. 1. Arcades of Mission San Juan Capistrano, ca. 1895. Courtesy Southwest Museum, Los Angeles, photo no. P20287. Photo by G. Wharton James.

range as vaqueros, shepherds, and shearers, and in other jobs involving crops or livestock. Some were also trained as catechists to translate prayers and religious dogma into native languages; others were the special servants and messengers of the priests, staying at their side from an early age. Each job necessarily entailed a highly regulated set of obligations and particular privileges.[29]

Spanish/mestizo settlers who worked and lived at the mission also performed the labor crucial to establish colonial society, but they had greater authority than any neophyte simply because of their non-Indian status. Eulalia Pérez's description of her work illustrates well the internal ordering of the mission.[30] As *llavera*, Pérez was in charge of the keys to the girls' dormitory and to the food storage rooms, though Pérez and her five daughters also cut and sewed most of the clothes worn by the mission population. Pérez measured out the daily rations of food and other goods, supervised their distribution, and every eight days doled out rations to the troops: beans, corn, garbanzos, lentils, ham, lard, and candles. To perform this distribution she had the help of an Indian servant named Lucio, who had the full trust of the missionaries. Some Indian families, especially those who lived in villages integrated into mission production, received their rations and ate at home, but the vast majority of Indians ate in the *pozolera* (place where *pozole*, a beverage of barley and sugar, was served).

The daily schedule recounted by Pérez began early in the morning. After she had unlocked the doors of the girls' dormitory, mass was said by Father Zalvidea, who spoke Gabrieleño (*hablaba indio*). Afterward, everyone went to the *pozolera* to have a breakfast that usually consisted of *pozole* and meat. They then began multiple jobs, but if they were field workers, at eleven they would have a drink of water with vinegar (or lemon) and sugar so they wouldn't get sick. At noon they had *pozole* with meat and vegetables. Work ended when the sun went down, and the workers went from the fields straight to the *pozolera*, where they had *atole* (corn flour gruel).

Nepantla: The Painful Ordeal of Mission Life

The political reorganization of Acâgchemem territory by the mission system had disrupted every aspect of native life by the early nineteenth century. Even so, although the Spaniards went far toward regulating outward behavior by imposing regimented time in the workplace and spatial confinement, in the end they were unable to eradicate all preconquest traditions, material culture, and historical, religious, and practical knowledge. The Acâgchemem, after all, who continued to speak their language among themselves, constituted the overwhelming population at the mission virtually from the start. The demographic balance around 1812 was typical in its proportions: that year found 1,361 Juaneños living at Mission San Juan Capistrano proper, together with approximately 30 Spaniards, including 6 soldiers of the guard, their families, and 2 missionaries. Thus, even when the mission population and production were at their height, precontact social relations persisted, not only in the countryside, but also within the mission compound itself.

Geronimo Boscana was a missionary at San Juan who wrote a *relación*, or narrative account, about the Acâgchemem between 1812 and 1822, when he presided over the mission; his observations testify to the persistence of indigenous practices and authority figures—such as healing and healers—over two generations after the initial conquest. For example, Boscana describes a dance he saw outside one village sometime around 1820.[31] It was, he said, enacted according to oral traditions and performed twice a year in a special locale. An unmarried girl disrobed and danced naked inside a circle formed by all the villagers. She put her hands under her breasts and sang a song naming the sexual parts of her body and of men's bodies. As she danced and sang she touched each part suggestively and shook herself. This dance of sexuality and procreation continued to be performed in the designated place and time of year even after the mission had extended its dominion over the countryside—indeed, under the very gaze of Boscana, who found it "obscene." Nevertheless, at the time he observed this performance, most Juaneños and Acâgchemem were slowly abandoning it and other dances, or at least no longer performing them in public.

The persistence of indigenous culture and practices within the mission compound was facilitated by persons who waged a quiet opposition to Catholicism and Spanish culture. The idea that new manifestations of *ayelkwi* (a concept that embraces both knowledge and power) were available from the Spanish friars had attracted male and female elders to the mission compound, where they continued their work not only underground but also in some cases openly. Boscana provides the example of a young woman who had been sick for nearly one year and had become so wasted away from dysentery and fever that her death seemed imminent. Having already administered the last sacraments to her, he was later astonished to find her in the garden clearing grass with a group of women. She told him that a healer, whom she identified by name, had extracted bear's hairs from her, which, she argued, had been the cause of her illness. Now, after only a short time, she was as robust and healthy as ever.[32]

The most systematic effort of the missionaries to disrupt the passage of indigenous forms of knowledge, authority, and power from elders to their children, and to more easily inculcate Christian norms, was the act of placing all neophyte children in *monjerios,* or dormitories, away from their parents from the age of seven or so until their marriage. An older neophyte was named as the "mother" in charge of the girls, and an *alcalde* or other male official was put in charge of the boys. Eulalia Pérez, the *llavera* we met above, was given the keys to the girls' dormitory every evening after they were locked in, and she in turn gave them to the priest each night. Pérez relates that at Mission San Gabriel a blind Gabrileño would stand at the door and call the names of each girl who was supposed to enter for the night. If a girl missed the roll call, her mother was brought to the mission from her village the next day and punished for detaining her child, and the girl was locked up for having failed to arrive punctually.[33]

Confinement and lashes were the most common forms of punishment against offenses that included challenges to discipline and authority, and violations against persons and property. The small rooms that served as jail cells were prominent features of each mission. As for lashes, the practice of flogging neophytes remained one of the greatest reasons to run away from the mission. The logic of punishment was integral to Catholic belief and practice. The priests themselves inflicted self-punishments as a regular course of bodily penance. Their practice of self-flagellation, called "the discipline," was almost as much a part of their spiritual life as prayer. Whipping generally continued to play a significant role in Spanish Catholicism into the early nineteenth century.[34] For example, Father Zalvidea, a missionary who had worked at San Gabriel and San Juan Capistrano, spent the last months of his life with nails in his feet and other self-inflicted wounds on his body: he was, he said, punishing himself for the sins he had committed in this world.[35] This belief in the value of self-inflicted pain to maintain social and individual spiritual order legitimated coercion and direct force.

(Miguel León-Portilla explains that indigenous peoples experienced a state of *nepantla,* a Nahuatl term meaning "to be in the middle," because their colonizers' use of force wounded the ethical and spiritual foundations of their world.[36] In response, indigenous peoples syncretized their cultural practices and collective identities with those parts of Christianity and Spanish culture that made sense to them, while elements of their culture that resisted syncretization were retained) For example, identities such as Quechla and Acâgchemem represented a long historical past; for Tac and others, that past was embodied in their language, maintenance of which made possible a constant but quiet resistance to the colonial process. For those who lived "in the middle," in a world where surveillance by missionary and guards enforced the dominance of the new system, Indian identities were negotiated and given meaning according to circumstance. The behaviors of acceptance and accommodation easily intertwined with overt and subtle forms of resistance.

The painful reality of living between contending social and cultural systems during this period is illustrated in the deaths of two young men, both raised at the sides of the missionaries, thoroughly instructed in the Christian religion, and excellent speakers of Spanish, such that they served as interpreters for the padres. One of these young men, who died at the age of twenty-three, refused the medicine and advice offered by the priest. Instead he called for a *curandero,* whose medicines, however, did not cure him. As the young man approached death, the *curandero* told him that his people's god was angry and had sent him an incurable illness because the young man had always believed in the missionaries. The second young man, a neophyte at Mission San Juan Capistrano, was also suffering a painful death. The priest and his parents and friends all tried to get him to take the final sacraments, but he adamantly refused, shouting blasphemies and desperate cries. When asked why he refused, he answered angrily, "Ya que he vivido engañado, no quiero morir engañado" (Having lived deceived, I do not want to die deceived). Boscana asserts that these two cases represented the rule, not the exception. Those who appeared most enlightened by Christian doctrine and practices, he stated, were the ones who surprised the missionaries the most when they abandoned Catholicism. All the missionaries in California, declares Boscana, would agree that the true believer was the rare exception.[37]

Colonial Identities: *Indio* and *De Razón*

The designation Juaneño was a colonial identity made possible because conquest left Indian populations vanquished. In the Law of the Indies, Indians held legal rights second only to those accorded Spaniards.[38] But by and large, with the exception of caciques and other former nobility of indigenous peoples (such as the king of the Luiseños, who dressed like a Spaniard), *indios* carried the lowest social status of all New World groups. In contrast, the African slave, who was brought by force to the Caribbean shortly after the European conquest of the New World began, had the lowest legal status but a higher economic and social position than that of the Indian. This distinction between legal status and social standing is crucial to understanding the mentalité of colonists in California.

The categories of "Indian" and "Spaniard" were ethnic and national designations imbued strongly with racial meaning; they undergirded the legal system that evolved to define people throughout the Spanish Americas by the late sixteenth century, a system centered on the concept of the *casta* that categorized persons by their purported racial heritage. (The term *casta* was also used to refer to persons of mixed blood.) Yet despite a legal codification that entailed fifty-six such categories in Mexico alone and that regulated marriage, work, and other aspects of people's lives, enforcement of the codes, or of *casta* identities generally, was never systematic. A person's or family's racial status could be negotiated over the course of a person's lifetime, and the regional meaning of race identity (indeed, of *casta* terms) was far from constant.[39] Many persons changed their racial status between the 1781 census of Alta California and that of 1790. In 1781, for example, Pablo Rodríguez was classified simply as an *indio,* but by 1790, probably because he had assumed a new set of characteristics—different clothing, mannerisms, habits of speech—he was categorized as a *coyote* (having an Indian mother and mestizo father). In this new classification, he and his descendants assumed a position closer to that of the Spaniard. María Guadalupe Pérez and María Rufina Navarro both changed their status from *mulata* (mixed African and Spanish parentage) to, respectively, *coyota* and *mestiza* (Indian-Spanish parentage), thus shedding the stigma of African descent for themselves and their children.[40] Thus people reclassified themselves toward a lighter (and higher) ranking, the census takers generally recording information on the basis of a person's word and appearance. The movement away from African ancestry in legal classification was astute from the standpoint of legal rights, for the eighteenth-century Law of the Indies had affirmed a relatively high legal status for *indios*—contradictory as this was to their practical social standing—but more severely restricted the rights of persons of African descent.[41]

The "Spaniard" had the best legal condition, with the peninsular Spaniard (one who originated in Spain) at the top of the social hierarchy. But even the "Spanish" identity changed as part of the ongoing negotiation of racial and social status that defined colonial society. Although strictly speaking "Spaniard" also signified "white," by the late eighteenth century the category included persons born in the Americas who had mixed blood. In colonial New Mexico, for example, "Span-iards" were considered men of honor, in comparison to "vanquished Indians," such that the differences between Spanish "aristocrats and landed peasants were of degree rather than kind."[42] Whiteness was thus not a singular or static category but included a range of color. "White" lineage could be purchased from the crown with gold or other goods through a decree called *gracias al sacar* (thanks to be taken out, re-moved, or freed).

Although the Spanish American system favored the idea of *limpieza de sangre,* or pure blood, race categories remained relatively flexible concepts, constituting, on the frontier, one of but a number of attri-butes that defined status (others included religion, wealth, and legitimate birth).[43] Nonetheless, in Alta California as elsewhere, people continued to define themselves as being of pure blood when they could. Eulalia Pérez, for example, introduced her narrative of life in nineteenth-cen-tury California with the statement that she had been born in the presidio of Loreto in Baja California; she then gave the names of her parents, emphasizing that they were *blancos puros:* pure—unmixed—whites.[44] Julio César likewise began his account of life in nineteenth-century Cal-ifornia by describing himself as an *indio puro nacido en San Luis Rey,* or pure-blooded Indian born at the mission of San Luis Rey.[45]

The importance of race within the configuration of status varied across the Americas according to time and place. By the early nine-teenth century, for instance, the settlers of Alta California most fre-quently used the polarized terms *gente de razón* (people of reason) and *indio* or *gente sin razón* (people without reason) to differentiate between "Spaniard" and "Indian." The term *sin razón* developed out of the the ological debates of the sixteenth century that addressed such questions as whether Indians had souls. These debates evolved through the Spanish Renaissance to define a notion of rationality that was strongly influenced by classical and ancient Christian philosophical judgments.[46] Not only were pagan Indians and neophytes deemed to be lacking in reason, but they also considered minors before the law and so were tried by the Church in a separate Inquisition court. Although the identities of *de razón* and *sin razón* originated out of religious discourse, and thus implied a modicum of theological approbation, they were used inter-changeably with the ethnic and national categories *español* and *indio,* and in this sense implied an insurmountable divide between civilization and savagery.[47]

In the baptismal records at Mission San Juan Capistrano, the missionaries referred to children's legitimacy or illegitimacy and to their status as either *indio* or *de razón*. *Casta* identity, in this area where Indians remained in the vast majority until the 1850s, received no mention. The use of the term *de razón* to identify the nonindigenous population was so widespread that in his response to a questionnaire from the Spanish Cortes that sought information about the *castas* of Los Angeles the missionary at San Gabriel stated, "How many these castes are and precisely which castes they are we do not know because, as we have said, they are all known as *gente de razón*."[48]

The prevalence of the identities of *de razón* and *sin razón*, Spaniard and *indio*, stems from the ongoing processes of conquest that defined the history of colonial California, and the regional histories of those areas—notably Baja California, Sinaloa, and Sonora—from which most of the soldiers and settlers came.[49] These areas were not only marked by the conquest of and conflict with indigenous peoples, but they had also been colonized by a broad range of ethnic groups, such that status was gained for many through the singular distinction between *de razón* and *indio*. In Baja California by 1790, after a century of colonization, the 844 non-Indian residents were classified as 29 percent Spanish, 21 percent African, and 50 percent *casta*.[50] These proportions are generally comparable to those of the population of colonial Alta California, reflecting the high degree of racial mixing that existed in the settlers' places of origin. Speaking of late-eighteenth-century Sinaloa, for example, a Spanish colonial official argued that it was difficult to trace specific bloodlines within that highly diverse population.[51] In any event, owing to the long history of conquests and relationships formed among persons of different ethnicities on this Spanish frontier, *casta* distinctions had declined markedly in significance among the *gente de razón*, to be replaced by other designations.

Californio: A Regional Identity

After independence had been won from Spain (1821), the national government of Mexico began to formulate land policy that promoted the rights of individuals over those of the Church and other corporate bodies. At the same time, it slowly expanded the definition and privileges of citizenship. In 1824, the *casta* system was abolished.

In 1826, all Indians were made full and equal citizens under the law, and in 1829 slavery was abolished. As citizens, neophytes awaited their imminent emancipation from the California missions. Throughout the Americas, in fact, as large, captive labor forces that had sustained colonial empires and young nations were proclaimed free, a central question arose: What did freedom mean? For the *gente de razón*, as represented by the territorial government, defining mission Indians' freedom required that they clarify their own territorial sovereignty vis-à-vis Mexico and articulate a regional identity. Their position represented one of three sides in the debates over freedom's meaning. Interested in maintaining Indians in subordinate positions, the territorial government managed, in efforts that spanned nearly a decade, to set very limited conditions of freedom for California Indians. The Mexican federal government, for its part, as well as the mission Indians themselves, also acted to define the terms of emancipation. For all involved, freedom was inextricably connected to two key questions: Who would own mission lands? And who would control the labor of Indians after they were freed from their obligations to the mission?

Mexican federal policy linked freedom to the larger effort to colonize the frontier by opening it up to landless and relatively poor Californios, to colonists from Mexico, and to foreigners who would adopt Mexican citizenship and Catholicism. This scheme was designed to foster a countryside inhabited by a diverse population of small farmers, cattle ranchers, artisans, and other workers. Yet it did not always work as planned. In Texas, for instance, this policy of colonization brought the eclipse of the Mexican population as Americans poured into the area, becoming the majority group as early as 1833.[52] In any case, Californios blocked such a policy, and their relative distance from the United States promised little interference on that front. Because Mexican law granted equal citizenship irrespective of race, the federal government's emancipation and secularization laws gave former neophytes the right to claim a share of mission land as citizens but, in contrast to colonial policy, refused to acknowledge their right to the precolonial territory that the Church had held in trust for them during the mission period.

This spirit of Mexican law governed the tentative declarations of emancipation in California beginning in 1825 with the arrival of Mexican governor José María Echeandía, whose explicit instructions were to design and implement an emancipation and secularization program. According to Echeandía's plan, the missions of both Baja and Alta California were to be converted into pueblos in which former neophytes, non-Christian Indians, Californios, and colonists all would reside. The rural ranchos of the missions were to be annexed to these pueblos, to fall under the jurisdiction of an elected *alcalde* and town council. The cultivated lands and livestock of the missions would constitute the property of these pueblos. Two plots of land, one for a house and one for crops, were to be given to each family according to its need, up to a maximum area. In addition, each family of former neophytes would receive a specified number of cows, sheep, and goats, one yoke of oxen, two horses and a mare, and instruments for carpentry and cultivation. Their land and goods could not be alienated or mortgaged for five years. Each pueblo would have common lands accessible to each inhabitant, water rights, and public buildings for government, schools, and social institutions. Once land was distributed to the neophytes, most of the remaining land would go to *de razón* settlers. The missionaries, who were relegated to the status of parish priest, would retain rights only to the church building and their living quarters. All undistributed property was to be placed under the care of an administrator, who was subject to the orders of the respective town councils and the territorial government. Any income from this public property was to be used to pay the salaries of teachers and to maintain public institutions.[53]

Echeandía announced impending emancipation at some missions upon his arrival in 1827. In response, many neophytes began to resist orders to work, mounting minor revolts against uncompensated gang labor. Their acts were interpreted by the *gente de razón* as indicating a lack of preparedness for freedom. As a consequence, emancipations were restricted at first to individuals who could be self-supporting because of the skills they possessed. In 1831, Echeandía expanded this to include men and women who had been in the mission ten years or more and were married, or widowed with minor children.[54] That same year, the California territorial deputation passed a full-scale emancipation edict, but debates over amendments to the law delayed its implementation. Two aspects of that law nevertheless remained intact in subsequent legislation: after emancipation, undistributed mission property became part of the public domain, and administrators continued to organize former neophytes to perform work on this land as a public service during specified periods of the year.

In contrast to the California territorial deputation's plan, the secularization and emancipation law devised by the Mexican Federal Chamber of Deputies, to be implemented by one José María Padrés, was intended to encourage the colonization of the California territory. According to this law, mission lands were to be divided among former neophytes and other Indians; soldiers in the garrisons of California to whom the federal government owed pay; Mexican residents of California who owned less than the minimum acreage allotted under the secularization plan; Mexican and foreign families who emigrated to California; entrepreneurs who brought people into the territory; and convicts who completed their terms of imprisonment in California and wished to stay.[55] Although this bill never emerged from the Mexican Senate because of the disruptions of a cholera epidemic and the overthrow of the reform-minded Congress in May 1834, it found its way in spirit into the instructions sent with a colonizing expedition of two hundred families dispatched in 1834 and headed by José María de Híjar and José María Padrés. Upon their arrival in California, they were to occupy the missions immediately, declare them pueblos, and open them to settlement.

Hearing of Híjar's orders, the California territorial deputation put its own law for full-scale emancipation into effect, beginning two months before the colonizing expedition was due to arrive. Their law contrasted sharply with Mexican federal policy in that it enabled only Indians, rather than the region's soldiers, settlers, or recent immigrants, to receive mission lands and goods. Moreover, Indians were to constitute the sole population of mission pueblos. Given these objectives, the deputation promised each head of a neophyte family and all neophyte males over twenty-one years of age one plot of land for a home and one plot to cultivate, a portion of mission cattle, other livestock, and tools. The children's dormitories were to be immediately disbanded and the children handed over to their fathers, together with instructions about "the care they should take of them" and "their obligations as parents."[56] Villages of twenty-five or more persons were recognized as separate communities. Their inhabitants were similarly entitled to private land, goods, and public lands. Smaller villages would be annexed to the nearest large village or pueblo for administrative purposes. The land and cattle thus distributed to Indians could not be sold, burdened, or alienated, and at death an individual's possessions would revert to the public domain in the absence of an heir. The right of former neophytes to political representation was restricted to voting for municipal officers in charge of the pueblos (the extent of whose duties, however, was not specified).

Having outlined the property and political rights of the former neophytes, the law at once limited their freedom by obliging them to perform "indispensable common labor" on undistributed lands for the "public good." One administrator, who would oversee common labor and the distribution of its yield, was to be appointed by the governor.[57] In contrast to Mexican federal policy, California territorial law was designed to retain the labor of former neophytes on mission lands. Moreover, the California territorial deputation's plan blocked the acquisition of mission lands by immigrants from Mexico and elsewhere, and it opened the way for *gente de razón*, now assuming the regional identity of Californios, to assume jurisdiction over mission territory as administrators of the secularized missions.[58]

The California territorial deputation defended this policy by linking the emancipation of the neophytes to its own demand for territorial sovereignty. The debate raised by emancipation over the meaning of freedom was wholly bound up with still more questions: How should the countryside as a whole be organized? And who should own the land? Resolution to these questions was formalized in the 1834 *Manifiesto a la República Mejicana.* A large collection of documents compiled, introduced, and woven together by California governor José Figueroa, the *Manifiesto* expressed, for the first time, a collective Californio political identity. Composed primarily of documents of the territorial deputation and official correspondence, the *Manifiesto,* which was widely circulated, read, and discussed throughout California, defends the territorial deputation's decision to flout federal secularization policy and prevent colonists (such as those accompanying Híjar) from settling mission lands. The arguments presented strongly support neophyte land rights; they also appeal to the federal government to recognize California's sovereignty.

These two issues intertwined to form a fundamental basis on which a "Californio" identity could be established. The U.S. Land Commission hearings of 1852 on mission property contain testimony by Californios that echoes the arguments made in the *Manifiesto* concerning neophytes' legal, historical, and natural rights to former mission lands.[59] The Californio José Joaquín Jimeno, for example, stated that "the Indians were recognized as the owners of the[se] lands," and others confirmed that "the government recognized the title and right of possession (derived from nature) of the Indians to the large tracts of Mission lands."[60] Emphasizing the importance of the document to the expression of a Californio political consciousness, the Territorial Deputation placed a note at the end of the *Manifiesto* that referred to Governor

Figueroa (who died while the document was in press) as "the protector of the Territory, the Father of our California."[61]

Ignacio Sepúlveda situated the "Californio" identity in the colonial institution of the mission, which controlled the countryside for over sixty years (1769–1834) and shaped the social relationships that defined the territory well into the Mexican period (from 1821 on). Californios, Sepúlveda states, "differ in many essential particulars from the other people of Mexico," largely because of the influence and example of the "Franciscan fathers."[62] He also linked Californio identity to racial status and bloodlines: "There are [a] great many families in whose veins circulates much of the *sangre azul* [blue blood] of Spain." Indeed, a pretense to aristocracy was not uncommon for the Spanish/mestizo population that came to identify themselves as Californios and Spanish Californians. Sepúlveda stressed that Californios stood apart because of their "traits of character, features, and mental gifts," characteristics cherished in preindustrial California, where language, bearing, and physical appearance constituted visible marks of status. Sepúlveda noted the geographic origins of most colonists: some had migrated from Sinaloa and Baja California, others from the interior of Mexico and South America, and a few came directly from Spain. Their provincial ways were consequently diverse, and their Castilian reflected distinctive regional characteristics.[63]

The *Manifiesto* claims historical justification for California's territorial sovereignty based on the principles underlying the Spanish colonial order, specifically the principle of paternalism toward the neophyte. It illustrates the political origins of the myth—one articulated many times throughout the late nineteenth century (as in Sepúlveda's account)—that a Californio territorial identity had been molded by this paternal good. The *Manifiesto* makes frequent reference to a Spanish law of 1813 that recognized the rights of neophytes to own land, arguing that Californios followed the logic of this unbroken tradition of rights—the "derecho que respeto el gobierno español durante su dominación y que nadie ahora les ha interrumpido."[64] Numerous times the *Manifiesto* states outright that the neophytes "are the owners of the land they cultivate and of the goods that their work produced."[65]

Californios' interpretation of freedom and definition of their territorial identity, based as these were on colonial law, remained closely tied to the ideas that had sustained the colonial regime. These ideas continued to support coercive forms of labor, albeit among a population now ostensibly free. The idea that the land was the possession of the neophytes, moreover, was later contradicted in various drafts of the territorial government's emancipation and secularization laws that declared mission lands to be national domain. Throughout the Americas, indeed, not only was it rare that former neophytes were actually given formal title to the lands distributed among them upon their emancipation;[66] but also—although the ideological justifications differed—coercive labor systems and a relatively landless group of freed people were common results following emancipation.

Juaneños and Other *Indios* Define Their Freedom

For Juaneños and other former neophytes, as for African-descent slaves (who were distinguished from the former by their legal status as chattel), freedom meant entitlement to land—where possible, to that land that they themselves had cultivated. Land ownership alone promised the material basis for other far-reaching liberties, such as the right to organize and control their own labor, the right to associate, to be educated, and to move about. In the United States, freedom was intricately connected to political representation, and there alone among New World nations, former slaves participated in the creation of state constitutions and laws that, for varying periods thereafter, defined liberties involving civil rights, property, and the social good.[67]

The first provisional proclamation of emancipation ordered by Governor Echeandía in 1826 was restricted to certain military districts (San Diego, Santa Barbara, and Monterey) and to those neophytes considered by the missionaries to be capable of supporting themselves. Nevertheless, the promise of liberty brought widespread resistance to work at other missions, and sometimes open revolt. At Mission San Juan Capistrano, for example, the missionary stated that if the 956 neophytes residing at the mission in 1827 were "kindly begged to go to work," they would respond by saying simply that they were "free."[68] This embrace of liberty was repeatedly articulated through the various stages of provisional emancipations up to 1834, when neophytes at San Luis Rey, who knew they were about to be freed, proclaimed in one voice, "We are free! We do not want to obey! We do not want to work!" whereupon thousands left the mission and returned to their rural communities—which in some cases their forebears had left two generations earlier.[69] Still others petitioned for their freedom. Governor Echeandía reported having received many such petitions, some from neophytes who self-consciously defined themselves as skilled craftsmen and workers—as masons, tilemakers, carpenters, soapmakers, muleteers, or *vaqueros*—knowing that these skills qualified them as self-supporting.[70]

When provisional freedom for some was replaced by general freedom for all, neophyte *alcaldes* requested that lands surrounding the mission proper be distributed to the neophyte community. In 1833 in San Juan Capistrano the *alcaldes* requested that the community be granted the land surrounding the mission, which the Juaneños had irrigated and were now using to support themselves.[71] (This sense of rightful possession was derived from the value Indians placed on their individual, family, and collective labor.) As one *alcalde* explained, "To stand by and watch these men [the appointed administrators] take over the missions which we have built, the herds we have tended, and to be exposed incessantly, together with our families, to the worst possible treatment and even death itself, is a tragedy!" Why, he went on, should former neophytes be blamed "if we defend ourselves, and return to our tribes in the Tulares, taking with us all the livestock that could be led away?"[72]

Meanwhile in the countryside, Juaneños and other mission Indians claimed and were granted villages, though again they rarely received legal title. In San Juan Capistrano, a relatively small mission territory, there were at least seven such villages. Although these lands were never formally ceded to the Juaneños after emancipation, their continuing claim to the land is documented by formal protests they made against encroachments. In 1841 the still resident missionary stated, "The Indian community came and informed me that efforts had been made to deprive them of Trabuco, Mission Vieja, and Yuguilli. If their land is taken away from them," he implored the governor, "how will they maintain their few thousand cattle?"[73] At San Gabriel similar protests were heard as title to those extensive mission lands was steadily claimed by Californios from 1833 on.[74] At San Luis Rey, by contrast, a number of titles were actually bestowed upon Indian villagers; as a result, villages were able to persist as cultivated areas with viable economies.

One such title was granted to María Juana de los Angeles, who petitioned for and received a grant of land from Mission San Luis Rey in 1845. Her husband was a Luiseño chief, and in the late 1830s he was granted possession of village lands by a mission administrator, but not formal title. At the time of her petition María Juana was a widow with a large family, cattle, horses, an adobe house, and a cultivated field and garden.[75] Many years earlier, in 1834, another group of Luiseños had actually received title to "Pueblito de las Flores," an area of twenty square miles (a league and a half in each direction). Less than a decade later the village had a population of thirty-two families and boasted fifty-four sheep, sixty-nine other livestock, several oxen, four milk cows, a cultivated area, and cornfields. Yet encroachments were beginning to be made on their land, in response to which the villagers lodged numerous complaints with officials in Los Angeles. Even so, in 1843 "some inducements" persuaded three villagers (including the first and second *alcaldes*) to consent to the transfer of the pueblo's land, buildings and all, to Pio and Andrés Pico, Californios who became large landowners during this period.[76]

(The former neophytes' response to freedom suggests the bicultural world in which they were forced to negotiate their status. They demanded liberty—freedom from the coercive labor system and land on which to sustain themselves.) Many also pointed to the skills they had learned at the mission in an effort to obtain their freedom. Neophytes in many missions claimed entitlement to mission lands based on the fact that their labor had made these lands productive. Both in the environs of the mission and in the countryside, former neophytes continued to produce field and orchard crops, to gather and eat indigenous foods, and to run cattle. In fact, they established a viable rural economy. Yet when rancho grants on the lands of San Juan Capistrano were made in the early 1840s, Indians' rights to their village lands went unrecognized.

Indeed, the villages became the objects of investigation by the territorial government, and individuals were increasingly vulnerable to being forced to work on public projects. In 1839, the governor stated that if villagers "reverted" to a state of dependence on wild fruits or neglected planting crops and herding, they would be returned immediately to their respective missions under conditions similar to neophytism[77]—conditions that were thenceforth written into the law and applied to any who remained within the reach of the mission administrators. Required to labor for the "common good" on undistributed mission property to sustain the territorial government, their own municipality, the infirm and aged among them, and the Church, former neophytes in the lands surrounding the missions found themselves subject to the same spatial order that had controlled their life and work under the mission system. Thus, the new political ordering of space continued to bind the former neophytes to many of the same conditions of coercive labor that had characterized their previous state. Julio César, a former neophyte from Mission San Luis Rey, emphasizes this continuity in his account of life at the mission during the late 1830s and early 1840s: "The order established by the missionaries was continued under the administration of Sr. Pico; there was a dormitory for the single girls and one for the boys. . . . This same regime was continued under the subsequent administrations of Estudillo and Ortega." As during the mission years, work was remunerated with food, clothing, and, as César stresses, lashes for punishment.[78] The most common form of resistance to the conditions of labor under the administrator was flight to villages in the countryside, following a precedent established during the colonial period.

Although Juaneños and other California Indians near the missions and pueblos found their freedom highly restricted, they nevertheless demonstrated a sharp sense of their rights and maintained community political structures that sustained an alternative ordering of authority and social norms. When Juaneños protested Californio encroachment on their village lands and unfair labor practices, they did so through their *alcalde*. José Delfin, an Indian *alcalde* from San Juan Capistrano, represented Juaneños living at the mission in 1839 when he charged one administrator with "wasting and misapplying the mission effects, in consequence of which the Indians, tired of working without benefit to themselves, were deserting." Delfin stated that the administrator, a man named Argüello, "cultivated fields for himself with Indian labor, put his brand on the best horses, and bought animals with mission brandy." He argued that the sixty former neophytes still at work demanded a just administrator with a smaller family (Argüello had twenty-two persons in his immediate family, plus relatives, living at the mission).[79] The authority of the *alcalde* was recognized everywhere an Indian community existed. In Los Angeles, for example, although vagrancy and convict labor laws were in force and the use of Indian labor for the "common good" and restrictions on Indians' residential options underlined the multiple constraints imposed on their freedom, nonetheless the city council felt obliged to honor the Indian *alcaldes'* authority. When ordering the labor of the town's Indian population for a given job on specific Saturdays, the town council was always cautious to insist that "the Alcaldes of the Indians shall meet and bring together the Indians without a [white] boss, so no one will be aggrieved."[80]

Interpretations of the history of emancipation and secularization generally refer only to secularization, a process that involves the redistribution of Church lands and goods. Secularization is considered an

event of singular importance because it made the division of the countryside into private ranchos possible. Yet the term *emancipation* focuses
instead on individual and collective freedoms. The laws governing the
associated processes were called "secularization laws" only during the
colonial period, as in the 1813 secularization law of the Spanish Cortes.
Laws formulated in the Mexican period, when the individual freedom
of the citizen received greater weight, either used both *emancipation*
and *secularization* in their titles or defined one process as having pri-
macy over the other, such as the California territorial deputation's "provisional emancipation" law of 1831. David Weber's focus is typical when
he writes, "In California land and cheap Indian labor from the newly
secularized missions, combined with new markets, gave rise to a class
of *nouveau riche* cattle barons late in the Mexican period" who went
on to acquire ownership of most of California's mission lands between
1834 and 1846.[81] Weber's interpretation emphasizes the history of Californios but leaves the agency and experience of Indians entirely unex-
amined. Howard Lamar follows this line of thought in an article that
otherwise astutely questions whether the West should more properly be
a symbol of bondage rather than of freedom, particularly when it comes
to labor systems.[82] Sherburne Cook, who examines the injustices of
white-Indian relations on the California frontier from a stance sympa-
thetic to native peoples, is content to argue simply that "secularization"
brought former mission Indians into the rapidly expanding system of
Indian peonage on the private ranchos. He goes on to discuss peonage
in an uncritical manner, stating that, under favorable conditions, peonage was reasonably satisfactory to the former neophytes because it
permitted them to live in their own communities on the ranchos, where
their tribal customs were maintained or in any event suffered less disruption than in the mission compound.[83]

Historians who have more recently examined the encounter between
colonizers and colonized in California likewise attribute an absence of
agency, or a certain passivity, to former neophytes when discussing the
dissolution of the missions. Doug Monroy, for example, states, "Probably five thousand died during the disarray of secularization. Most,
however, merely went someplace else and then aimlessly dawdled when
they got there." According to Monroy, colonization "thoroughly dis-
organized Indians" by displacing them from their lands. "Once the
missions were gone, they had little left of either their original cultural
ways or the new discipline that made them social beings."[84] Leonard
Pitt similarly writes that secularization was a "painful experience" for

the Indians themselves, when "the neophytes were torn tragically between a secure, authoritarian existence and a free but anarchic one. . . . Even by the 1850s, the neophytes remained a demoralized class, alternately prey to disease, liquor, violence, submission, and exploitation."[85]

George Phillips presents the most sustained analysis of how the actions of southern California Indians contributed to define emancipation. He argues that their unwillingness to work for an administrator after emancipation was significant in bringing about the decline of the missions. By focusing on the emergence of new political leaders among southern California Indians in the Mexican period, Phillips provides a unique view of the political and cultural life of village Indians.[86]

It is difficult to identify examples of Indian agency in Mexican society because of the nature of the Mexican documents themselves, which tend to further a history of *nepantla,* or cultural woundedness. While they record incidents, uprisings, and statements *about* Indians, they rarely allow Indian voices themselves to be heard. The social reality of Mexican California remained divided between the two groups of *indio,* on the one hand, and Californio, on the other. This division in turn made Indian invisibility possible and sustainable. The 1836 and 1844 California censuses, for example, list *indios* separately, by first name only, and all are assigned the occupation of *sirviente,* a blanket designation that denied the multiple skills they practiced on the ranchos.[87] Similarly, land grant appeals from the time of Mexican independence forward ignored the presence of Indian villages and the indigenous peoples' possession and use of the land. Although Indian villages might persist on land grants, they effectively lost their claim to the surrounding territory.

Despite their precarious legal and civil status, Acâgchemem and Juaneños maintained a syncretized material culture through the nineteenth century. After their emancipation many returned to their former villages near San Juan, where they cultivated gardens and orchards and raised livestock; others, meanwhile, cultivated land in San Juan, living in the many structures built around the mission. Only some individuals and families moved to ranchos or the pueblo of Los Angeles.

In the end, the absence of full Indian rights can be traced to the very definition of a "Californio" territorial identity, which asserted the right of the region's *gente de razón* to exercise sovereignty over all political issues in the region. The California territorial deputation set restrictions on mission Indians' freedoms and rights to land just as other legislatures had done in response to the emancipation of other unfree workers. A free labor society did not emerge in postcolonial, postemancipation California, and the distinctions between *indios* and Californios persisted, furthering the stark social divisions that had long defined colonial society in this territory. Nevertheless, many Indians lived in villages that were relatively independent of the control and oversight of rancheros and *pobladores.*

CHAPTER 2

Rural Society, 1840–1880

Property and Inequality
in the Mexican Countryside

Few Indians received legal title to the land they inhabited. Moreover, the governor rarely recognized Indian land rights when granting ranchos. Hence, the protests former neophytes made against granting the rural lands of San Juan Capistrano to Californios went unheeded, and most of the former Acâgchemem territory was incorporated into Californio ranchos by 1841, when San Juan Mission was formed into a pueblo.[1]

The 1841 petition of Juan Abila and Concepción Abila de Sánchez, a brother and sister, illustrates the lack of attention given to Indian land claims in this process of dividing the former mission into ranchos.[2] When applying for the grant of Rancho El Niguel, the Abilas followed the common procedure for procuring a rancho. They sent a petition and *diseño* to the governor, who examined the documents and then forwarded them with his approval to officials in Los Angeles. Petitioners had to certify that they were born (or naturalized) Mexican citizens, that the land had not been included in previous legal concessions, and that they were prepared and able to stock the land with the required number of horses and cattle. The *diseño* had to include the names of neighboring ranchos, the boundaries and approximate size of the desired parcel, and rough designations of topographical landmarks (map 4). During the

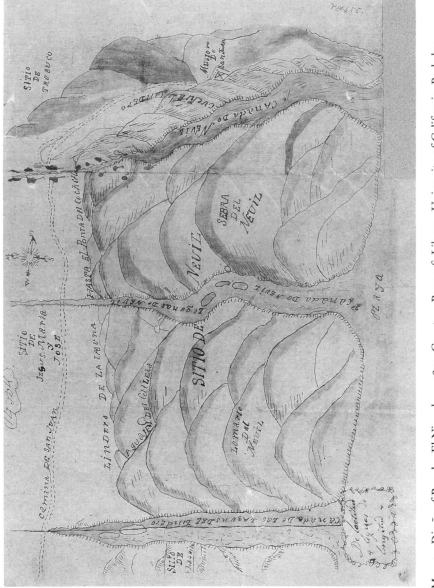

Map 4. *Diseño* of Rancho El Niguel, ca. 1841. Courtesy Bancroft Library, University of California, Berkeley.

colonial period, petitioners for grants also had to prove that Indian villages did not exist on the land, with verification provided by the missionaries of adjoining mission territory. Mexican law, however, did not require formal recognition of Indian villages; instead, Indians had the right to inhabit and use their land once it was encompassed within rancho boundaries, but title was possessed by the grantee. The Abilas' *diseño* noted the borders formed by the ocean (or *playa*), the prospective *ejido* lands of San Juan (land parcels given to each family or individual), and the boundaries of Rancho San Joaquín. Most of the *sitios* noted on the *diseño* were Juaneño villages, but the map rendered them as simple topographical features, even though Indian villagers used the land for horticulture and raising livestock. After the grant was approved in 1841, and the land surveyed on horseback with a rawhide cord in the presence of a magistrate and neighboring rancheros and *vecinos* of San Juan as witnesses, the Juaneño and Abila herds would mingle on this 13,316 acre rancho only at the discretion of the Abilas. In 1842, the Abilas built a house on the rancho for themselves and their children from their re spective marriages.

By 1843 the boundaries of the large ranchos of El Niguel, San Joa- quín, Mission Viejo, and Trabuco encompassed all the villages and graz- ing sites of the Juaneños (see map 2). The new owners had first become familiar with these lands as administrators of the mission or as members of former administrators' families. They had branded young mission cattle as their own when administering the property and carved out their desired places in the countryside—a countryside they knew to be already inhabited. José Sepúlveda, who had received a grant of mission land in 1837 when his father was administrator of San Juan, was given two more leagues of mission property in 1842. Juan and Concepción Abila, the petitioners for El Niguel, were Sepúlveda's relatives through marriage. Another of Sepúlveda's in-laws, José Serrano, was granted Rancho Cañada de los Alisos in 1842. Santiago Argüello, the fourth administra- tor of the mission properties, who had gone on to act as inspector of the missions and who argued for San Juan's transformation into a pueblo, was granted Rancho Trabuco in 1841. And the administrator Agustín Olvera was granted Rancho Mission Viejo in 1842. The only grant of San Juan's lands that was not made to the family of a former administrator was that of Rancho San Joaquín, which became the pos- session of Tomás Yorba, a son of the colonial grantee of the Rancho Santiago de Santa Ana.

Members of families who had been granted ranchos in the colonial period received a significant number of grants in the Mexican period; the Yorba family story presents a classic picture of one of these wealthy rancheros. In 1836, on the grant of the Rancho Santiago de Santa Ana, two population centers existed comprising seventy-four *gentes de razón* and eighty-one *indios*. The Indians on this rancho planted, cultivated, and harvested the crops in fields and orchards irrigated by channels they had dug; they also worked as *vaqueros* and shepherds and made up the work force for domestic service and production. Their contribution, however, went unacknowledged in the formal census records, which listed only the family groups, full names, and occupational titles (landowners, rancheros, artisans, or servants) of the *de razón* inhabitants.

As was typical, the non-Indian artisans on the Rancho Santiago de Santa Ana were not California-born. Asunción and María Loreto Castro were *plateros,* or silversmiths, who resided with their family; all had been born in Sonora, Mexico. Simian and Dolores Sabaleta were *zapateros,* or shoemakers: Simian had been born in San Luis Potosí, Mexico, and Dolores in San Diego, Alta California. Their youngest child had been born on the rancho itself. Mariano Dominguez was a *comerciante,* or merchant, born in Sinaloa, Mexico. Alvino Cristan was the *cigarrero,* or cigar roller, who, like Simian the *zapatero,* was from San Luis Potosí. Ramón de León was a *sombrerero,* or hatmaker, who had been born in Manila, Philippines. Their presence illustrates the strong connections that existed between California and other areas of the former Spanish empire.[3]

This rancho, which was unusually large and well populated for 1836, represented a highly developed center of rural production. Its existence, moreover, provided an important base from which a local elite managed to expand its land ownership. In 1834, Bernardo Yorba, son of the colonial grantee of the Rancho Santiago de Santa Ana, petitioned for a grant of property adjoining this rancho. He had several children from two marriages, he said, and needed land on account "of the small extent of land which we occupy"—by which he meant the Rancho Santiago de Santa Ana itself.[4] A missionary from Mission San Gabriel argued against Yorba's petition before the town council of Los Angeles. When mission Indians had made their recent rodeo to round up cattle and brand young calves, he said, Bernardo Yorba had ridden in their company, as he, too, had cattle grazing on this land. But Yorba proceeded to separate his cattle from mission cattle, then claimed possession of all the grazing lands—lands that, the priest protested, in fact belonged to the Indians of San Gabriel Mission. The Los Angeles town council, however, ignored the priest's argument. Instead they lauded Yorba as an exemplary citizen and one of the most industrious Californios in business, and declared that he had every right to the property.[5] The council approved the grant, and by 1836 the Rancho Cañon de Santa Ana had a substantial population that included Yorba, his wife, seven of his eventually twenty-two children, seven other Californio rancheros, two non-Indian servants, and eighteen Indian servants.[6]

While the scale of production on Bernardo Yorba's rancho never approximated that of the missions, a portrait of his work force in the early 1850s suggests the range of tasks performed. A large number of workers, for example, were engaged in producing hides and tallow for commercial trade. For domestic consumption and local trade Yorba employed woolcombers, two tanners, one soapmaker, one harness-maker, and one head shepherd; a butter-and-cheese man milked from fifty to sixty cows a day; a cook, a baker, and a winemaker provided for the large household's daily meals. Among the resident artisans were a plasterer, a carpenter, a blacksmith, two shoemakers, one jeweler, one dressmaker, and four seamstresses. The rancho also employed a school-master, two gardeners, two errand boys, and an overseer.[7] Many of the *vaqueros*, shepherds, sheepshearers, and farm laborers were Indians, and their numbers grew at the time of the roundup and slaughter. Itinerant artisans also worked and lived at the rancho while they produced particular goods.

The rancho home, as the center of production, was not a private space, but one where business was transacted, artisans and servants labored, and many workers interacted with members of the immediate and extended family. In the largest households, such as that of Bernardo Yorba, private spaces such as bedrooms opened directly onto the spaces of social life: the central courtyard, the garden, and the reception room. In Yorba's home a family patio, set off from the servants' quarters, contained a private courtyard and reception room that connected to rooms used by the family.[8]

Family members held rancho land through the joint ownership of undivided parcels, as shares-in-common. Heirs to rancho grants could not legally sell or divide the land. Children generally established their own ranchos on the original grant or secured an adjoining claim, as Bernardo Yorba had in 1834. Although the lands of the ranchos were extensive, the multiple sites needed for grazing the proliferating herds and planting the crops of a growing number of heirs eventually strained the limits of even the largest holdings.

The 1845 will of Tomás Yorba underlines this relationship of heir to delimited property held through shares-in-common. On the vast expanse of shared grazing land on the colonial grant of the Yorbas' Rancho Santiago de Santa Ana, Tomás Yorba's brand was fixed to three thousand head of cattle, nine hundred ewes and rams, one hundred mares and stallions, and a good number of burros and mules. His title to these lands, which he passed on to his wife and four children, did not clearly specify which rural lands he claimed; rather, he cited simply a "right to the part which belongs to me as heir of my father, in the lands of Santa Ana en Medio and Santa Ana Abajo," the two ranchos on this grant. In contrast, the property on which he had built structures and cultivated crops is clearly described. He claimed possession of a house in Santa Ana en Medio "of adobe roofed partly with planking, and partly with carrizo reeds, divided in[to] 18 rooms, including the soap factory . . . two vineyards with fences of cribbing, which are covered with staked grape vines in fruit, and some fruit trees, also an extension of land with a stake fence."⁹ Yorba's detailed description of the material used for roofing and fencing suggests his close relationship to the materials of the countryside. Elsewhere in his will he delineates boundaries on the rancho according to the markings of nature: a sycamore tree here, a river there, a rock over there.

Although on a few ranchos goods were produced for a fairly lavish daily diet and diversified trade, most ranchos produced only subsistence goods and traded hides and tallow for particular items, especially cloth. The production of hides and tallow enabled Californios who owned land, or who had access to communal land in the towns, to engage in trade with foreign merchant vessels and with the few ranchero and pueblo merchants. Ships from around the world traded along the California coast. Although high tariffs were imposed on foreign goods to stimulate manufacturing within the territory—and thus produce an income for the territorial government—industry did not develop. In 1835 a single New England merchant house dominated two-thirds of this foreign trade; a description of one of its ship's cargo illustrates the range of manufactured items that were commonly traded by the mid-1830s. This ship, according to Richard Henry Dana, brought "spirits of all kinds (sold by the cask), teas, coffee, sugars, spices, raisins, molasses, hardware, crockeryware, tinware, cutlery, clothing of all kinds, boots and shoes from Lynn, calicoes and cottons from Lowell, crapes, silks;

and, in fact, everything that can be imagined, from Chinese fireworks to English cart wheels."[10]

A striking contrast can be drawn between society in New England and California from this account of merchandise. In New England, the availability of affordable cloth had freed women from the labor of weaving the family's cloth, and industry enabled daughters to take work in the Lowell textile mills. Similarly, technological developments and the output system, in which shoes and boots were sent to farming and fishing villages for task work, had begun to transform rural family economics and ultimately encourage artisans and other villagers to move into factory towns.[11] California, however, was not defined by a market economy in farming or manufacturing; instead, its principal goods of trade were hides, tallow, horns, and skins produced under preindustrial conditions. Dana notes that the same merchant vessel in 1835 carried back to the eastern seaboard forty thousand hides, thirty thousand horns, and several barrels of otter and beaver skins.[12] Dana, a Harvard University student who shipped as a sailor on this vessel, recorded his disdain for Californios because they did not engage in capital ventures. Californios, he argued, "are an idle, thriftless people, and can make nothing for themselves. The country abounds in grapes, yet they buy, at a great price, bad wines made in Boston and brought round by us. . . . Their hides, too, which they value at two dollars in money, . . . buy shoes (like as not made of their own hides, which have been carried twice round Cape Horn) at three and four dollars."[13] Yet the Californios, for their part, saw this situation to be a sensible one given the social ordering of the countryside: if what they had was hides—and in copious quantities at that—why not trade them for the manufactured goods they desired? As an abolitionist, Dana wrote against slavery and the exploitation of sailors and California Indians. Yet perhaps not surprisingly, given his attitudes discussed above, he condemned the Californio regional population for their work culture (as he perceived it), favoring instead the New England family farm and capitalist industrialization. His book *Two Years Before the Mast* was widely read and contributed to the building of derogatory ideas about Californios, whom he presented as men and women, undifferentiated by social class, who did not work but, rather, lived off the labor of Indians.[14]

Significant social distinctions between Californios did indeed exist, however, and are delineated in the types of goods purchased and the various methods of payment recorded at the store of Tomás and Vicenta Yorba, located in the Yorbas' eighteen-room adobe on the Rancho Santiago de Santa Ana. The store's accounts, spanning the period 1841 through 1845, the year of Tomás Yorba's death, were reconstructed by Yorba's brother Bernardo. In this rural world where people made verbal agreements to transact business, Tomás's scribbled notations reflect the close interconnections, characteristic consumption patterns, and varying means of diverse social strata.[15]

Sugar, a delicacy of eighteenth-century Europe, was a product commonly purchased by the wealthy landowners. In contrast, *aguardiente*, a low-quality alcohol, was most often purchased by workers. Although beans and rice were occasionally sold, in general food items were rarely available for purchase, as field and orchard crops and meat provided the bulk of the table fare for both rich and poor. The most frequent purchase, of wealthy landowners and Californio workers alike, was cloth: finer cloth—woollen cloth, printed cotton, embroidered muslin, silk, and linen, plus thread of all qualities, stockings, and silk handkerchiefs— for the wealthy; less expensive varieties of cloth, as well as shoes and pants, for workers. The prices of the more common goods suggest that these were made specifically for the trade in inexpensive ready-made garments, such as the "slave shirts" sent to the American South and the cheap cotton garments that the missionaries bought for Juaneños, Luiseños, and other mission Indians.[16] Landowners had artisans craft their clothing and footwear; in the case of the wealthy, resident seamstresses carried out the task of appareling the family, using only the finest of cloth.

Dress distinguished social position. The care required to maintain fabrics such as velvet and silk emphasized social difference. Many of Tomás Yorba's own clothes, for example, had a higher value than did the relatively modest furnishings and utensils he possessed.[17] Similarly, *rebosos* (shawls) were available in his store at a variety of prices, reflecting a wide range of quality; and they were paid for in a variety of ways, again suggesting a range of attire and wealth among the local population. Vejar, the owner of a small land grant, for instance, bought a *reboso* for 3 pesos' worth of hides, which his servant delivered in exchange for the order. The wealthy landowner Pio Pico, in contrast, bought several *rebosos* that cost anywhere between 18 pesos (six times the price paid by Vejar) and 40 pesos. Pico, moreover, paid for his purchases not in hides, but partly in silver and mostly in lumber.

Workers generally exchanged labor for their purchases of cloth or other goods. One of the store's debtors sent his son to work on the rancho for 3 pesos a month to help pay off his account. During those months pants, shoes, and bolts of white cotton cloth were added to the family's account, for a total debt of 24 pesos, 5 reales. Finally, after the *matanza* (killing), the boy's mother paid off the debt with twelve hides, thus freeing her son from work on the rancho.

Owning cattle enabled *vaqueros* and workers to purchase goods even when they were not landowners, because they at least had hides to trade. However, most workers, who received 8 pesos a month plus some quantity of soap and meat, paid their accounts in labor. The notation "paid by labor as servant" frequently accompanied debts extending from 32 to 164 pesos, amounts that would have taken months or even years to work off; only a few of these workers were Indians. The schoolteacher paid by "teaching children." Artisans paid by practicing their craft or in silver.[18] In this 1840s economy, in short, although the price in pesos was listed, trade and labor were the most usual compensation, rarely silver and gold. Tomás Yorba's accounts indicate a large degree of indebted labor among workers, primarily Californios, whose debts far surpassed a year's wage. They also depict a rural world where exchange took place within a system of acknowledged obligations and debts, and among a population so familiar to Yorba that he recorded them not in a formal ledger, but only on scattered pieces of paper.

The wealthiest rancheros were easily distinguished from the majority of rancheros, who lived near their resident Indian, Californio, and Mexican workers, with itinerant workers producing extra clothing and staples for basic consumption as needed. In most rancho households, Californianas engaged in daily and seasonal work with their mothers, sisters, and other female relatives, as well as one or more Indian women. A few Californios were artisans, and some worked as servants, but the majority worked as either rural laborers or *vaqueros* on ranchos they had no hope of ever owning. In the adobe home shown in figure 2 a large or extended family who worked as *vaqueros,* farm laborers, artisans, seamstresses, and laundresses might well have resided. The size and contents of the home are representative of a majority of California village and rancho households. The trunks and their contents, the clothing, hat, bedding, tables, small shrine, and pictures on the wall were significant possessions in a society where goods were either traded or made by hand.

The importance of land to sustain the modest economies of most Californio families prompted settlers in San Diego to petition the government to open the lands of the Mission San Juan Capistrano to their settlement. Before the pueblo was formed from mission lands, the

Fig. 2. Interior view of an adobe, San Juan Capistrano, ca. 1880. Courtesy Seaver Center for Western History Research, Los Angeles County Museum of Natural History, photo no. GPF7219.

governor asked the one hundred or so Juaneños living there if they favored this transformation. Seventy voted in favor, aiming thereby to free themselves from any further obligation to work at the mission under the administrator. Thirty old men and women opposed the change, possibly because they did not want to live among Californios. The pueblo was formed in 1841 and remained the only California mission that was made into a Mexican pueblo.

Californios and Juaneños received land in the town. Every Juaneño family received a *solar,* or lot for a house, and each of the approximately hundred Juaneño adults received a *suerte,* or land on which to plant.

Fig. 3. Patio of Zeferino Taroje, ca. 1860. Courtesy Seaver Center for Western History Research, Los Angeles County Museum of Natural History, photo no. GPF4894.

They chose these lands in the eastern part of the pueblo. Forty Californios, many of whom were the men who had petitioned to settle there, also received *solares* and *suertes* ranging from 1.8 to 10.8 acres (measured in *varas en cuadro,* a *vara* being a little less than a yard). If the *poblador,* or town dweller, abandoned his or her land, it reverted to the government.[19]

Thus a small population of Californio and Indian subsistence farmers, shepherds, and laborers grew up around the former mission. The home depicted in figure 3, for example, was acquired by Zeferino Taroje, the last Indian cantor at the mission, in the 1841 distribution. It was built by Juaneños in 1794. The patio is closed off from the main street (seen through the patio doorway), an arrangement that enabled women and men to produce household goods outdoors. Goats and chickens could roam free, and corn and other garden produce were cultivated here as one of the multiple activities that provided for family subsistence.[20]

The public lands enabled *pobladores* to engage in diverse subsistence and trade economies. They grazed livestock in public pastures and raised crops in their fields and on pueblo common land. Some raised animals, selling and trading them and their meat as well as goat milk and cheese and sheep's wool. One man raised bees and traded their honey. Another grew tobacco and rolled and sold cigars. Indeed, for the next two decades residents continued to lay claim to such things as "solar calle Trinidad," "solar en la plaza" (house lots on Trinidad street or on the plaza), "mejores en terreno de San Juan" (goods on land in San Juan), "casa, viña, y demas en San Juan" (house, vineyard, and other things in San Juan), and "casa en la jaboneria" (house in the mission soap factory).[21] The material culture of the pueblo continued to be shaped by the buildings of the former mission, which provided multiple living spaces to own and rent, and by the public spaces of the commons and the plaza.

As the town grew its built and social spaces began to reflect the hierarchies of wealth and status that defined Californio society. During the 1850s most of the families who owned the ranchos that had been carved from Acâgchemem and Juaneño land acquired town lots. By then, most of the mission buildings and land had been purchased at public auction by John (Juan) Forster and James McKinly.[22] Forster was an Englishman who had married into the Pico family, an elite clan with significant political power (his wife's father was the last Mexican governor of California) and wealth. Thus Forster, like others who had arrived in California from Europe and the United States during these years, was fully incorporated into Californio society through family, language, and the practices of daily life. But the wealth that these migrants brought to California and generated in the territory enabled them to acquire land and buildings, invest money, and begin to sharply reorganize the economy in the American era.

Territorial Conquest

The American occupation (1846) and subsequent acquisition of the California territory through the Treaty of Guadalupe Hidalgo (1848) produced rapid and dramatic change. Indian peoples throughout California were drawn into the "cycles of conquest" that had been initiated by the Spanish.[23] Indeed, the California Indian population declined by 80 percent during the 1850s.[24] For Californios this conquest brought the rapid implementation of a new logic in law, business, and finance that caused devastating losses of land, property, and place. And while the state constitution (1850) declared Spanish and English to be official languages, and the rights of Mexican citizens were guaranteed by treaty and state law, persons of Mexican descent were in fact viewed according to a spectrum of race perceptions, with Indian and "white" at either extreme. All Mexicans, including those who were integrated into Californio society through marriage, shared these losses, but those who had traveled from elsewhere to work on ranchos and in the pueblos often chose to leave Alta California altogether.

The Treaty of Guadalupe Hidalgo that ended the Mexican-American War embodied two key aspects of U.S. domestic and foreign policy: it deterritorialized Indian peoples even as it recognized the national sovereignty of Latin American nations. The basic protection of Mexican citizens' land rights, whether or not they assumed U.S. citizenship—to which all had a right—was stated in articles 8 and 9 of the treaty: "Property of every kind . . . shall be inviolably respected." Yet article 10, which stated, in part, that "all grants of land made by the Mexican government . . . shall be respected as valid," was stricken by the U.S. Senate, thus leaving the validity of particular grants open to interpretation.[25] Article 11 concerned the Indian peoples, who were granted no land rights whatsoever. This article begins by stating, "A great part of the territories which, by the present treaty, are to be comprehended for the future within the limits of the United States, is now occupied by savage tribes"; it then declares the United States responsible for policing and controlling those tribes, preventing their raids into Mexico and their warring against citizens within the United States. In conclusion, article 11 asserts that in the process of removal of the Indians and settlement of the land by U.S. citizens, "special care shall . . . be taken not to place its Indian occupants under the necessity of searching new homes," the fear being that they might then invade Mexico.[26] The phrase "new homes" implicitly denied their rightful possession of land or claim on ancestral territory. The absence of civil and property rights for "savage tribes" contrasts sharply with the acknowledged rights of "Mexican citizens"; indeed, only the land rights of the hispanicized Pueblo Indians of New Mexico were recognized by the U.S. government. During the occupation of New Mexico and California by U.S. troops in 1846, one method for forging alliances with the territorial populations involved the military's promises to control native populations and to "open" lands for settlement.[27] Later, a committee of the U.S. Senate confirmed the federal government's right to declare indigenous lands public domain and to take possession of them "as the absolute and unqualified owner." "The Indian," the Senate committee argued, "had no usufructuary or other rights therein which were to be in any manner respected."[28]

The policy of denying California Indians recognition of the land they claimed formed part of a larger set of Indian-white relations. When the U.S. army occupied California territory in 1846, the resident Indian peoples became wards of the U.S. government. In 1847 they were required to carry a passport or permission from an employer when they moved about, and they were prohibited from gathering in crowds. The Los Angeles town council required all Indian domestic workers in the city to reside at their workplace and restricted the movement of other Indian workers. Similar surveillance and policing were established in other towns because of the fear that Indian populations in the territory would coordinate a revolt in response to perceived political instability.[29]

In 1850, a team of federal commissioners appointed by the president and authorized by the Senate went to California to negotiate treaties with the Indian peoples that had already suffered devastating losses of lives and land in the gold mining area of northern California.[30] As a result of this effort, eighteen treaties "of friendship and peace" with California "tribes" were drawn up and signed by "chiefs" who relinquished most of the land in the state in return for recognition of Indian title to designated reservation land. Most of the so-called tribes were only village groups, and their "chiefs" were generally village heads. (It will be recalled, in view of the following, that even chiefs did not have the authority to cede tribal or village lands, which were divided into collective and private property.)

The first and second articles of all these treaties are representative of the government's land policy. The treaty signed with "mission Indians," for example, specified that the U.S. government had gained ownership rights to Indian land through the Treaty of Guadalupe Hidalgo. Article 1 of the treaty signed by the Luiseño and other bands in the region of San Juan Capistrano and San Luis Rey began with the following statement: "The several nations above mentioned do acknowledge the United States to be the sole and absolute sovereign of all the soil and territory ceded to them by a treaty of peace made between them and the republic of Mexico." Article 2 further elaborated the position of these "nations of Indians," who by signing the treaties acknowledged themselves to be "under the exclusive jurisdiction, authority, and protection of the United States" and "furthermore [agreed to] bind themselves to conform to and be governed by the laws and regulations of the Indian bureau."[31] The treaties in fact ceded almost the whole of the state, and not even the lands set aside for reservations were acknowledged as rightfully possessed by the various peoples; rather, they were treated as a gift by the U.S. government "to promote the settlement and improvement" of groups referred to variously as "tribes," "bands," and "nations."[32] The United States reserved all rights to minerals found on the land and the right to establish military posts and to build structures and maintain employees such as teachers and farmers on the lands. As in similar treaties of cession, the goods to be given Indians during the first two years of their relocation were also itemized.

The California legislature sent a report to Congress opposing the treaties and recommending the removal of California Indians to the "Indian territory"—that is, the area that would become Oklahoma. Pressure exerted by California's congressional representatives subsequently caused the treaties to be rejected by the Senate. That same year, 1850, the state legislature passed its own "Act for the Government and Protection of the Indians," which instructed local authorities to determine how much land each existing village needed. Then, in 1853, the legislature passed a preemption act, which opened all land whose title was unverified by the land court to settlement as public domain. This act simultaneously sanctioned squatting on Indian lands and on most Spanish and Mexican rancho grants. It also affirmed the federal government's treatment of Indian lands as public domain.

In 1873, twenty years after the passage of this act, a federal Indian agent, John G. Ames, described how the process of preemption had destroyed the integrity of village life and property in the majority of Indian villages in southern California. The common belief among new settlers was that these lands were indeed "public." The residents of the village of San Pasqual thus "complained of the encroachments of their American neighbors upon their land, and pointed to a house near by, built by one . . . who claimed to have pre-empted the land upon which the larger part of the village lies." Ames found that the American had paid the land office registrar for this land and was "daily expecting the patent from Washington." The man, Ames said, "owned [that] it was hard to wrest from these well-disposed and industrious creatures the homes they had built up." Yet he argued, "if I had not done it somebody else would, for all agree that the Indian has no right to public lands." Ames further noted that among the properties included in this man's preemption claim were many with well-cultivated orchards and vineyards.[33]

The federal government rarely recognized the Mexican land grants of the few Indians who held them. In 1851 the federal government required its land commissioners, who were sent to determine the validity of Spanish and Mexican grants under the newly legislated California Land Act (see below), to determine in addition which lands were held, used, and occupied by Indians. The law did not require Indian villagers to present land titles, nor did commissioners have to validate the usufructuary or other rights Indians claimed to rancho lands. The relatively few native peoples who had received legal title to their lands during the Mexican period did sometimes present these claims before the land commission; the vast majority were rejected for lack of sufficient documentation.[34] In San Juan Capistrano, the claims of Indians who had acquired land in the 1841 formation of that pueblo were similarly ignored, despite evidence that the land commission had data substantiating these Juaneños' titles.[35] Indeed, the vast majority of Indian landholdings went unacknowledged by the land commission.

With the breakup or sale of California ranchos, villagers who resided on those lands were often evicted. Moreover, the floods and drought of the early 1860s that dealt the cattle industry its death blow caused a decline in farming and herding among southern California Indians as well. All these pressures encouraged a scattered migration. Meanwhile, squatters, Indian agents, and others acquired Indian land whenever they could. During his travels in 1873, Agent Ames found that in southern California "many Indians are at present living upon [Mexican] grants which have been confirmed by the United States," but he acknowledged that their future on those lands was precarious because of the poor state of most rancho economies. The greater part of the lands claimed in accord with their natural rights, he said, "has been taken up under the pre-emption and homestead laws, so that of the many leagues once set apart for the specific benefit of these Indians, and designed as their perpetual possession, not one now remains to them."[36] He discussed, for example, the village of Santa Ysabel, whose population of 125 was harvesting their fields of grain at the time of his visit. "The land which they occupy is claimed under a (Mexican) grant," but the owners "hesitated to undertake to eject the Indians for fear of violence on their part in resisting, as they [the Indians] dispute any ownership more sacred than their own, and insist that they should not be disturbed in their possession."[37] Villagers from Kúpa, in the mountains to the southeast of San Juan Capistrano, brought suit in the late nineteenth century against Warner, a new settler, to keep themselves from being evicted from their old village (see figure 4). After losing their case in 1901, they were evicted in 1903, but the federal government granted them 3,438 acres on what had become the Pala reservation, primarily inhabited by Luiseño Indians (see map 1).

It was, indeed, the Indians' resistance and concerted efforts to attain legal title to their lands that produced, in 1865, the first reservations in southern California. Established by executive order in two areas, these reservations were intended for all southern California and some northern California Indians. Indian opposition to forced resettlement was naturally great: much of this reserved land was rocky and rugged, adequate for farming only by the four villages already on the land. The executive order was consequently canceled in 1871. The continued deterritorialization of Indian farmers and ranchers and of Indian villages was widely publicized, and in 1875 the president again withdrew a number of small Indian villages from the public domain by executive order. Some lesser-known villages were not included in this order; their continued loss of farming and grazing land remained the object of steady publicity, which finally, in 1891, led to the congressional Act for the Relief of the Mission Indians. Here, at last, was an order that allotted reservations "for each band or village of Mission Indians residing within said State, which reservation shall include, as far as practicable, the lands and villages that have been in the actual occupation and possession of said Indians."[28] The reservation lands set aside under these various laws were owned by Indian bands, whereas lands granted to individual Indians under the Indian Homestead and Public Domain Allotment acts of 1883 and 1887, respectively, were owned by those individuals. The title to the reservation lands, however, is held in trust by the United States through the Bureau of Indian Affairs.

Juaneños were affected by the American occupation and territorial conquest in the following ways (and here I will go over, again, the four decades subsequent to American annexation). By 1860, twelve years into the American period, the first population census of consequence was taken. Indians who lived in San Juan and Santa Ana townships (whose boundaries embraced the ranchos on map 2) and who were enumerated

Fig. 4. Village at Kúpa (Warner Hot Springs), ca. 1895. Courtesy Southwest Museum, Los Angeles, photo no. N34355.

in this census constituted 19 percent of all households. Although they were the third largest group (after Californios and Mexicans), the way information was recorded about them in the census depicts the marks of their colonization: they had Spanish first names and no surnames; the occupations of 38 percent of their household heads went unrecorded; and they owned only 1 percent of the land and 0.6 percent of the assets (including cattle, household items, and silver or gold).[39] Thirty percent of the households were headed by women who still lived in San Juan on the plots of land that had been distributed in 1841. These women worked in the homes of Californios, and did subsistence farming and goods production as they cared for their children and the many elderly Indian people who similarly remained on their land in San Juan. Husbands, fathers, daughters, sons, and other relatives returned to visit these family homes from their places of work on the ranchos and in other pueblos of California. Many Indians lived in the homes of Californios as servants and workers, and sometimes as wives. Seven percent of Californios were married to Indian women, as were 19 percent of

Mexican men. Indian men who lived on the ranchos and headed their own households worked overwhelmingly as laborers. Only 6 percent worked as *vaqueros,* a better job that was primarily held by Californios.

The Indians represented in the census were only a portion of the total Indian population. Unlike Indians who lived in their own villages, the ones counted lived among Californios and Mexicans. Shortly after this census was taken, the entire population began to leave the area for villages to the southeast of San Juan. In 1862, a smallpox epidemic took 129 Juaneño lives in one month alone—and this in a population of only some 227 Indians.[40] Villagers and workers began to be thrown off the ranchos when these were subdivided and sold after 1863. New strains of disease, the loss of village lands on ranchos and in town, and a general brutality toward native peoples caused the majority of remaining Juaneños to reestablish themselves among the Luiseños, with whom they shared linguistic and cultural similarities, family ties, and colonial histories.

Many of the Luiseño villages that accepted Juaneños were mentioned in the first unratified Senate treaties with the eighteen California tribes (see above). The treaty with Luiseños was signed in the village of Temecula and involved representatives of Pala, Pauma, San Luis Rey, La Cañada Verde, and La Puerta de San Felipe.[41] Some of these villagers, but not all, were able to hold on to their land until 1891, and their villages were recognized under the Act for the Relief of the Mission Indians (see map 1). Nevertheless, San Juan remained an important town for Juaneños and other Indians connected to it through their history and family ties, and by the latter part of the nineteenth century individuals and families often moved back and forth between these villages and San Juan for work, residence, family events, and festivals.

In contrast to the policies that led to Indians' deterritorialization, the Treaty of Guadalupe Hidalgo protected Mexican citizens' civil and property rights; but an ambiguity regarding even Mexican citizens' land rights was foreshadowed when article 10 was struck from the treaty, and that ambiguity became quite pronounced in subsequent land laws and litigation. In 1851 the U.S. Congress called the legitimacy of all Spanish and Mexican land grants in California into question by establishing a land court through which all grant owners were required to prove clear title to their land. The California Land Act (1851) went against the spirit of the Treaty of Guadalupe Hidalgo, and a huge number of lawsuits between 1853 and 1890 challenged the right of the United States to conduct such an inquiry. Most of this litigation began with the submission of documents proving title, beginning in 1852, and litigation ended only on receipt of the patent—a process that took an average of seventeen years. In the meantime, California state law enabled squatters to preempt uncultivated land until the titles to grants had been confirmed. When patented, the grantee was obliged to pay squatters for the cost of improvements they had made on the land. These land laws, together with policy that largely dismissed Indian land rights, set in motion in California a process that amounted to legalized territorial conquest. Because litigation necessarily involves lawyers, the California Land Act required a large outlay of cash; for many Californios, the only option was to borrow the money or mortgage property.

One underlying problem for Californios was a contrasting perception of land and land ownership in Mexico and the United States. Under Mexican law, granted land was to be held communally as inalienable property. In American law, however, land was generally considered a commodity to be bought and sold by individuals or partners and to be used to produce capital through rent and improvement. With American law now holding sway, the legal constraints on landowners who held shares-in-common were loosened. Now a sharer could sue for a division of property into individual parcels once the land had been cleared. This allowance facilitated the sale and subdivision of the ranchos.

Another fundamental problem was that in California, wealth and social structure were built on the single industry of cattle production, which created a dependence that also made rancho society vulnerable. The profits derived from cattle increased substantially during the early 1850s, when animals not used for hides were herded north and slaughtered for their meat; hence in 1860, despite the pressure exerted by land litigation, the economy and society were still oriented around this business. Most of the land (61 percent) in San Juan and Santa Ana townships was owned by Californios, and because of cattle, Californios also possessed 72 percent of the wealth.[42] Most of this property was concentrated among the few landowning families. Rancheros and farmers (who also had cattle, but whose non-market-oriented farming was more extensive than that of "rancheros") in fact represented just over a quarter of the Californio heads of household, yet they owned half the land and slightly over half the assets possessed by Californios as a whole. The six rancheros, representing 9 percent of the Californio heads of household, possessed the most extensive land holdings and wealth. (See appendix 1.)

The land monopoly that promoted the growth of the cattle industry was made possible by territorial politics, through which Californios placed themselves in charge of the former mission lands; this same land politics also enabled the vast majority of Californios to own more land and goods than either Indians or Mexicans. One-fourth of all Californio heads of household worked as *vaqueros*, as did many of the male family members of these households. In contrast to Indian and Mexican *vaqueros*, who were virtually landless, most of the Californio *vaqueros* who headed households owned some land. Similarly, 44 percent of Californio heads of household worked as laborers; they rarely owned land, though most of them had some assets such as livestock, silver, or valuable household items. This property again distinguished them from Indians and Mexicans, who, though similarly employed as common laborers, were virtually propertyless.

On the one hand, Californios shaped an economy and society that indeed benefited the majority of the regional non-Indian population; on the other hand, the profit they invested in the cattle industry represented fixed wealth, which would systematically undermine the structure of their prosperity. Whereas Californios who had sunk their all into cattle were entirely dependent on that industry, the migrant population favored regenerative wealth. By bringing land into the market economy, which enabled individuals to profit from its escalation in value, and by investing in a variety of ventures oriented to a national market (which in turn raised land values), they rapidly established an economy over which they had dominion. They maintained their authority by enacting the laws necessary to protect that economy and propel it forward.

The sharp differences between the forms of wealth that Californios and new migrants possessed could already be anticipated from a look at the first wave of European settlers to this area, a group of stockholders in a German vineyard society. They found the locale after Juan Pacífico Ontiveros hired George Hansen, the deputy surveyor for Los Angeles County, to survey his Rancho San Juan Cajón de Santa Ana for the land commission in the late 1850s. Hansen bought a relatively small portion of the 35,970-acre rancho for the stockholders, having been commissioned by them to find good property. In 1859 they arrived by steamer to the site named Anaheim, encircled by a stockade of willow cuttings.[43] By 1860 these settlers from the German principalities, Poland, and Russia constituted 14 percent of the area's household heads, but, because there were so many men and childless couples, their households (which did include Californio, Indian, and Mexican workers) made up only 10 percent of the local population.

Although they were less than a tenth of the population, the new migrants owned 25 percent of the land and 12 percent of the assets. Their land was distributed fairly evenly among them, and most possessed at least some capital. Their occupational profile also provides some idea of the changes they would initiate locally. Twelve percent of the newcomers worked in urban and professional jobs that were virtually unknown in rancho society, and three occupational groups owned 82 percent of the total property: businessmen, farmers, and artisans (all of whom also employed farm laborers). Only 3 percent worked as rancheros, 7 percent as *vaqueros,* and 7 percent as laborers—in sharp contrast to the pattern among Californios, Mexicans, and Indians. Two of these laborers, moreover, owned more property than the average amount possessed by farmers in Anaheim. Thus, not only did their jobs reflect occupations uncommon in this area during the Mexican period, but their activities were imbued with a different social meaning because, unlike Californios, Mexicans, and Indians, almost all of these immigrants, no matter what their occupations, had capital to invest.

Their ability to invest in land and other economic ventures contrasted sharply to the situation of most Californios, the majority of whom lost their ranchos during the 1860s (see table 2). The final blow to already-strained assets was dealt when the majority of their cattle died between 1861 and 1864, years of drought and flood.[44] Many were ruined by the unregulated and high interest rates that fed off an economy that was cash poor. The new migrants, with their regenerative wealth (money to loan and to invest in land, farming, livestock, and other capital ventures), gained substantially during this decade.[45]

By 1870 European immigrants possessed 51 percent of the land value and 47 percent of the assets;[46] Anglo-Americans were right behind them, with 36 and 39 percent, respectively. Together, then, these two groups, which constituted just over half the population, were in control of some seven-eighths of local wealth. The dramatic rise in land values between 1860 and 1870 emphasizes the triumph of the new economy: by 1870 land was valued at $591,000, up from the 1860 value of $172,000—a comparatively low figure reflecting the period before land was brought into the market as a source of capital gain. The physical reorganization of the countryside mirrors these vast changes. In contrast to the rural rancho society of 1860, by 1870 the countryside had three American towns and hundreds of American farms.

It is worthwhile to trace specific losses of ranchos by families and dates. The owners of rancho lands had submitted their documents to prove their titles in 1852 and generally had to wait another four to six

Table 2. *Wealth in Land and Assets by Group, Santa Ana and San Juan, 1860 and 1870*

		No. of Heads of Household	Land (% of total)	Assets (% of total)
Californio	1860	73	62	72
	1870	92	11	9
Mexican	1860	101	6	10
	1870	102	1	4
Indian	1860	53	1	1
	1870	2	0	0
European	1860	41	25	12
	1870	147	51	47
Anglo-American	1860	5	6	4
	1870	175	36	39
Other	1860	13	0	1
	1870	20	1	1

SOURCE: Federal Manuscript Censuses, 1860 and 1870, Santa Ana and San Juan Capistrano townships.

years for confirmation. Their cases proceeded through the land board to the district court and were often appealed by the attorney general's office. Although the appeal was usually rejected before the case made it to the U.S. Supreme Court, land court decisions favorable to Spanish or Mexican grantees were often contested numerous times even after the patents were granted. Most landowners in San Juan and Santa Ana townships received formal approval of their grants around 1858. The first patent for land, however, was not issued until 1866, while the last was issued in 1883. Hence, legal expenses, falling prices for cattle after 1857, and severe floods and drought between 1861 and 1864 caused the swift sale and subdivision of the ranchos. The 1857 sale of land to the German Vineyard Society, for instance, was a direct result of the burden of litigation experienced by Juan Pacífico Ontiveros. Then in 1860, Teodosio Yorba and Inocencia Reyes de Yorba sold their rancho, Lomas de Santiago, to a German colonist for $7,000.[47] They placed their cattle on the Yorba family's Rancho Santiago de Santa Ana, but by 1863 the drought had reduced their once-vast herd to forty-three head. Yorba died a relatively poor man in Anaheim.[48] José Sepúlveda, owner of the Rancho San Joaquín, had gotten into enormous debt after 1855, but for nine years he was always able to pay back his loans and the high rates of interest. Finally, at the height of the great drought in 1864, he, too, was forced to sell his rancho; the purchasers were James Irvine and his partner, who began to raise sheep and, later, to open some of these lands to tenant farmers. They also purchased Lomas de Santiago.[49]

Parcels of Rancho Santiago de Santa Ana had been sold as shares-in-common to numerous Americans and Europeans or transferred as payment to lawyers by the many heirs of this colonial grant during the drought. Although new owners were legally considered successors to the original owners until the land was patented, as successors they were able to appeal for the right to divide the property. In 1868, nineteen of the wealthiest heirs and American successors petitioned for permission to divide the rancho, whose aggregate boundaries stretched 54.23 miles and enclosed an area of 78,941 acres. The largest parcels of the newly subdivided rancho were allotted to the legal representatives of three Californio defendants.[50] Such transfer of land to American lawyers in payment for their services in land cases enabled many lawyers and law firms to act as land speculators and town developers. In 1869, William Spurgeon, an American merchant, purchased property from Zenobia Yorba de Rowland, Ysidora Vejar de Rodriguez, and Rafael Gradios in order to establish a town; he immediately plotted twenty-four city blocks.[51]

The Meaning of Ethnicity in the American Countryside

The towns of Santa Ana, Orange, and Tustin were founded between 1869 and 1873 on land that had been part of the vast Rancho Santiago de Santa Ana. By 1880, Orange had approximately 200 households (as did Anaheim by then), Santa Ana had 174 households, and Tustin (like San Juan) had 50 households. Anglo-Americans had become the majority of the population by the mid-1870s, and these towns in which they resided were characterized by a marked lack of ethnic diversity. The vast majority of them had been born in one of the six states from which a large number of land-hungry farmers had migrated—New York, Missouri, Kentucky, Illinois, Pennsylvania, and Ohio. In addition, they were overwhelmingly of American ancestry for at least one generation back: 96 percent of the Anglo-American heads of household in 1870 had parents born in the United States, 94 percent in 1880. In 1870, moreover, over half of these households had no woman present; that proportion declined to one-fifth by 1880, a year in which 97 percent of the married heads of household had an Anglo-American wife. In both 1870 and 1880, these households contained very few persons who were not Anglo-American (18 percent and 15 percent, respectively)—in contrast to households headed by European immigrants, which, through 1880 at least, tended to be ethnically and nationally more diverse. Anglo-American households also had significantly more family members who worked for a living and fewer nonfamily members within their homes than did European immigrants. Anglo-American family farms and businesses were usually operated by immediate and extended family who had migrated together or in succession, and they tended to employ other Anglo-American workers, though as the relative proportion of these workers declined, Anglo-American farmers hired Californio and Mexican laborers.

Farmers represented the single largest occupational group in the areas where Americans predominated. Fifty-five percent of Anglo-Americans and 38 percent of European immigrants farmed in 1880, introducing specialized crops and market-oriented production. Another 20 percent of both groups worked in jobs not performed in Californio society, such as small service-oriented businesses, professional occupations (such as medicine, dentistry, law, and teaching), and transportation. In sharp contrast, only 3 percent of Californios and 2 percent of Mexicans in 1880 worked in jobs that did not appear in the 1860 census. Included here were cooks and servants, who had been listed in their employers' households in 1860 but had often taken up separate residence by 1880.

Californios and Mexicans, in other words, had a different job structure in their communities relative to Europeans and Anglo-Americans (table 3). In 1880 almost half of the Californios and an overwhelming majority of the Mexicans (70 percent) worked as laborers, as compared to only 5 percent of the Anglo-Americans and 7 percent of the European immigrants. Many of the Anglo-Americans preferred to work as poor dirt and share farmers rather than as laborers, a leaning also present among Californios, who constituted one-third of the homesteaders in San Juan in 1875.[52]

Employment preferences reveal only part of the meaning of these occupations, however. Workers in each group continued to live in communities where they shared linguistic, cultural, and historical affinities with their neighbors, for and with whom they worked. In the American towns, skilled laborers worked primarily out of their home workshops

Table 3. *Employment of Heads of Household by Selected Occupation and Group, Santa Ana and San Juan, 1860–1880 (% of total)*

	Californio			Mexican			European			Anglo-American		
	1860 (N=73)	1870 (N=92)	1880 (N=97)	1860 (N=101)	1870 (N=102)	1880 (N=68)	1860 (N=41)	1870 (N=147)	1880 (N=90)	1860 (N=5)	1870 (N=175)	1880 (N=214)
Artisan	1	4	2	12	7	10	29	12	10	20	15	7
Businessman	—	1	3	4	4	—	17	9	10	—	4	3
Farmer	18	18	17	1	11	7	25	35	38	20	47	55
Laborer	46	41	48	71	63	70	7	18	7	60	13	5
Rancher	9	8	6	—	—	1	3	2	6	—	5	2
Vaquero/Shepherd	25	3	7	10	4	3	7	10	6	—	5	—
Housekeeper	—	23	8	—	9	7	—	2	3	3	3	—
Launderer	—	—	6	1	—	—	—	—	—	—	—	—
Other	1	1	3	1	2	2	12	12	20	—	8	20

SOURCE: Federal Manuscript Censuses, 1860, 1870, and 1880.

with the aid of their families and a few employees. Professional seam-stresses, or a wife or daughter, generally made the family clothing, while the milliner (an occupation for women in the American towns) and the harnessmaker were kept busy by the small circle of town residents. Al-though one man declared himself a real estate agent in Santa Ana in 1880, generally land and investment matters were overseen by the suc-cessful merchant.

Work in these towns was still defined in relationship to rural pro-duction. Plots containing crops for family subsistence were scattered throughout town, and gardens and orchards supplemented most family incomes. Small markets, shops, seasonal work, and artisanal work out of the home defined what remained a primarily rural society. Although the Southern Pacific railroad reached all of the American towns and Anaheim sometime between 1876 and 1878 and connected them to Los Angeles, and a streetcar system built in the late 1870s joined the Amer-ican towns and Anaheim, in that decade most passengers and mail still went by stagecoach. San Juan, meanwhile, remained disconnected from the growing urban network of transportation.

In that village, Californios, Indians, and a few Mexicans constituted 86 percent of the village population of 113 households in 1880. The vast majority of the town lots were owned by families who had been granted pueblo lands or ranchos in the vicinity of the mission upon its trans-formation into a pueblo in 1841. The Catholic Church had reclaimed the mission proper in a land case, with Abraham Lincoln signing the property over to the church in 1864. Once the land was patented, the Church resumed proprietorship over the mission buildings, orchards, and fields. The pueblo population was concentrated around the mission and plaza, where merchants of different ethnic and regional back-grounds sold in bulk, lent money, and sometimes purchased the prod-ucts of farmers. Rancheros, who had built houses in the center of the pueblo during prosperous years, often remained in the village after they lost their rural land. At some distance from the mission were larger lots, farmed by families who had expanded cultivation from the original seven to eleven acres they had been granted in 1841. These town lands generally were held as shares-in-common by family members through the late nineteenth century.

While Anglo-Americans and European immigrants constituted the majority of the population in the countryside surrounding San Juan village by 1880, Californios persisted there longer as rancheros who re-tained at least portions of a rancho to farm, and many became homesteaders in the mid-1870s. The three ranchos, El Niguel, Cañada de los Alisos, and Boca de la Playa, remained in the possession of the original Californio ranchero families through the 1860s. Abila sold parts of El Niguel to a Californio creditor, but in turn he purchased a share of Boca de la Playa, which subsequently became the possession of his daughter and her German-American husband from Anaheim. Cañada de los Alisos remained in the Serrano family's holdings. Sometime in the mid-1870s El Niguel, Boca de la Playa, and Cañada de los Alisos were sold; most of the heirs to these ranchos, however, retained property in the town or township into the twentieth century. The new owners of these former ranchos kept most of the land they purchased, or were granted in homesteads, in relatively large parcels, raising sheep and farming, often with tenants. Over the years the homestead lands and town lots of poorer farmers passed into these men's hands, aggrandizing their holdings as the century drew to a close.

These large parcels meant that most land was not subdivided for individual farms and towns; hence, in the countryside and village of San Juan the population rose only slightly between 1860 and 1880, from 113 households to 185, almost half of which were located in the village proper. Only a few Anglo-Americans and European immigrants had settled in San Juan village, though they gained successively more village land as they bought it up or received it in payment for credit. These groups were more numerous in the sparsely settled township of San Juan, constituting three-fourths of that population by 1880. In those communities where Californios lived, the persistence of a significant number of laborers, and the almost constant proportion of rancheros, represented a continuity from an era when the accumulation of property by a few Californios had fostered a growing population of Californio and Mexican laborers within rancho society. This persistence is extremely important because it took place within a site-specific context. In the townships of San Juan and Orange, Californio and Mexican workers continued to engage in supplementary subsistence production of field and orchard crops, and they worked for Californio farmers and ranchers, with payment in traded goods and wages.

Nonetheless, the decline of the cattle industry and the sharp drop in work for *vaqueros*—the occupation of 25 percent of Californios and 10 percent of Mexicans in 1860—suggests the vast changes in rural society that occurred with the sale of the ranchos. Remember that Californio *vaqueros* commonly owned some land, and many expected to inherit more land upon the death of their parents. They also had a better social position than laborers because they had greater access to the skills required to work with cattle, which, in turn, provided them with greater access to the trade in hides. It was among the *vaqueros* and rancheros that the cumulative effects of rural change were most immediately apparent. Many *vaqueros* became laborers, while others continued in seasonal work as, for example, itinerant *vaqueros* and sheepshearers.

By 1880 most Californios lived in San Juan village, but two small communities of Californios persisted elsewhere: in the countryside to the northeast of the town of Orange (where some members of the Yorba and Peralta families still lived, farming and growing livestock, and ultimately founding the town of Yorba) and in Anaheim. Their households were organized according to certain characteristics that remained relatively constant between 1860 and 1880: most Californios were married to Californianas;[53] and apart from Indians, who resided in 40 percent of Californio households in 1860, most of the household members were also Californios and Californianas. Hence, while 41 percent of Californio households had persons from other ethnic or regional backgrounds in 1860, when Indians were present, that number dropped to 13 percent in 1870, then rose slightly, to 19 percent, by 1880. (See appendix 3.) Californio households were always larger than other households because of the presence of extended family, servants, cooks, farm laborers, and *vaqueros*. The households of workers also had many family members and other workers in residence. When Indians left the area during the 1860s, the average size of Californio households declined, but they still remained larger than the households of other regional and ethnic groups. (See appendix 3.)

These patterns of large households and intermarriage between Californios emerged from a regional history in which members of local *de razón* families commonly moved for work between presidios, pueblos, and missions, while in the Mexican period individuals, and sometimes whole branches of families, moved to the countryside. These people, moreover, established close relationships with blood kin and nonrelatives alike through a *compadrazgo* system of obligation and mutual respect. The world of Californios was, in other words, closely interconnected, even across significant geographic distances.

The Californianas who married Mexicans, Indians, European immigrants, and Anglo-Americans brought their husbands into this close world of family and fictive kin, across the full range of social class and status group (see figure 5). While Californio men tended to marry Californianas, the latter were more likely to marry outside their regional

Fig. 5. The children born to twice-married and twice-widowed Vicenta
Sepúlveda Yorba de Carrillo. In the top row (left to right): Chloromiro
Carrillo, Juan Yorba, Ramón Carrillo, José Antonio Yorba, and Garibaldo
Carrillo; in the second row, María Ygnacio Carrillo Harris, Chapita Yorba
Smythe, Vicenta Sepúlveda Yorba de Carrillo, Ramona Yorba, and Edelfrida
Carrillo Alvarado; seated, Encarnación Carrillo Richards, Natalia Carrillo
Rimbau, and Felicidad Carrillo Kirby. Five of Vicenta's seven daughters
married newcomers to this region. Courtesy Bancroft Library, University of
California, Berkeley.

group. This only made sense: men migrated in higher numbers and
were often single. In 1860, 46 percent of Mexican men were married to
Californianas and Indian women. Twenty percent of European men
were married to Californianas; 8 percent were married to Mexican
women and 4 percent to Indian women. Ten years later, the proportion
of European immigrants married to Californianas had dropped to 9
percent. By 1880, the balance had again shifted: now a mere 7 percent
of European men were married to Californianas, while 34 percent had
Anglo-American wives and were clearly forging closer ties with the now
majority Anglo-American population.

By 1880 Californianas were again primarily marrying Californios and
Mexicans, but the integration of newcomers into Californio regional

society, including Mexican spouses and their relatives, is reflected in the parentage of Californios and Californianas. Whereas in 1860, before significant migration, 88 percent of their fathers and 90 percent of their mothers were Californios and Californianas, respectively, by 1900 those numbers had dropped to 64 percent and 76 percent. By 1910, the proportions had fallen still further, to 52 percent and 65 percent, respectively.[54] Here it should be noted that in San Juan, where a smaller population of Mexicans settled because of the large Indian population in the pueblo and villages, Californio parentage remained significantly higher through 1910 than among Californios and Mexicans who resided elsewhere in Orange County. Most of the parents who were not Californios were Mexican; however, before the 1870s, Californianas, Indian women, and Mexicanas had formed unions with European immigrants and Anglo-Americans. The resulting households were incorporated into California society and often remained in the vicinity of San Juan and Anaheim, towns characterized by a far greater diversity of regional origins and ethnicities than were the American towns.

Two factors in particular distinguished households headed by European immigrants from those of Anglo-Americans and other groups: although they were on average smaller than Californio and Mexican households, they had significantly more workers residing within them, and they continued to include many Californios and Mexicans. These households existed principally in Anaheim and San Juan; in 1880, Californios and Mexicans made up over 15 percent of Anaheim's population, and 86 percent of San Juan's. In the mid-1870s, in fact, Anaheim was described by Helena Modjeska, a Polish immigrant, as "inhabited mostly by German colonists and Spaniards."[55] Both San Juan and Anaheim remained more ethnically diverse than the American towns, though by 1880 Anaheim was connected to them by transport, economics, and marriage ties.

In these new towns, various processes of community-building were at work for each group. Californios and Mexicans, of course, participated jointly in the culture of Greater Mexico. They had a common language, common traditions, and common beliefs, as well as shared work and related social practices. The Europeans and Anglo-Americans shared ideas and cultural norms related to capital, investment, and work; they introduced sociocultural practices related to economic behavior that increasingly defined the town and countryside. By 1870, they represented slightly more than half of the total population; by 1880, Anglo-Americans had become the majority.

By 1880, then, the social geography of the countryside surrounding San Juan was defined by the predominance of particular regional and ethnic groups. Anglo-Americans constituted the largest sector of rural and urban society, exerting economic and political sway because of the capitalist transformation of the countryside. Their presence, however, did not subordinate either San Juan or the rural communities of Californios to a singular Anglo-American culture. The existence of some landownership among Californios, and the initial interaction between Europeans, Californios, Mexicans, and Indians, sustained an ethnic heterogeneity within this area, even as American towns and farms rose to dominance. European immigrants tended to live fairly close together. Likewise, Californios and Mexicans resided near one another in communities shaped by the social ties forged, and in some places built, during the Spanish and Mexican periods. The relatively few Chinese and Latin American immigrants lived primarily in the towns of San Juan and Anaheim, both of which were more ethnically diverse than the American towns of Santa Ana, Orange, and Tustin. While the English language predominated in the American towns, Spanish was the main language in San Juan, and German and Spanish were far more common than English in Anaheim.[56]

Ethnic communities, including Anglo-Americans, were extremely important in shaping the new rural landscape. Mexicans from California and elsewhere, Indians, Europeans, and Anglo-American migrants represented distinct and often contending sectors of society within this still strongly "frontier" area. Their competing voices, cultural practices, and perspectives were rooted in the physical landscape. Nevertheless, territorial conquest effectively removed most of the Indian populations from this countryside; they moved to villages distant from the areas of settlement, and sometimes resettled in San Juan after 1880. Californios persisted, but they lived in ever smaller, more precisely defined areas of the countryside and in San Juan. San Juan was rather different from other California pueblos in that its population was not overwhelmed numerically by an Anglo-American migration, as were Santa Barbara, Los Angeles, and San Diego by 1880 or 1890, when barrios formed in the old urban cores of these pueblos and city space became increasingly dominated by American planning ideals.[57] San Juan's history is more like that of towns somewhat removed from the center of American society; its built space of public land and older houses and buildings provided a stable place for many families of workers and former Californio landowners. But the town's lasting connections to outlying Indian villages was, perhaps, more typical of other former Mexican pueblos in California than historians have heretofore imagined.

Gendered Stories of Conquest

Land is not considered private property until the title to it is confirmed and patented. As the proceedings to obtain a patent might consume years, almost a life time, the result is that the native Californians [of Spanish descent] who were the land owners when we took California, are virtually despoiled of their lands and their cattle and horses . . . there is no denying that our laws are doing all that can be done to drive them into squalid hovels, and thence into the penitentiaries or the poor houses. (María Amparo Ruiz Burton, 1885)

Así es que después de haber trabajado tantos años, de haber poseído bienes, de que no me desposeí por venta ni de otro modo, me encuentro en la mayor pobreza, viviendo del favor de Dios y de los que me dan un bocado de comer.

So it is that after having worked for so many years, after having had possessions which I did not relinquish through sale or otherwise, I find myself in the greatest poverty, living by the favor of God and from handouts. (Doña Apolinaria Lorenzano, 1878)

In these passages two women describe the results of the U.S. territorial conquest that wholly reshaped California and the larger Southwest between 1848 and 1880. The first passage is drawn from the novel *The Squatter and the Don,* written by María Amparo Ruiz Burton, under the pen name of C. Loyal, to protest the new land laws and the invasion of squatters that brought most rancheros to financial ruin by 1870.[58] Ruiz Burton's aim was to generate sympathy for the Californio land-owning elite, whom she represents as misunderstood class allies of the Anglo-American national elite. In the passage quoted, we hear the voice of an American who is appealing to President Ulysses S. Grant to intervene in a land case involving title to a Mexican grant, the possession of which is being contested by a Californio family, the Alamars, and a group of American squatters. Ruiz Burton argues that the Californios' loss of land and subsequent impoverishment were brought on by Congress when it passed the California Land Act of 1851, which required every holder of a Spanish or Mexican grant to prove title to it in an American land court established for this purpose. She provides an astute analysis of the land politics of territorial conquest that is quite similar to the one I presented earlier. She argues, for example, that the plight of Californio rancheros was aggravated by state laws that enabled settler-farmers to preempt land while the title was being confirmed. For Ruiz Burton, this process of dispossession was made all the more disagreeable by the squatters themselves, who disdained the Californio elite as "greasers" and greedily seized their land and killed their cattle.[59] Her analysis of the squatters' race prejudices against Californios forms an important part of her critique of territorial conquest. This melodramatic novel was a document of its period: it sharply criticizes the corruption in government, especially the alliances forged between railroad interests and elected officials, that unfavorably affected particular elite and popular sectors alike.

Ruiz Burton's family history reveals the extent of the ruptures caused by territorial conquest and the capitalist transformation of the countryside. Ruiz Burton's grandfather and great-uncle participated in the colonization effort in northern Mexico and the California peninsula in the late eighteenth century. Her grandfather, a lieutenant in the Spanish army, later served as governor of Baja California in the early Mexican period (1822–1825); her great-uncle commanded the presidio of San Diego. Both received land grants (1804 and 1823, respectively) for their service in the army. Her family extended over the geographic area of both Lower and Upper California. They lived in the social world of the military elite, the milieu from which most politically and economically prominent Californios emerged.

Ruiz Burton herself was born in 1833 in Baja California and educated by a private woman tutor from Spain. Her training and her position in a social hierarchy based on racial status and landownership undergirded her portrayal of a Californio identity. In 1848 she traveled on an American ship to Monterey, Alta California, with her mother, brother, and other families. Married the next year to a Lieutenant Burton from the invading American army, she settled in San Diego in 1852 when her husband was transferred to the American military garrison there. In 1854 they began to homestead on Rancho Jamul, land they acquired after it was returned to the public domain when the title of its original owner was rejected by the American land court.[60] In 1859, Burton was transferred to the eastern seaboard; leaving her mother and brother on the rancho, María Amparo moved with her husband to Washington, D.C., and then from post to post during the Civil War. She socialized with President Lincoln and others from the American political and social elites.[61] Burton died in 1869, whereupon María Amparo Ruiz returned to her rancho in San Diego to administer her property. She ran cattle, which she fed on castor leaves that were resistant to drought; the castor beans she sold to a paint company. She also built irrigation channels, grew wheat and barley on the slopes of her rancho with the help of tenant farmers, rented the hillsides out for beehives, and used the lime produced on her land for the Jamul Portland Cement Manufacturing Company, which she formed with her son in 1869. She also managed land and warehouses that she owned in Ensenada, Baja California.

Ruiz Burton's legal battles to retain her lands in the United States and Mexico, which began in the 1860s, illustrate how the internationalization of capital affected land ownership and tenure patterns in the Southwest and Mexico in the late nineteenth century. In 1871 she won her claim to the Rancho Ensenada de Todos Santos from the Mexican courts, but Mexico's 1883 Law of Colonization later enabled part of this rancho to be claimed by the international land developing firm of George Sisson and Luis Huller. She continued to fight, however, and finally won claim to most of that land, only to see her title reversed in 1889 by the Supreme Court of Mexico. Meanwhile, on the north side of the international border, she received a patent to Rancho Jamul in 1876, but subsequently lost almost all of this rancho land to 160 squatters and creditors who filed against her estate during the 1880s. Throughout these years she was involved in land litigation in local and state courts as well as in the U.S. Supreme Court and the highest courts in Mexico. She traveled to Washington, D.C., to lobby Congress in defense of the land claims of Californios generally. Her novel was an attempt to present her case to a wider public in the name of all Californio landowners. She wrote it while living in a small, rented house in San Diego; she died in 1895, ten years after its publication, virtually propertyless.[62]

The land politics that Ruiz Burton presents in the novel are described solely from the point of view of the Californio elite. The idea, much less the defense, of Indian land rights was as little a part of her story as it was of the Treaty of Guadalupe Hidalgo, which ceded Mexico's northern territory to the United States in 1848. Ruiz Burton portrays the Californio elite's high status largely through the vehicle of the Alamar women. In so doing, she demonstrates an astute understanding of the dynamics that constitute "class" both as a subjective, assumable social identity and as an objective relationship. All of the elite women in her novel, Californios and Americans alike, have strong and "reasoned" voices; all these women recognize in their regional and national counterparts a female comportment that follows class norms. The Alamar women have carefully manicured manners, behavior, and appearances; the daughters are virtuous and obedient, and they are highly protected by male family members. Their class position is indicated in the retort of one American woman to a squatter's derogatory remarks about the Alamars: "Inferior? It is enough to see one of those Alamar ladies to learn that they are inferior to nobody."[63]

The Californio and American elites did intermarry, as Ruiz Burton's story illustrates, but unlike most Californianas, including Ruiz Burton herself, the fictional Alamar women do not work or engage in other economic activity. Rather, they maintain the family's elite status through their "pride," even when most of their land and cattle are lost. The novel's male characters, by contrast, whose status is closely tied to their economic behavior, either become emotionally paralyzed or commit suicide once they must work as farmers and day laborers.

Ruiz Burton also uses oversimplified racial categories to define the Californios' elite standing. She refers to the Alamars and other Californios as "Spanish people," "native Californians of Spanish descent," and "Spano Americans," collective identities that overlook the complex social and racial ordering of the California society in which she grew up.[64] The only nonelites of Californio society in her story, in fact, are male Indian workers: Mexicans and Indian women simply do not figure in. In this manner she eliminated the possibility that Californios were a racially mixed people.

Apolinaria Lorenzano was the unmarried owner of three ranchos, two of them granted her by the governor of California as a result of her long decades of work at the San Diego Mission; the third she purchased.[65] She had a house and stock on one of the ranchos, but spent little time there, relying instead on a Californio mayordomo to administer the property. Thomas Savage's preface to Lorenzano's memoir, which she dictated to him in 1878, suggests how she fit within this closely woven regional society. People, he writes, "spoke of her in the highest terms of praise. She was known by many [in San Diego] as Apolinaria *la cuna* [the foundling], and by most as *La Beata* [the pious]." Savage notes that Lorenzano was "cheerful and resigned to her fate"; in her old age, blind and dependent on the charity of the county and friends, she was "loath to speak" of the loss of her land. She said she "didn't want even to think of it."[66]

Lorenzano played a central role in the life of the presidio and mission at San Diego. She was orphaned in San Diego after her mother died in Mexico. She worked from an early age, teaching in a small school established by a widow, where *de razón* girls learned to read, pray, and sew. She was a nurse, matron, and teacher of sewing and reading at the mission, and she earned money during her entire adult life by doing sewing and embroidery.[67] Shortly after the American invasion in 1846, Lorenzano went to live in San Juan Capistrano and then Santa Barbara, leaving the care of her properties to Juan Forster, who in turn placed them under the care of a mayordomo. Unlike many unmarried women and widows, she never assumed direct administration of her lands. She spoke merely of having her *terrenos* (lands) blessed upon receiving them, and of naming each property for a saint. She apparently lost her land in the late 1850s; she lamented the loss, but declined to tell her "long story" of how it had happened.[68]

The lives of Ruiz Burton and Lorenzano illustrate the social differences among Californio landowners and the potential meaning of those differences in the American period. Ruiz Burton was from a colonial military elite family and married an American in 1849. She continued to accumulate land in the early American period, modernized the production of cattle and other procedures on her ranchos in the 1860s, and fought vigorously and tirelessly against the laws and persons that threatened her properties. Lorenzano, in contrast, represents the relatively poor landowners of the colonial and Mexican periods who worked with their hands or labored for others. Unlike the vast majority of rancheros, rich and poor, she did not reside on her rancho. (Residence was a provision for keeping grants under Mexican law, and her absence from her land may be one reason for her ultimate dispossession.) But like some members of almost every Californio family, regardless of their social standing, she lived her life in presidio-pueblos and mission-pueblos; and like many Californios in the social upheaval after 1848, she moved about—from San Diego to San Juan Capistrano, and later to Santa Barbara, from where she told her story.

These two stories represent more than just tales of personal loss; they introduce the effects of conquest on women landowners and the multiple ways Californianas defended their land by acting on a long tradition of women exercising their property rights. I want now briefly to examine that tradition because it informed the entire process of territorial conquest. Women's sense of entitlement rested, in part, on the fact that Spanish and Mexican law gave them the right to control their property and wealth and to litigate on questions related to their person, their families, and their holdings. Daughters had the right to inherit property equally with male siblings; upon marriage, women retained as their own the property they brought into the arrangement, and if they were widowed they inherited half the property and wealth accumulated during the marriage. Adult women could conduct their own legal affairs, write their own wills without the consent of their husbands, serve as attorneys for elderly relatives, be guardians of their children and grandchildren after the death of their spouses, and adopt children with government permission. As Sylvia Arrom notes, women had acknowledged roles in the public sphere; they "were neither confined to the domestic sphere nor defined exclusively as wives and mothers."[69] Women were engaged in various levels of work and commerce, in positions ranging from landowner to servant. Across the social spectrum, their rights to land and compensation for their labor were most fully exercised by unmarried and widowed women, though some married women with property managed it apart from that which they owned jointly with their husbands.

Californianas negotiated their positions from within a complicated gender order and on distinctive grounds relative to Indian women. Spanish and Mexican law had two categories for women: "decent" women—virgins, nuns, "honest" wives, and widows; and "vile" women whose sexual conduct placed them outside the protection of law when it came to defending their rights against seduction, rape, and other offenses involving their persons or reputations. If a woman was deemed "vile" she could lose her right to child support, and a widow could lose the guardianship of her children and the inheritance she gained from the marriage.[70] These laws established social contours in which Spanish-Mexican women acted under the surveillance of others, and if they acted outside the prescribed morality they could not exercise the full range of rights or be granted respect.

Moreover, these laws expressed the logic and practice of placing whole categories of women outside the protection of society. As Antonia Castañeda has shown, the categorical debasement of Indian women as a conquered people went "beyond the devaluation based on sex that accrued to all women irrespective of their sociopolitical (race, class) status."[71] Ramón Gutiérrez analyzes the way in which the terms *Spanish* and *Indian* acquired meaning through the construction of oppositions. Indian women working as servants and slaves in New Mexican households, for example, purportedly "bore illegitimate children, failed to establish stable unions, were frequently sexually assaulted, and [were] reputedly licentious." Hence, "to be a Spanish woman, regardless of one's class, was to be concerned for one's sexual purity and reputation."[72] Spanish women were meant to confer legitimacy, lineage, and purity of religious, ethnic, and racial background; together with land-ownership, these constituted the operative distinctions within the honor-status hierarchy that shaped colonial society.

During the Mexican period Californianas continued to have greater privileges, benefiting from the land politics that enabled a significant number of them, but very few Indian women, to own land and preside over the family economy on the ranchos. Over sixty-six women were granted ranchos in the Mexican period (after 1821). Single women and widows predominated among these original grantees, but many more women shared title to a rancho with their brother or another male relative, and the number of female landowners was higher with every generation thanks to their inheritance of family land, even though an increasingly smaller portion of the total population owned large acreage.

Upon widowhood, for example, Isabel Yorba, a member of the colonial grantee family that owned the Rancho Santiago de Santa Ana, petitioned for a land grant around the presidio of Santa Barbara for herself and her four adopted children. She owned a significant number of cattle and horses and established a business on the grant.[73] Vicenta Sepúlveda, widow of Tomás Yorba, another heir to the Rancho Santiago de Santa Ana, continued her husband's petition for land after his death and in partnership with her brother-in-law Bernardo Yorba. Jointly granted this rancho, Sepúlveda also kept up the business she previously had run with her husband on the Yorba family's colonial grant.[74] And recall that around San Juan Capistrano itself, the widow Concepción Abila petitioned with her brother, Juan Abila, for the Rancho El Niguel. Another widow, María Juana de los Angeles, a Luiseño Indian whose husband had been a chief of the Luiseños, was one of the relatively few Indians granted legal title to the village land where they had lived for years. She raised her large family on that rancho, cultivated a large field and garden, and raised cattle and horses.[75] The widow Eulalia Pérez raised her children at Mission San Gabriel, where she cooked and was in charge of the production and distribution of multiple goods. She, too, was granted a rancho from Indian land claimed by the mission.[76] These profiles of widowed women clearly suggest that adult Californianas cared for their children and others by establishing themselves within the rural economy as landowners, supervising the production and trade of cattle, hides, and other goods, and engaging in subsistence farming. They also engaged in village economies, tending smaller plots of land and manufacturing foodstuffs and goods for trade, a subject I will return to in the next chapter.

Women were central and visible actors in the economy, yet this role required that they negotiate particular arrangements of power, which varied according to their status. Married women were expected to give nearly total obedience to their husbands and to relinquish their sovereignty over most legal transactions, property, and earnings.[77] For their part, elite and landowning men often acted, spoke, and understood and represented themselves as the single governing figure in their family. According to their accounts, the world they created was ordered by their absolute authority as husbands and fathers.[78] The wills of Tomás and Bernardo Yorba (mentioned above) exemplify this sense of dominion over the persons and property of their wives and children. Tomás Yorba's will bequeathed to his wife all the jewelry he had given her as a wedding gift, even though it was already her property by law. She was a woman who knew the law; she ran their trade business and ranchos after his death.[79] Bernardo Yorba likewise left to his wife half the household furnishings as well as the trunks and personal possessions that she had brought into their marriage. The law gave her unquestioned rights to that property, but, he stated, he wished to bequeath these items "by way of gift and in virtue of her widowhood."[80] This sense of proprietorship over the persons and contents of the household was pronounced: Yorba likewise willed to his children and a relative living with the family the trunks that contained their own possessions.

These two elite men articulated the patriarchal logic that Californianas negotiated to establish their position within society, and which they often subverted. Bernardo Yorba's widow, for example, was unimpressed by his sentiment: she immediately sued to divide the estate in order to separate her land, and the land of her two children, from the property of her many step-children, all of whom held portions of the land through shares-in-common. Yorba's particular interest in the legal division of this rancho may have derived from her precarious authority over her twenty step-children, many of whom were adults. But her actions had precedence in the meticulous protection of property by other widows and women in charge of their families. She could divide the land because Bernardo Yorba's death transpired in the American period, after the rancho title had been cleared. Her ability to sue for division illustrates the shift in the terms by which women negotiated their positions in that period.

One of the ways Californianas established their new position in the late nineteenth century was by asserting their role in California history. As Genaro Padilla argues in his reading of more than a dozen personal narratives spoken by Californianas in the 1870s, these women systematically constituted themselves as crucial historical and political agents, at the same time recreating in their accounts the matrix of loving relations that gave depth and substance to other women. Each woman placed herself squarely at the center of all major events; they situated their lives in the public realm rather than in the home or through the patronymic affiliation.[81] In their narratives, widowed and single women landowners and married women did not differ substantially in their relationship to authority and property. Felipa Marrón spoke of "nuestro" (our) rancho when referring to the property she occupied with her husband and family, and of "mi serviente," or my servant. The world of work that took her family from one location to another was determined by her soldier-husband, the onetime administrator of Mission San Luis Rey. But the structure of her narrative makes her the central agent in defining the course of events in her life, which included administering to the missionary Zalvidea during his prolonged illness and death and helping to suppress a robbery by Digueño Indians. She uncovered the plan for the robbery because she knew Digueño and overheard a discussion of the plan. Marrón, like other women who dictated their memoirs in the late nineteenth century, viewed herself as a force in the larger world of political events. Women described their actions within a social milieu that, though perhaps framed by family, was not dependent on family relations.[82]

Californianas' sense of entitlement to property and to a place in public memory derived from social practices unfamiliar to many Anglo-Americans. Prior to 1850, American common law deprived married women of direct ownership of land in their own name; widows held land by virtue of their connection to their deceased husbands. In the area that became the United States, women landowners could be found primarily in the former French and Spanish territories, and among Indian women. Most Anglo-American women saw control of their family's land passed down from father to son.[83] Thus, following the American law, Ruiz Burton's American husband named his lawyer as guardian of their property upon his death, and until she had this decision reversed her business dealings and land litigation were heavily encumbered.

Informed by their own traditions, Anglo-American writers and settlers poorly interpreted the roles that Californianas and Indian women played in public life. A gendered politics of conquest was one result of this (mis)reading of social roles, which in turn helped to further numerous false assumptions about Mexican and Indian peoples, regional history, and society. Consequently, Californianas and Indian women had particular burdens as they negotiated more than one gender system in the American period. They were vulnerable as women in U.S. society, where women were not accorded equal status in law or custom, and they were vulnerable to the anti-Mexican prejudices of Anglo-American migrants. Ruiz Burton was aware of these vulnerabilities when she set her elite Californiana characters apart from the world of business and landownership and asserted Californios' European lineage, despite the contradiction of such a portrayal with the actual social order of the time.

Californianas acted within a tradition that was far removed from Anglo-American law and custom; this history explains the relatively high number of female heads of household in Californio communities. In 1860, Californianas headed just under 10 percent of Californio households; by 1870, they headed one-quarter of those households (figure 6). This upward trend in female-headed households was common among women of Mexican descent throughout the Southwest.[84] Possession of land and property often motivated women to head households rather than to live under the guardianship of a male relative or spouse. As a group, as we have seen, Californios—even when mere laborers—tended to possess more property than other local groups; similarly, Californiana heads of household as a rule owned more property than did women of other backgrounds. In terms of land value, Californianas' share of land (relative to land held by female heads of household of all backgrounds) rose by 11 percent between 1860 and 1870, a decade in which the number of Californiana heads of household also increased dramatically. And although their other real assets declined in the same period, to constitute only 57 percent of assets owned by all female heads of household, Californianas continued to possess assets more often than did other women household heads. This greater degree of property ownership and the social acceptability of women's not marrying also explains why Californianas tended to be younger and were more often single than other female heads of household. In 1880, fifty-seven percent of Californiana household heads were widowed and 14 percent married, whereas the vast majority of Anglo-American and European female heads of household (72 and 75 percent, respectively) were widowed, while the rest (28 and 25 percent, respectively) were married.[85]

These differences reflect not only traditions of gender that influenced

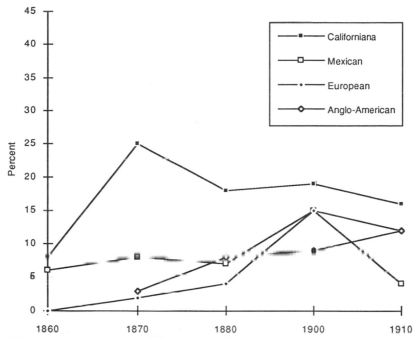

Fig. 6. Percent female-headed households by group, 1860–1910. *Source:*
Federal Manuscript Censuses, 1860–1880, 1900, 1910. *Note:* The populations
represented are adults born an average of forty years before the year specified.
The 1860–1880 figures include all of the area encompassing the 1860 boundaries of Santa Ana and San Juan townships; the 1900 and 1910 figures include
all of Orange County.

personal choice, but also the occupational, geographic, and social order
of each group. Californianas had the largest households, with the vast
majority of their family members working in jobs connected to common
labor and farming. Although in 1870 many Californiana heads of household still owned some land and had assets, ten years later they increasingly worked washing the clothes and linens of other people: in 1880,
6 percent were engaged in such work, while by 1900 that number had
risen to 18 percent. Anglo-American and European female-headed
households, which were located overwhelmingly in the center of American towns and in Anaheim, tended to be smaller and to comprise only
immediate family members. By 1880, these women were engaged largely
in urban employment, working as dressmakers, milliners, or teachers,

or in new forms of agriculture tied to expanding markets, such as or-chard nurseries (though a few depended on their sons' wages or boarded farmhands for extra cash). These women did not become wealthy from these female-typed jobs; nevertheless, through such work they gained skills that were acknowledged as valuable in this new economy.

CHAPTER 3

Village Society, Ethnic Communities, and Memory

I began this book with the story of Modesta Avila, who had placed an obstruction on the Santa Fe Railroad tracks after they were laid near her doorstep in San Juan Capistrano. Avila not only defiantly reported her actions to those men in Santa Ana who represented the new legal authority and economic order, but she later held a dance to celebrate receiving the money from the railroad. I argued that Avila, who was born in 1867, in the midst of the American conquest, was motivated by her generation's experience of land loss. Now I would like to expand that story and explore its meaning more fully.

Avila had been born in that house. In 1889 she was living there with her sister. Her father and other members of her family lived on the same property in another house some three to four hundred yards from the tracks. Her father and two brothers were laborers, and her mother had a small income from boarding and caring for a young child she had taken into the family. They probably tended a subsistence plot on the three-acre lot that Modesta claimed as her own. The family's labor supported eight children. In 1880, at the age of twelve, Modesta was the only family member in her household who could read and write English. By writing "This land belongs to me. And if the railroad wants to run here, they will have to pay me ten thousand dollars" on a sign placed on the obstruction, she employed the power of literacy in the new society—where the written word had long been in the service of conquest through land records and legal documents. She used literacy to inscribe and affirm her sense of entitlement to profit from land that she claimed.

Yet sometime before 1889 the family had sold the land. Perhaps they continued to reside on the property because Modesta's eldest brother, Vicente, had married into the Jiménez family, recent immigrants from Mexico who had purchased this and two adjoining town lots.[1] Thus Modesta Avila defiantly asserted a right to land that no longer belonged to the family, and then held a dance to celebrate receiving money that she in fact never was sent. Why? Her indignation over the usurpation of the lot—a space that symbolized the intersection of culture and history, family and community—ran deep and was widely shared. As Genaro Padilla states, the loss that Californios and Californianas felt so deeply was a cultural loss, in which their homeland was seen to have been "stripped of its land and social economy, its language," its daily practices, and aesthetic production.[2]

On one level, Avila's defense of "her" land reveals the persistence of the idea among Californios that landownership was central to prestige, status, and their identity as a regional group. This identity emerged at the very moment when the locus of authority over the secularized mission lands was being determined. Implicit in this identity was the submergence of the Indians' land rights, in an ideology based on paternalistic protection. Yet Avila's action was more than just her expression of a sense of entitlement to the land: for the fact that she demanded a considerable cash compensation is significant.

Avila's story thus represents one woman's sharp awareness of property rights and land value in a commercial economy. It was an uncommon story, though it did relate to a more common process in which Californianas acted by means of symbolic protest, in their economic behavior and through the courts, to define their rights to land and their right to act in the economic sphere. Their entitlement to property had its origins in Spanish and Mexican law but developed as Californianas in ever greater numbers became paid laborers and managed property as heads of households.

Avila's protest can be interpreted in another way as well: land guaranteed an often poor but still viable means of subsistence for the small farmer and for those who worked as field workers, laundresses, seamstresses, cooks, domestic workers, midwives, laborers, traders, vendors, and artisans. The Californianas' protests can be read as a defense of an economy in which the landowner could still eke out a living from the soil, as long as it was supplemented by other work, work that brought both respect and some traded goods or money. A family's field, garden, and orchard harvests, supplemented by seasonal work and sporadic employment, enabled individuals and indeed the whole community to weather unfavorable market forces.

Yet even though Avila's story illustrates an active defense of Californio property, it did not become part of the legends that shaped the town's collective memory. Instead, the oral tradition of the late nineteenth century centered on the close social and ethical relationships among town residents, in tales of a popular religious nature that stressed, for example, the importance of a person's word (rather than the written contract), the tenuousness of Indian survival, and the sanctity of the town as a collectivity of longtime residents. There were also stories of injustices, cautioning against newcomers and pointing to the vulnerability of the community and its citizenry in the changing circumstances of the times.

Another kind of popular history emerged in the 1910s through the 1920s, as the mission was made into a monument to the "glorious Spanish past." This interpretation presented a secular history that had its counterpart in the Anglo-American lore of the Dons and Doñas of Old Mexico. But told by Californios and Indians in an era when American ethnic consciousness was strong, it represented an appropriation of mission history to contest unfavorable attitudes toward "Mexicans," a term used generally by migrants of Euro-American descent to define all Spanish-speaking and Indian residents of San Juan.

A third set of collective memories, taken as oral histories from among the town's elderly population after 1970, represent yet another way the town's past and sense of community were given meaning. These wholly secular stories affirmed the ways in which the sharing of goods and close human relationships between families helped to shape small-town life in the period before 1940.

The town itself constituted the material basis of collective memory. In 1880, 80 percent of the village population of 71 households was composed of persons from the former Mexican territories, and in 1910 they still made up 60 percent of a population that had grown to 133 households. Religious, social, and cultural practices that developed out of colonial and nineteenth-century society persisted well into the twentieth century. Here ethnicity was forged by a shared small-town life and the various meanings that were given to the community's history at crucial periods of change in the town structure. That structure grew out of the mission site that was made into a pueblo in 1841, and until about 1910 the lots that former neophytes and Californios had been granted, along with pueblo lands and communal water rights, defined the town's social geography. The trend, however, was toward the development of American land-tenure patterns. Farmer-merchants and farmer-speculators acquired land, often in partnerships, invested capital to make improvements, and introduced new crops and livestock. As Avila's story shows, the incursion of new economic forces and the scarcity of capital and cash caused continued land loss among the former neophytes and Californios.

In the small town of San Juan, the face of capital and the wheels of commerce were highly personalized in the few merchants and large landowners who increasingly monopolized the farming sector. Mendelson is a case in point. At the time he discovered Avila's obstruction on the railroad track, Mendelson was not only a merchant and a farmer, he was also an agent for the railroad and the mail service in San Juan Capistrano. As a Polish Jew, he was not accepted into the inner circles of the wealthy merchants and farmers of Anaheim; however, he represented his age as immigrant, migrant, and merchant. Mendelson's migration to California had followed a well-traveled path. He left Poland for the United States sometime before 1864, perhaps already married to Clara Mendelson, a native of the German principality of Wartenberg. They were in Mississippi during the latter part of the Civil War and the early years of Reconstruction. By 1871 they had moved to Missouri, and from there to California, where they settled in San Juan by 1873.[3] They probably arrived by overland passage from Missouri, the second most common state of origin for migrants to this area in 1870 (and still the fourth most common in 1880).

Mendelson appeared as a plaintiff in numerous suits for land and money in payment for debts owed to him.[4] He acquired or attempted to acquire acreage in San Juan and its surrounding area, much of which was held in shares-in-common. Hence, Mendelson often found himself confronting numerous heirs in his suits; when successful, he forced the division of lands held in common.

Even as Mendelson threatened the land tenure system that was so fundamentally important to Californio families in the San Juan area, his household in 1880 reveals his own family's integration into this rural society. Mendelson employed, and had residing in his home, a Californio who clerked in his store, a Californio (from the Yorba family) who worked as a laborer, and a Chinese cook. By the early 1890s Mendelson's son had become a lawyer who represented Californios, Indians, and Mexicans in civil and criminal cases.

Mendelson's relationship to the town and its residents, in short, was ambiguous. That ambiguity—or perhaps more accurately, the duality of an existence that was directed toward both changing the community and being absorbed into it—is suggested, on the one hand, in the argument made by Avila's lawyer that Mendelson had a grievance against Modesta Avila and, on the other hand, in Avila's father's insistence that they had no quarrel. The larger story that unfolds in the following pages is mostly about this rural society of Californio and Indian farmers, workers, and town dwellers; nevertheless, Mendelson's story cannot be omitted, for it defines well the important role the new immigrants played in changing that rural economy and society.

The Pueblo

In the first decades of the American period (beginning in 1848), San Juan's landscape was still structured according to the physical ordering of the Mexican pueblo, with a central plaza and the imposing mission forming the town center. The mission continued to exert not only a cultural but also a strong economic presence through the mid-1880s. The account book of Father Mut, resident priest at the mission from 1866 to 1886, reveals details about the commercial life of the town, the importance of subsistence production, and the kind of work people were doing.[5] Father Mut, for example, never purchased fruit, and only a few times over his twenty-year tenure did he purchase vegetables, beans, wood (for the stove and heating), garlic, onions, potatoes, wheat, or flour. Irregularly, but more frequently, he bought corn, and hay for the horses, which were grown locally and could be purchased to fill out a slim harvest. Otherwise mission essentials were either raised in the mission fields or by the Indians of Pala, Temecula, Pauma, El Rancho los Cahuillas, and San Luis Rey.

Indians from these villages who either resided in San Juan or came occasionally to work were paid by Mut for their labor as cooks, servants, workers in the fields and orchards, and woodcutters. An Indian woman from the village of Pala went to San Juan each week to cook the priest dishes made of frijoles, maize, and chiles that she brought from Pala. These were grown in the village gardens and, together with acorn mush, were staples of the Indian diet. Acorns, in fact, continued to be gathered seasonally well into the early twentieth century.

Mut bought many goods from local people, who supplemented their subsistence economies by selling or trading garden and orchard products, fish and game, and services. Among Mut's regular purchases from local people and, increasingly, at the stores of local merchants were soap, wine, candles, lard, and butter. In 1868 he began to buy goods in bulk—coffee, sugar, oil, and starch. His purchases of meat, fish, pork, ham, and bread for daily consumption emphasize the fact that the regular slaughter of animals and such activities as baking were no longer undertaken at the mission, but rather were provided for by the *carnicero, panadero,* and fish vendor. See, for example, the goods in Mendelson's store (figure 7). The local economy of the small town of San Juan sustained a range of small shops and trades. With the exception of the baker, most artisans and merchants worked in other jobs and farming as well.

To get a picture of San Juan's local economy and social order during these years, one must consider not only what Mut purchased and from whom, but also the workers that he, having relatively greater ready cash than most town residents, employed. A washerwoman, a seamstress, a cook, and a servant received a monthly wage, and Mut also hired part-time Californio or Mexican artisans: a *zapatero* for shoes, but also, at various points, a clockmaker, a locksmith, a carpenter, and a person to whitewash the church. He received money from parishioners in payment for performing marriages, baptisms, and funerals, and over a number of years he rented church pews to wealthier families. In turn, he sometimes paid the cantor and the *acolitos,* or choirboys, for a sung mass. Mut's stipend from the church, tithes, and special collections was supplemented by the selling and renting of mission property and products, though these brought but a modest income. Between 1875 and 1879 alfalfa was the mainstay of the field products that Father Mut sold; from the mid-1870s to 1886 he also occasionally sold beans, wood, and orchard products. The rent of land brought far more money during these years than did his sale of goods. He rented orchards or fields in San Juan and San Luis Rey to various persons, and in the early 1880s he took on some Chinese tenants, who then resided in small numbers in San Juan. He also rented rooms of the mission to families and individuals; although some paid cash, most renters exchanged work for their stay.

Mut left the mission in 1886, at a time when the mission property and large town lots granted in 1841 were being sold off (see map 5). This transfer of church property was typical of a general shift in land-ownership between 1875 and 1889, from relatively long-established local

Fig. 7. Interior of Mendelson's store, ca. 1887. At left is Max Mendelson's son, Marcus; the Chinese man in the center is possibly the family's cook or one of the Chinese farmers who rented land in San Juan to raise vegetables. Mendelson sold boxed and barreled goods, ribbon, paper products, soap, candles, lard, coffee, tea, and sugar, but no local agricultural products, which people grew themselves. Courtesy Seaver Center for Western History Research, Los Angeles County Museum of Natural History, photo no. GPF4227.

owners to newcomers with capital. In this process, Californios and Mexicans slowly lost land to larger owners, forfeiting their holdings to satisfy debts or selling for needed cash. Although a few parishioners bought parcels of church land, by 1889 J. E. Bacon, a merchant and one of the aforementioned newcomers with capital, had purchased most of the mission lands, as well as eight town lots and part of Rancho El Niguel, on which he now grazed thousands of sheep. M. A. Forster (recorded as "Foster" by the tax assessor in 1886), the son of John (Juan) Forster, also possessed substantial property, including town and rural land, on which he had farm machinery, eight hundred head of cattle, and a good number of thoroughbred horses and mules. Domingo Oyharzabal, a

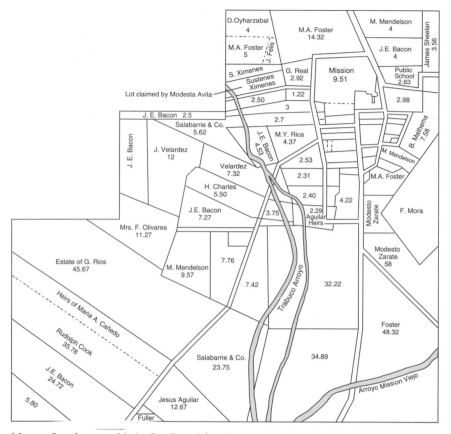

Map 5. Land-ownership in San Juan (showing property owner's name and acreage), from tax assessment map, ca. 1886. Some of these properties (chiefly the unlabeled lots adjacent to the mission) were owned by the church; others were granted to Juaneños and Californios in 1841. Merchants increasingly acquired town land and the size of Juaneño and Californio lots progressively diminished. Courtesy Orange County Archives, Santa Ana, California.

French Basque who came to San Juan via South America and San Francisco, owned four town lots and thousands of acres of sheep pasturage. The merchants Salaberrie and Co. and Max Mendelson owned three lots each, plus thousands of dollars in merchandise. All five of these large owners also had acquired partial interest in other lots through purchase or as satisfaction of debts.[6]

In the 1890s, the largest transfer of acreage took place among the merchant-farmers and a small number of the newcomers. By 1898, for example, most of the Bacon property had been purchased by Oyharzabal, Salaberrie and Co., or L. F. Moulton. The last-named had also acquired large parcels of rural land for sheep and farming. Mendelson had sold portions of his property to Henry Stewart, his partner in other real estate transactions.

The merchant-farmers' investment in land improvements brought about enormous changes in the local economy. By the late 1890s the merchant-farmer and the farmer-speculator generally possessed tens of acres of nut and fruit trees, assorted farm machinery, and many wagons, horses, cows, chickens, and other animals. Both groups had substantially diversified their farming ventures. Like small farmers, they used some of their lots for subsistence-style dry farming, including beans, wheat, barley, corn, and alfalfa; yet at the same time they applied themselves to the economically dynamic sector of high-value crop farming and, in the process, changed not only the orientation of agricultural production but land values as well.

The value of the unimproved property of the widow Refugia Rios, for example, had increased by a mere $15 between 1886 and 1898, whereas one of Oyharzabal's town lots, on which he planted trees and introduced irrigation, had increased in value by $1,450. Because few Californio farmers and landowners had acquired new sources of wealth after the devastation of the cattle market during the 1860s, many were simply unable to invest in new crops, diversify their farms, or irrigate their land. Generally, they owned little more than a wagon, a few horses, a cow or mule, sometimes a dozen head of cattle or a dozen chickens, their household furniture, and possibly a watch. Those individuals who did have capital to invest, by contrast, tended to be from families with a non-Californio head of household, like the Forsters, who were integrated into Californio society but had business connections and skills that facilitated their success in the American business and legal world.

Village Society

Farming was a precarious venture, and farmers from the former Mexican territories were not the only ones to fare poorly when debts went unpaid after a poor or failed harvest or when family circumstances required cash, which was scarce. These farmers were, however, particularly vulnerable when they relied solely on California-style business practices to arrange their accounts, or when the actions of one sharer of property held in common forced the division or loss of family land.

The story of Rosa Pryor is that of one former ranchero who persisted as a farmer in the American period yet continued to employ the logic of exchange to which she was accustomed, that of Mexican California. When Pryor was widowed in the mid-1870s, she and her children became heirs to 6,658 acres of land in Rancho Boca de la Playa, valued at $9,987. Yet a relatively small amount of money still owed on a $1,000 loan to pay taxes, secured by mortgage on their land, had not been paid. Although the subsequent course of events is unclear, her tax assessment profile for 1889 suggests that this debt probably accounted for a decline in Pryor's landholdings to only 463 acres a decade later, at which time her material assets comprised only cows and horses.[7] Nonetheless, she continued to maintain the farm as a modest enterprise. In 1890 she employed three Californio workers, and her two sons and one daughter also helped her with the farming. Rosa Pryor made the decisions about planting and about the purchasing of supplies. Her story comes to light because she was brought to court by Max Mendelson for an alleged two-year debt accumulated on goods bought at his store.[8] Pryor herself did not read or write either English or Spanish, so her children wrote up her orders, and they or her workers would go to Mendelson's store to make the transactions. She bought her goods on credit, and Mendelson often recorded the purchases in her account book long after the transaction had been completed.

Born in 1836 into the Avila family, which had owned Rancho El Niguel since 1841, Rosa Pryor was accustomed to functioning in a society where the word, rather than the written account, was binding; hence, she trusted Mendelson's accounting. Whether or not Pryor had been cheated is not known, but she lost the suit and paid Mendelson the stated balance of her account.[9] Fortunately, she did not lose any of her remaining property. Still managing the farm in 1900, she lived with one of her sons, who was by then the town constable, her daughter-in-law, and a Californio boarder who worked for her as a farm laborer. Her other son resided nearby with his family and was similarly engaged in farming. Subsequently her children placed land into orchards. The family remained relatively prosperous through the 1930s.[10]

The story of Espíritu María R. de Olivares, a widow who administered the farm left to her in the will of her husband, typifies that of the poor farmer working on unimproved land held in shares-in-common. This land was originally the property of Antonio Olivares, who upon his death in 1877 bequeathed it equally to each of his eight children. One of these children was Espíritu's husband, Francisco Olivares. After their marriage she and Francisco lived for three years with Espíritu's mother, whose property Francisco farmed; they then moved into Francisco's family's two-room adobe, where they lived with three of his sisters. Another sister, who maintained a large vegetable garden for the family's subsistence, also lived on the property in a wood-frame house with her husband. Espíritu had known the Olivares family ever since she was a small girl in San Juan. Upon Francisco's death in 1886, Espíritu assumed responsibility for the cultivation of the approximately eleven acres of family land, only some of which was irrigated.

The first year, she hired Lucio Yorba to sow a crop of corn on a share basis: each received half the crop, which amounted to one wagonload of corn for her and one for Yorba. The next year she hired Diego Mendoza, who had lived in San Juan for thirty years (and had also worked for Rosa Pryor), to sow the crop in exchange for room and board at the Olivareses' home. The following year she took on Ramón Padilla, who had lived in San Juan for ten years, to sow the crop on a share basis. These workers were drawn from the many Californio laborers who shared the poverty of landowners such as the Olivares family. None of the three continued the arrangement after the year's end; they moved instead to Santa Ana to find more lucrative pay—a common pattern in the 1890s and 1900s. Thereafter, José Higuera sowed corn and barley under Espíritu Olivares's continued administration of the farm.

The Olivares case is marked by the difficulties of dry farming and the often poor yield from crops grown on unimproved lands. Subsequent disruption to this poor farming household may have been introduced in part by the widow, who appears to have lived in a common-law marriage with Higuera in the adobe home with her sisters-in-law and her three children, one of whom was born well after her husband's death and bore her surname. When Higuera attempted to buy the land from the Olivares sisters, they, along with all but one of the other siblings, sold their shares to Mendelson and Oyharzabal instead, between October and December 1891. In a suit brought by Mendelson and Oyharzabal for possession of these parcels, Espíritu argued for her right to full title of the land. She lost the case, however, and when it closed she and a second heir were left with but a one-eighth share each. In 1900, Espíritu Olivares and her brother-in-law were still farming in San Juan; sometime during the 1900s, though, Oyharzabal acquired almost all their land. By 1911 he had improved it, bringing this land and adjoining acreage into productive cultivation.[11]

The situation of Delfina Manriquez de Olivares, born in San Juan in 1896, is typical of relatively poor farming families who owned substantial rural acreage. Her family had lived in San Juan beginning with her great-grandfather, and relatives on both sides owned land in and near the town into the twentieth century. Despite their property, Delfina later argued that "at that time [ca. 1900] the people were awfully poor; we all were poor . . . but we always had enough to eat."[12] Delfina was born on her family's ranch, where her father planted beans, corn, tomatoes, chiles, and other subsistence vegetables. With the help of an Indian woman named María Gomez, who was paid in kind, Delfina's mother canned their field and orchard products for the family's consumption. Unlike prosperous farmers, the Manriquezes had no cattle or sheep. M. A. Forster, for whom Delfina's father sometimes worked, lent them a cow so they would have milk, cheese, and butter. The Manriquez family made little, if any, money from the farm. The family's only cash income—indeed, the only cash income of most of San Juan's Californio and Indian families—came during walnut season. With that money they would go in a wagon to Santa Ana, stay overnight with an aunt, and buy shoes and clothes for the year. Delfina's mother worked as a midwife and was sometimes paid in cash, sometimes in kind. In this her mother followed in the footsteps of her grandmother, who had nursed ill villagers.[13]

Californio landowners who persevered as farmers commonly turned to the extended family to provide material sustenance in the form of cash, labor, goods, and even a home. The case of Daisy Yorba, whose family home in San Juan, including all their possessions and cash, burned to the ground, reveals just how important family resources were, for Daisy's family was able to resettle immediately in the maternal grandparents' home on former rancho property some distance from San Juan. Her father continued to grow vegetables, corn, and fruit trees for family use, but he also had a walnut orchard, which produced a cash crop that made him one of the better-off Californio farmers in the area. That income enabled Daisy's mother to rent a home in Santa Ana during the 1910s so that Daisy and her brother could attend high school.[14]

The Aguilar family represents a second example of the usefulness of extended family resources for Californio landowners; yet among the Aguilars, as with Espíritu Olivares, property held in shares-in-common added a dimension of precariousness for family members who relied for their income on the parcel. A. G. Aguilar had borrowed money from Max Mendelson, possibly to improve family land. He was unable to repay it, and in 1898 Mendelson sued him for the amount of the debt. The repayment that Mendelson sought consisted of Aguilar's half-interest in two large town lots and his fifth-interest in a third town lot, for a total of thirty acres of unimproved land. Although the family owned land, they were far from well off. Nevertheless, they paid back their brother's debt—a substantial amount for the time, $381.51, which they could only have raised through the sale of some of their land and by working for wages.[15]

Part of the land of Josefa Serrano de Ríos was also entangled and lost, because of both family dealings and the incursion of the railroad on her property. Her story, reminiscent of Modesta Avila's, illustrates yet another Californiana's increasingly defiant sense of entitlement to property. In the late 1870s, Serrano de Ríos had given her brother, José Serrano, power of attorney over her legal transactions so that the sale of their land in Rancho Cañada de los Alisos, San Juan township, might be concluded. In the mid-1880s she purchased a rural lot in the township from James Field; on this land she planted fruit trees and crops. Serrano de Ríos had lived there for four years when she went to the bank to secure the deed to her property, only to discover that it had been sold by her brother, who had accepted a deed of conveyance for it from Ricano Dominguez. Dominguez had, in turn, given the Pacific Improvement Company, a subsidiary of the Santa Fe Railroad that aggressively bought and developed real estate, permission to cross the land with a rail line. In a first court case, Serrano de Ríos sued not only José Serrano and Ricano Dominguez, but the Pacific Improvement Company as well.[16] She lost the case but immediately filed another one, this time against the Southern Pacific Railroad, which had cut down her fruit trees to build the tracks. In this second trial she articulated a strong sense of her perceived property rights and demanded damages from Southern Pacific for cutting down her trees, payment of rent on the land they had crossed, and a share of the railroad's profits. Like Avila, Serrano de Ríos wanted economic compensation from the railroad; also like Avila, she did not receive it.[17]

These stories demonstrate the persistence of preindustrial social and economic practices, in a society where money, though scarce, was needed for taxes and select goods, yet where land was still held in shares-in-common and people's debts or desires to sell could divide the property and drive the family into dependence on wage labor. On the part of women in particular, the defense of property became more acute as they began to work as farmers and wage laborers and to manage their families as heads of households. Land was the foremost medium of investment, profit, and exchange; at the same time, land also provided for subsistence and enabled the members of poor farming families to pursue other jobs such as midwife and *curandero* that brought not only status, but also goods in trade or a little cash.

Ultimately, these stories demonstrate the defense of a social world that was emerging following the collapse of former rancho society. These Californianas and Californios faced the same conditions as other farmers throughout the nation; capitalist agriculture was transforming rural society and bringing small farmers into a market controlled by merchants and the banks and steered by new systems of distribution, most notably the railroad.[18] The populist movement represented national protest against these conditions of monopoly in the last decades of the nineteenth century. But in the small town of San Juan, the history of territorial conquest shaped the experience of change and defense of property. Anglo-Americans' race and gender prejudices deeply colored their interpretations of Modesta Avila and others who protested the inequalities produced during capitalist development.

In their trials, opposing lawyers belittled Avila, Serrano de Ríos, and Olivares by drawing on these prejudices. Avila was prosecuted not only for her defiance of railroad interests but also for her unconventional gender behavior, which made her doubly vulnerable before the law. Her "reputation" was cited unfavorably more than once during the hearings; indeed, her boyfriend's employer threatened to fire him if he was seen with her again, and then did so. A general sense of mockery pervaded the testimony of some witnesses as well as English-language newspaper accounts of her case. The *Santa Ana Weekly Blade,* for example, reported her appeal to the California Supreme Court under the heading "Modesta Again," and it cheered the fact that the "decision by that tribunal will set at not any further proceedings."[19] Moreover, possibly because she was a woman who acted publicly in a defiant manner, she did not become part of the regional Spanish-language oral tradition, which interpreted similar acts admiringly as a form of banditry or resistance to the new forms of economic and political power.[20]

Serrano de Ríos, who took the railroad to court for crossing her land, defined herself before the court as a "native Californio of Spanish descent." This self-identification corresponded to her feeling of group identity as heir to a rancho. Emphasizing her heightened sense of land

and property rights, Serrano de Ríos explained that she had given power of attorney to her brother because she knew so little about "deeds, transfers, mortgages, and transactions," though subsequently she purchased and assumed the management of new property. Even though she was married by then, she acted alone to purchase the land and to bring the two suits to court. However, the defense defined her as being "of the Mexican race" and argued that she was "illiterate, ignorant, and helpless, and unable to read and write," thus implying that her case could not possibly have legitimacy. These accusations, of course, sharply contradicted her actual behavior; nonetheless, they formed part of the legal record against her.[21]

In Olivares's trial, testimony centering on her illicit union with Higuera, the last man to work her farm and the person who had attempted to purchase the land from the other heirs before they sold it to Oyharzabal and Mendelson, was introduced by the plaintiff's lawyer to damage her case. Indeed, the relationship may have been a source of discontent within the family, though poor yields or Espíritu's management of the farm may have been sufficient to cause the other shareholders to sell their portions. In the decade after the trial, Olivares continued to live and farm with her children, without Higuera.[22]

Deena Gonzalez's study of Hispanas (meaning women of Spanish-mestizo descent in New Mexico) in Santa Fe offers a complementary example of this process of territorial conquest. The number of Hispanas who wrote wills and deposited them before a local magistrate in Santa Fe rose dramatically after 1877. For more and more women, Gonzalez argues, "the act of writing a will offered a measure of control over their circumstances."[23] While the language of the wills expressed timeless concerns, such as the desire to leave the world with debts and affairs settled, it also exposed a situation in which "a community's ideals and mores [were] out of alignment with the realities of many women's lives." Many Hispanas stated in their wills, for example, that they had been "watched over" by a husband and the Church; yet some 90 percent of all female heads of households had children who carried these women's own surnames. In other words, these women were not marrying their children's fathers.[24]

Olivares and other women in San Juan fit this pattern of forming unions out of wedlock. Such relationships, in fact, were not uncommon among poorer women, but they are often difficult to trace. Some women were mistresses, and their children constituted the second family of a married man. Bernarda Cabacicci de Romero is one such case.

This woman, whose father was Italian and whose mother, María Estones, was a full-blooded Indian, left her husband and children for a man named Lasero Morrillo. The four children were then raised by various persons in San Juan. Morrillo had a wife and continued to live with her, but Bernarda remained with him in a separate household and bore their children.[25] Although the practice of taking a mistress was widespread until the early part of the twentieth century, formal documentation of these relationships is scarce. In one year only did the census record "mistress" as the relationship of a woman to the head of the household, though even then only mistresses who lived with the man were noted.

Seven such mistresses were listed in San Juan in the 1880 census. Declaration in itself suggests some acknowledgment of the legitimacy of this practice as economically and socially viable. One Californiana was the mistress of a Californio laborer; another lived with a laborer from Mexico; and a third was the mistress of a Mexican teamster. The three Indian women included in this category—two being the mistresses of Californio laborers, the third of a shepherd from the principality of Baden—resided in households distinguished by having one or more boarders, more children, and, in one case, another Indian woman who worked as a washer woman. The seventh woman was a Mexican who lived with a Mexican shoemaker. Although such relationships were not highly visible in formal documents, older residents from San Juan discussed without antagonism women who lived out of wedlock with men or who had illegitimate children.[26] These women were generally acknowledged to have another set of rights that were rarely recognized by law. Sarah Deutsch also found that women who refused to marry or were unwed mothers formed a respected part of their communities. They tended to be poor.[27] Because legitimacy constituted an element of status, these women and children were vulnerable to being marked.[28] However, Deena Gonzalez suggests that women who fulfilled even two of the more significant roles expected of them (such as childbirth and religious devotion) could be well regarded.[29]

Women, who headed some 35 percent of Californio and Indian households in San Juan in 1900, had always fared poorly in the wage labor market. Between 1880 and 1910, for example, they labored almost exclusively as laundresses, work that accounted for 6 percent of the total employment of Californio heads of household in 1880 and 18 percent by 1900. Fewer than 10 percent of San Juan's women who headed households worked in other jobs; these included a few of the farmers discussed earlier, a dressmaker, and a landlord.[30] As Deena Gonzalez found for New Mexico, the majority of these women lived with adult daughters and other relatives; few lived alone. When they were not the sole wage earner in the household, their children, relatives, and boarders worked as farm or day laborers, the single most common occupation of Californio and Mexican males.

Indian women in San Juan generally had relatives, sometimes land, on reservations; it was often through their marriage to a Californio, Mexican, or European man that they came to live in the town. Luce Robles's story describes her family's relationship to San Juan. In 1852, at the age of four days, Luce Robles's husband had been baptized at the mission, the son of mission Indians. His father had been born on a mission rancho in 1828 and was baptized and given the surname Robles in 1830. Luce Robles's own parents, neophytes from Santa Inez and San Juan missions, were married at the mission. Her family moved to Pala sometime after the 1862 plague, but they maintained their connection to San Juan. Her parents arranged her marriage to Robles, who lived in San Juan. She raised four children in a small adobe home by the mission, where she cooked and cleaned for the priest. She nursed a man named José Felix through an illness and his death; he willed her his property, also by the mission, to which she moved and on which a son-in-law built another house. Grandchildren and great-grandchildren were raised on that property, which continued to be passed down.[31] Luce Robles remained closely connected to the village of Pala after her marriage. She remained in both worlds, speaking Juaneño at Pala (where she held land) and among her relatives in San Juan, and Spanish with her children and grandchildren. Despite having been inheritors of mission land in theory, her family did not possess land in the mission town, but inherited it from a Californio.

Another Indian woman, Victoria Doram, raised her family in a house inherited from her Indian godparents, who raised her. Her family's stable residence did not prevent her from engaging in the kinds of work that Californiana and Indian women often performed to sustain their families. Her husband, fifty years her senior, worked as a migratory sheepshearer from the late nineteenth century into the 1920s. He would leave San Juan with her godfather and four other Indian men and move north through Bakersfield to the Oakland–San Francisco area, on into northern California, swing into Nevada, Idaho, Wyoming, and Montana, and work his way back through Nevada and eastern California to

Arizona and Calexico. He would be gone six months at a time, while she was left at home with eight children. She took in washing at home and also worked washing dishes at the Mission Inn restaurant. She raised a family vegetable garden as well as chickens for eggs and meat, goats for milk and slaughter, and ducks. The whole family would go seasonally with their mother, uncles, and cousins to pick apricots, peaches, and walnuts.[32]

Juaneños

In 1860 Juaneños constituted nearly a third of San Juan's population; however, most left San Juan in the early 1860s for villages to the southeast to join relatives who had relocated. The divergence between the histories of Indian residents in San Juan and those in the interior villages grew sharper over time, but parallels did persist, especially economic ones. The Juaneños and Luiseños had been engaged in agriculture, stock raising, and wage or seasonal work long before 1846, and they continued to harvest acorns and to grow native crops in their gardens as in premission times. From the 1850s through the 1870s reports state that corn, wheat, barley, beans, melons, olive and fruit trees, grapes, and other subsistence and cash crops were cultivated at Pala, Pauma, and Temecula, and livestock was tended.[33] After 1891 most Indians began to engage in the production of other cash crops, such as tomatoes, yams, onions, chile peppers, squash, and watermelons, plus some citrus and nut crops, with honey, poultry, cattle, and horses also being raised for market.[34] These new cash crops and orchard products, together with the seasonal wage labor available in towns and on farms, defined the economies of these Indian villages around the turn of the century. Figure 8 shows home-grown chiles drying on racks, a common practice in this area since at least the mid-nineteenth century. Recall that a cook from Pala would go to Mission San Juan to prepare the priests' meals, often bringing garden vegetables from the village to use.

In 1901, Clinton Hart Merriam described the villages of Rincón, La Jolla, and Pauma, including their economies: "In all three settlements the people live in well-made adobe houses . . . [which are] scattered about, usually an eighth or a quarter of a mile apart." Wells and small streams were used to irrigate peach and fig orchards. "Fig and tobacco trees grow about the houses, and great masses of the giant tuna [prickly

Fig. 8. Esperanza Fiedelio, drying peppers at Pala, ca. 1935. Courtesy Southwest Museum, Los Angeles, photo no. P883. Photo by Josephine Cook.

pear] cactus are often nearby," bearing fruit to eat. "Most of the families cultivate wheat and barley—barley for the horses and wheat for themselves. . . . In the late fall, all of these old Indians go to Palomar Mountain to gather acorns of the black oak from which they make mush and soup, usually mixing fresh meat or pork and chili with acorn meal."[35] Acorn mush was still the staple food for the majority of the mission tribes in the southern part of the state. The bonds between the villages to the south of San Juan were affirmed through fiestas for religious, seasonal, and life-cycle celebrations. At the date of his visit, for example, Merriam observed that "most of them have just returned from a fiesta at Saboba, and in a week or two they are going to another, to be given by the Indians at Cahuilla or at Pichanga."[36]

Merriam also noted the high death rate, which exceeded the birth rate, especially among youths. "The children are very apt to develop tuberculosis," he reported; "they die between the ages of sixteen and twenty-five." He gave the example of a girl who had recently returned from Carlisle, Pennsylvania (one of the first Indian schools in the United States). When she arrived she had a dreadful cough, and within a year she died. Indian schools and illnesses associated with poverty shaped the painful experience of many Indians at the turn of the century in the United States. The majority of Indians in the villages spoke Spanish, but the children who had been sent to Indian schools spoke English.[37]

The close ties between San Juan pueblo and these villages were the consequence of many familial relationships, both blood and fictive, as well as historic ties among Californios, Mexicans, and Juaneños, including those between villagers and the priests at the mission. The Catholic bishop owned title to Pauma village, and Father Mut commonly went from San Juan to Pauma and Pala to administer the sacraments and say mass.[38] Likewise, Indian workers moved between these villages and the mission church for work and to sell goods. Within San Juan, Indians, like Californios, raised crops, worked in the herding and care of cattle and the shearing of sheep, and performed unskilled labor.

Yet despite their daily presence in community life, and even though many of them were joined to non-Indian families through both formal and informal relations, they remained a distinct social group. The children from marriages between Indian women and Californio, Mexican, European, and American men, significantly, identified themselves as being of Indian descent when their mother maintained a strong relationship to villagers in the interior and to indigenous practices, beliefs, and languages.

Indian identity was never a question merely of blood lines. Ties were also forged in a common cultural life centered on the church. In California, as elsewhere in the former Spanish colonies, Catholicism had incorporated aspects of local beliefs and practices to constitute a religious life that Indians and Californios could share. Indians were associated especially with the supernatural and healing. When someone in San Juan had an illness thought to be caused by a spell, a healer would be sent for in Pala, who would come to town to diagnose and cure the illness.[39] Evelyn Villegas tells of the *curandero* Calac, a man who lived in Pala and whose abilities to effect cures took her grandmother, uncles, and other relatives on many occasions from San Juan to Pala for exams.[40] Her grandmother also sought the spiritual advice of a *curandera* in that same village, who could read the past, present, and future by means of a conch shell. In addition, several Californiana *curanderas* lived in San Juan; these women employed medicinal and spiritual forms of healing that may have been passed down to them by an Indian relative. Polonia Montano, for example, maintained a small chapel, complete with saints and candles, in one room of her adobe home in San Juan, where Indians and Californios went for rituals and to pray for healing and other kinds of help.[41]

Most notably, however, it was the processes of land loss and population dispersal to the villages southeast of town that shaped the distinctive identity of the Indians of San Juan. One creation myth, told by a man named Eustaquio to the priest John O'Sullivan at San Juan Mission sometime during the 1910s, emphasizes a shared history and promotes a sense of unity between these groups even as it preserves their differences.[42] Eustaquio lived near the mission with his wife, Micaela; his people were from the mountains beyond the village of Pala.

According to this myth, people first appeared in the world around the lake at Elsinore and were called Pai'yachea. Then the sun, moon, stars, rocks, trees, wind, snakes, and other animals, who were both evil and good, were created. Naháchis, the good one, "who was like a god among them," rose from the swamp and did not want to become an animal or a tree or a stone; rather he said, "Poor people, how long are they going to live? I shall go on a journey and name the places and return here again, and then the people will live longer." This he did, establishing a sacred order among the places of the earth and their separate peoples for the purpose of their survival. On his journey Naháchis received particular foods from various peoples, whom Eustaquio refers to by name, mentioning, for example, the "Cahuilla tribe" and the place of the Cahuilla, which was "afterwards . . . called Cupa, but people now call the place Warner's Hot Springs" (see figure 4).[43]

The origins story contains the memory of the colonial encounter as well, for despite his desire "to give more life to the people" Naháchis could not ensure their continued existence. He came to a place where some girls were bathing. "One of them was Wahow'kee, the toad; but she was *gente*, that is, people, too. She had very long hair and was the most beautiful of all; but when the wind blew her hair aside, and Naháchis saw that she had the form of a toad, he said something that made her angry and her relatives too." So they made him something to eat from a root that caused him to become ill; he continued his walk back toward Pai'yachee but died before reaching there, and his body assumed the shape of a stone. "Because he did not finish the journey back to Elsinore, the people do not know how long they will live and so they have to die."[44]

The memory of Naháchis, however, remained alive. The people of Temecula, for example, who "used to grow grain," would send a messenger up to Naháchis (the stone) to strike it gently with a stick or small stone so that the wind would blow and they could winnow their grain. And Padre Guillermo ("whom people called Padre Blanco" because he wore the white gown of a Dominican) blessed the stone and (re)named it José. The journey of Naháchis joined different Indian peoples, including Juaneños and Luiseños, in a common origins story through naming. Unfortunately, this unity could not ensure their survival.

The Changing Meaning of Place and Time

Historical place was also given a new meaning in stories that configured San Juan as a sacred place, which in turn affirmed the sanctity of an otherwise diverse community. Californios and Indians, whose residence in San Juan often extended back for generations, remained the largest groups in town through the 1930s.[45] Together they provided fertile ground for the development of collective memories that were fortified, when not engendered, by the presence of the mission.

The mission's influence was especially strong from 1880 through the 1910s. Its built space, of course, embodied the past and facilitated continuous cultural practices that shaped notions defining San Juan as a community. As an institution, too, the mission fostered a sense of community through such inherited responsibilities as bell ringer and cantor, which were handed down from father to son or other male relative, and the related jobs of midwife and guardian of the children, which likewise were often passed from mother to daughter. José de Gracia Cruz, a Juaneño born in 1848, lived his whole life in the town and had relatives living in San Juan and in the Indian village of Temecula. He inherited the job of bell ringer from his father, who taught the young man the appropriate rings for feast days and other public occasions. The work of father and son extended from the 1840s through the 1920s.[46] Paul Arbiso, Gracia Cruz's nephew, became the bell ringer at the mission sometime after his uncle's death in 1924. Arbiso explains how each major rite of passage, from birth to baptism to marriage to death, was announced to the community. If a person "passes away and the people don't know it, just by the sound of the bells they know if it's a man (three rings) or a woman (two rings). . . . Then, if it's a little baby, they ring the little bells." Referring to the closely connected social life within this small area, Arbiso said, "If the town knows that that man has been sick, they know when he's passed away."[47] The words of bell ringer Arbiso suggest how the town might have been notified of the death of the person whose funeral is shown in figure 9.

The mission cantor, who led the congregation in verse, passed along other important traditions as well. Thanks to the accounts of two cantors in particular, we can gain an insight into the changing manner in which this inherited repertoire of songs and chants was transmitted, as well as the distinct context of religious celebration in San Juan in the mid-nineteenth century. Between 1840 and 1870 the cantor of the pueblo was Benancio Ríos, who in the early 1860s began to teach the religious songs to his son orally, as he had learned them. The son, however, "despaired at ever learning the whole stock of traditional songs and prayers" and so wrote them down. Their inscription was also necessary, the young Ríos stated, because of the "falling off of reverence and deference for religious ceremonies and traditions among [my] countrymen due to the influence of new American settlers of not the best type." These Americans "jeered" at the processions, chanting, and traditional celebrations.[48]

This manuscript of songs and chants was passed on to the cantor Ramón Yorba when he replaced the young Ríos in 1886. Yorba added a note to the book to authenticate the fact that the songs and chants, whose origins were in "Ancient Spain or Mexico after 1530," had originally been taught to the *indios neofitos* of the mission by the Franciscans. The manuscript thus presents a record of three moments in the history of cultural change in San Juan, from oral tradition to written notations—indicating both a response to the waning of old forms of celebration and a personal orientation toward the written word—to documentation of historical origins. In his otherwise English text, interestingly, Yorba used the Spanish words *indios neophytos* and *padres* without translating or underlining them—that is, without treating them as foreign words—for these terms remained lodged in a collective memory that was accessible only in Spanish. He did, however, underline and, when necessary, gloss other Spanish words that were less laden with historical meaning. In describing the role of the cantor during the mass, for example, he wrote (with underlining), "These practices are still in full effect among the *paisanos* of San Juan Capistrano, especially at the *velorios* or wakes."

Fig. 9. Funeral procession leaving Mission San Juan Capistrano, ca. 1880. Courtesy Southwest Museum, Los Angeles, photo no. P20290. Photo by C. C. Pierce.

This sense of community was affirmed not only in the persistence of past practices, but also in celebrations that shaped and renewed a historic attachment to place and brought people who had migrated away back to the pueblo for family events, such as the fiesta shown in figure 10. Through the 1880s, when town land was still owned primarily by the church and its parishioners, the congregation was referred to as *el pueblo*. Thus, when the priest Mut noted in his account book "colectas entre el pueblo para la semana santa," he articulated the sense that the congregation was synonymous with the town and that town life was marked by the church calendar of feast days and holy observances.[49] The two most prominent religious celebrations, in fact, focused specifically on the community: the week-long fiesta of San Juan, celebrated

Fig. 10. Family fiesta, San Juan, ca. 1880. Courtesy Southwest Museum, Los Angeles, photo no. N30590.

in early October, and Judas Day, celebrated on the Saturday of Easter week. On Judas Day it was the custom to steal by night wagons from all the households and arrange them in a line, with the effigy of Judas on the front wagon leading the procession. Something valuable that represented each household was also placed in the wagons. One year, for example, the lace petticoats of a reclusive town resident were stolen from her trunks and used to dress Judas, and four bags of wool belonging to Marcus Mendelson, Max's son, made their way from his store into the procession.

Many stories told from the 1860s through the 1910s cited miracles as proof that San Juan was a favored place within the spiritual universe. In one such tale, the midwife and *curandera* Polonia Montano, the "captain of the children of the pueblo" who officiated at children's births and deaths, is attributed with miraculous powers. During a prolonged drought that coincided with the 1890s depression, Montano was called on to pray for rain. For three days in succession she walked to the sea with children from San Juan. Singing hymns and litanies and reciting the rosary, they carried a dais on which a crucifix and a picture of Saint Vicente decorated with *milagros* (miniature metal figures) had been fixed. On the third day, so legend has it, it began to rain even before the procession returned to town.[50]

Another legend concerns the mission's statue of the Virgin Mary. Because the mission had no regular priest between 1890 and 1910, a visiting priest decided that the statue should be taken to Mission San Gabriel for safekeeping. As the statue was carried away from San Juan a crowd of townspeople followed behind, shedding tears and crying out their lamentations. Then, when they tried to erect the statue in the church at San Gabriel, it would not stand up but repeatedly toppled over. A priest, observing a miracle in this inexplicable occurrence, ordered that the statue be returned to San Juan. Almost too heavy to bear as it was carried away from San Juan, the statue was now light enough for the bearers to run with it out of the Mission San Gabriel.[51]

Some legends were based on favorite saints who originated in Sonora and Sinaloa, the homelands of many colonial settlers; others stemmed from the repertoire of oral tradition that included stories like *la llorona* that were common throughout the cultural area of Greater Mexico; and still others had a Californio regional origin. Many of the stories told about San Juan were meant to shape morality and to define proper social relations. Some tales contrasted the Californio's sense of *vergüenza*, or shame, which placed utmost importance on the integrity of a person's word, with the deceitfulness of newcomers. One such story tells of an alligator trapped on land and saved by a man who carries it on his back into the river. The alligator keeps insisting on being carried farther into the water, until finally the water comes up to the man's neck. Then the alligator catches the man with his claws and says, "Now, I shall eat you. I am very hungry." In the nick of time, a coyote saves the man. The man repays the coyote with chickens but then turns his hounds on the coyote, who gets away but vows never to do a favor for anyone again. The story's narrow escapes suggest that one should persevere even despite the treachery of deceit. The coyote presents the moral: Don't get involved with the newcomer, whose word cannot be trusted.[52]

These tales told as memories during the 1910s reinforced notions of history and community and drew morals about how to act in the present. But not everyone believed that the old traditions had meaning under the new circumstances. Some felt, for example, that the calendar of seasonal work in increasingly industrialized agriculture replaced the religious calendar. The bell ringer Gracia García, for example, related that one morning he had met a woman who was on her way to pick walnuts. He warned her, "It is going to rain, for tomorrow is *el día de San Francisco* [Saint Francis's feast day]." She said that "used to be," but those miracles no longer happened. It did rain, though, Gracia García told O'Sullivan, thus affirming the continuity in the relationship between sacred time and seasonal time. Indeed, O'Sullivan found that older townspeople did think it to be at least historically true that it always rained within the octave of the feast of St. Francis, the result of St. Francis striking the cord on his habit against the heavens.[53]

Oral Culture and Tradition

Stories like these are particularly significant because Californios and Indians in San Juan lived in a culture with a "high oral residue," a concept which implies that orality and literacy shape culture and community in very specific ways.[54] A "primary oral culture" is one without either writing or written texts. In an "oral residual culture," by contrast, writing is performed and written texts are created, used, and have influence. Knowledge is often stored in writing rather than memory, as when cantor Ríos decided to write down the sacred chants that his father had passed to him orally. Nevertheless, writing is not "fully interiorized" in an oral residual culture; it has not shaped, at the deepest levels, local culture and local society.

Orality involves a different relationship to memory than does writing. In oral culture, knowledge of past and present is often transmitted via the mnemonic devices of formula and rhyme. Formulaic thought and expression ride deep in the consciousness and unconscious; they do not vanish as soon as one used to them takes a pen in hand. In contrast to the highly individualized, interiorized, and privatized culture that marks literate society, an oral culture fosters communal relations: it unites people in groups. Words derive their meaning from context more readily than in literate society, where meanings tend to be fixed, singular, and abstract. Orality promotes the recording of such things as history and morality through tales and legends, which in turn are fairly adaptable to changing circumstances. Oral residual culture promotes, in short, a sophisticated verbal ability, a strong sense of collectivity, and a vibrant collective memory within the historical community.

The concept of "residual orality" describes both a form of communication and social interaction; it also suggests that the content of cultural life is different from that of societies organized around writing. The literacy rates of Californios in San Juan depict a society that continued to be infused by oral culture and in which there existed a layering of cultural sensibilities informed by orality and literacy (see figure 11). These rates are for adults born roughly forty years prior to the specified census year. Thus in 1860, the rates reflect persons born at the very end of the colonial period; through 1880, a significant portion of the individuals represented were born in the Mexican period. By 1900, the majority would have been born in the American period, when a few years of elementary schooling were easier to attain. The rise in literacy over the period 1860–1910 points to the complex cultural world of literate and bilingual Californios and Juaneños in the twentieth century, for they had to negotiate not only the oral culture of their elders, but also the dominant English-speaking and literacy-oriented culture.

Adults who grew up during the Mexican period acquired many forms of religious, historical, and practical knowledge via oral means. They lived in a culture where a person's word was sufficient to confirm a commitment or deal. Living by one's word was to uphold one's honor. The simple sign of the cross, rather than a signature, similarly was used to declare a commitment or to affirm consent on written documents, such as the petitions for ranchos tendered during the 1820s through the 1840s. Between 1860 and 1880 Californios' literacy figures rose. By 1880 roughly two-fifths of the men and slightly less than one-third of the women could read.[55]

Those who could read would read aloud to all. The nineteenth-century tradition of reading aloud melodramatic novels, published in Spanish in the form of *folletos* (pamphlets), was pervasive; it also illustrates how literary culture was incorporated into oral tradition. The explicitly political dimension of this integration was already suggested in chapter 1 in relationship to the influence of the *Manifiesto a la República Mejicana*. This manifesto, published in 1834 using the first printing press in California, documented the debates between the California deputation and the Mexican government over emancipation and secularization policy. Defining as it did a Californio territorial identity, the work was read aloud publicly and widely discussed. Its arguments were articulated

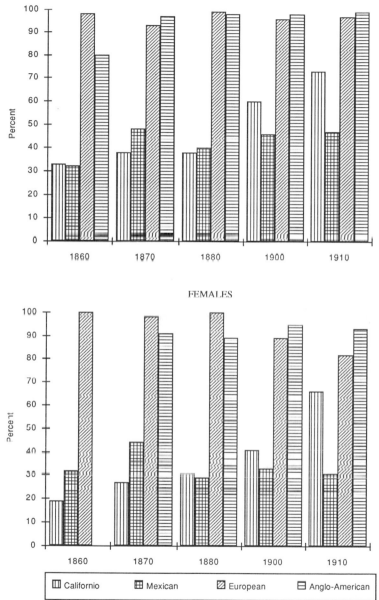

Fig. 11. Literacy by gender and group, 1860–1910. *Source:* Federal Manuscript Censuses, 1860–1880, 1900, 1910. *Note:* The populations represented are adults born an average of forty years before the year specified. The 1860–1880 figures include all of the area encompassing the 1860 boundaries of Santa Ana and San Juan townships; the 1900 and 1910 figures include all of Orange County.

time and again in the early American period to defend Californio and ecclesiastical land ownership.

Books and pamphlets were also imported to or printed in Alta California prior to 1848. Spanish-language newspapers began to be published during the 1850s. All of these publications would be read aloud by a male or female family member, neighbor, or friend. In San Juan as elsewhere in Mexico and the former Mexican territories, moreover, the *escriban,* or writer, was paid to write every kind of correspondence or document that needed to be put on paper, including memos to the governor or town council, business correspondence, and love letters. The man or woman who read aloud, together with the *escriban,* formed part of a public world. They negotiated between written and oral culture, bringing the former into the latter—one dynamic way in which society underwent change.

Literacy was neither the only nor an especially privileged route to cultural knowledge, yet it did mean greater access to political and economic power. This fact helps to explain the higher percentage of literate men versus women, and the tendency of the landed elite to secure formal education for their children. Recall that Ruiz Burton, inheritor of colonial grants and other land, had been educated by a female tutor from Spain when she was a young girl. Apolinaria Lorenzano learned to read on her own, which allowed her to work in a school for girls, teaching them to read, write, pray, and sew.[56] Modesta Avila was from a poorer family and the only one in her family who could read and write in 1880; one way she used that literacy was to create the sign on the post telling the railroad of her intentions. She was among a growing number of Californianas who were learning to read and write. Almost everyone born after 1880 had significantly greater access to formal education than theretofore, and Californianas in particular benefited from this change, most likely because it had become the practice that both men and women would work for pay or goods, and Californianas were frequently in charge of the family economy.

In the American period public schools began to replace the private tutors, priests, and schools in Mexico that had previously shaped the parameters of formal education in California. From the 1890s on San Juan had a permanent public elementary school, and a Catholic elementary school was established after 1910. For schooling beyond the sixth grade, however, students had to relocate to Santa Ana until 1920—an impossibility for the vast majority of Californio and Juaneño families. Moreover, even though elementary education was increasingly common, in working-class and immigrant families older siblings often attended school for fewer years, going to work for the family economy as soon as possible; this enabled younger children, like Modesta Avila, to attend school longer. The influence of the schools (in which, notably, Californio and Indian populations dominated; see below) is visible in the substantial rise in Californios' literacy in 1900 and again in 1910: by the latter date almost three-fourths of the men and fully two-thirds of the women could read and write (see figure 11).

Despite the rise in literacy among Californios, adults who came of age around the turn of the century still lived in a social world in which Spanish was the primary language and comparatively few elders were literate. These Californios were thus steeped in the ideas, cultural traditions, and social norms from the larger world of the Spanish colonies and Mexican California. But through their school learning, they also gained access to the ideas and perspectives embodied in the English language. This access to two traditions was especially important in the early twentieth century, when immigration from Mexico prompted the development of a Spanish-language regional culture. Immigrants introduced new cultural elements and reinforced older ones. The overall culture, however, was one with a high oral residue, in which younger and older Spanish-speaking persons from San Juan alike could share.

Literacy allowed greater access to power. This seems apparent when we look at the literacy rates of the European and Anglo-American populations in San Juan, which were high and relatively constant and symmetrical by sex. In fact, most of these newcomers came to California because of the written word: pamphlets, brochures, and books described a glorious landscape, promoted virtually unlimited commercial and farming possibilities, and praised the climate's beneficence for the ill. This English-language literature was also highly unfavorable to the population of colonial and Mexican California. Thus literacy played an important role in shaping the initial encounter and conflict between new settlers and the region's longtime population. The migrants' far greater ability to create and interpret written documents, and to manipulate an economic and political system based on the written word, made territorial conquest that much easier. Even in the late nineteenth century, when these populations displayed sharply different literacy rates, the English-language and Spanish-language presses battled over the meaning and interpretation of events, making the written word central to the processes that shaped the new society. Because the migrants had come to this region from all over, they had varying relationships to orality and oral culture. They were, however, linked by their literacy and the access to economic and political power that such implied. Ultimately, then, these divergent patterns of literacy help to explain the distinctive form and content of culture and access to power that distinguished the various ethnic communities within San Juan.

Rural Society After 1910

Subsistence and dry farming on relatively unimproved lands (meaning land that did not have substantial irrigation, was not fertilized, and was not planted in the new market crops) left most Californio, Indian, and Mexican farmers in San Juan in a state of poverty. In the late nineteenth century, as we have seen, some of these families hung on as farmers and landowners by engaging in a variety of jobs in addition to their farming. These included such work as midwifery, seasonal fieldwork and the storing of crops, small business and trade ventures, artisanal work, and providing services such as washing. The economy, in other words, was still highly localized, despite the emergence of larger merchant-farmers; most goods and services were provided by fellow townspeople or nearby farmers, when they were not the product of household labor.

The new economy associated with commercial agriculture, however, slowly and inexorably changed the meaning of rural poverty. In the early twentieth century, the disparity between Californios who owned land but invested comparatively little for improvements and the large owners of town land who invested thousands in irrigation, orchards, and sheep increased dramatically. Between 1900 and 1911 alone, the value of town land rose more quickly than it had during the previous twenty-five years; those who remained in possession of their land thus had to secure an income sufficient to pay the higher taxes on this more valuable property. Some did: between 1900 and 1910, the percentage of Californios who farmed (exclusive of other work) rose from 19 to 21 percent. But others did not. As the sale and forfeiture of town and rural land proceeded, more year-round and seasonal jobs were created by the largest landowners, to which the dispossessed increasingly turned. This shift, in turn, had a negative impact on the generally poorer Californio farmers.

What is meant by the new rural poverty? The increasing availability of jobs for wages in agriculture, and the decreasing recourse to a family economy rooted in diverse jobs, seasonal farm labor, and subsistence agriculture, tied work lives more closely to year-round wage labor (though garden and orchard produce, along with chickens and small livestock, continued to provide an important part of most families' sustenance through the 1930s). This "family" kind of economy is characterized, for example, by the work of "old man Luis Cojo," a fisherman who sold fish from a mule-drawn two-wheel vending cart that he guided throughout the town but who also cut gravestones and painted buggies for extra income.[57] Independent workers and artisans like Cojo contributed to an aspect of town life that never entirely disappeared; nevertheless, that sector of the local economy became progressively less viable as commerce and wage labor expanded.

Some families began to seek year-round wages earlier than others, which led to seasonal movement out of town for many families. By 1900 the vast majority of the Californio and Indian populations in San Juan were working in the seasonal walnut harvest, and they soon began to work other crops in Orange County as well. These seasonal jobs enabled them to continue to reside in San Juan, where many owned a family home. When, during the late 1910s and early 1920s, walnut orchards in San Juan began to be changed over to citrus, women and young adults likewise transferred their seasonal employment to the citrus packing plants established in the latter part of the 1920s.

The actual percentage of unskilled Californio laborers did not increase substantially between 1880 and 1910 (from 50 to 52 percent), but the nature of their work changed. After 1910 work for wages was the most common kind of labor, in contrast to work in exchange for goods, skilled labor, garden produce, or a share of the crop. Joseph Yorba, for example, had worked on his uncle's farm as a young boy. With the exception of one acre, the family lost that property around 1900, when his mother sold twenty acres to obtain bail for one of her brothers who had been jailed for gambling, and she gave another brother the family adobe home. By 1910, then, Joseph Yorba's immediate family was landless; yet with income from the paid labor of two sons and their father, they were able to buy a house. Yorba's father and older brother paid the monthly mortgage, while Joseph, who, in his mid-teens, earned one dollar a day for nine hours of work, paid for the household's food.[58] Their employer, M. A. Forster, had walnut and orange orchards, raised horses, cattle, and hay, and farmed lima, black-eyed, and pink beans. The young Yorba and his father worked year-round in these crops. Joseph Yorba remained a laborer all his life. As an adult he worked hauling and threshing barley and beans, and he later became a union worker in a mine near San Juan.

Paul Arbiso's grandparents, to cite another example, had lived in San Juan during the Mexican period. His relatives on his father's side of the family were laborers in the late nineteenth century, and his mother's family had owned an 1841 grant of town land, which some family members had farmed. By the late 1880s, however, most of that land was sold to Randolph Cook, who subsequently made substantial improvements on the property. In 1906 Arbiso was orphaned without an inheritance, and he began to work on the Cook ranch, where he harvested and pressed barley. As a youth, too, he worked washing dishes at the Mendelson hotel. After World War I, and for most of his married life, he worked for the Williamses, a local farming family.[59]

These changes in farming and farm work took place elsewhere in Orange County as well. (See the decline in the percentage of Anglo-American and European farmers in appendix 4, and compare the jobs prevalent in 1900 to the late nineteenth century employment patterns shown in table 3.) In 1910 the crops grown by the small and tenant farmer—grains, hay, and potatoes—accounted for 60 percent of the value of the county's agricultural products; one decade later, the value of these crops had dropped to 25 percent of the total, while citrus and nut crops had risen from less than 40 percent to 75 percent of the county's total agricultural output. The increased production and value of these industrialized crops accounted in large part for the sharp rise in the county's agricultural product, from $2.5 million in 1900 to over $6 million in 1910 and over $25 million by 1920. By 1930, more than 70 percent of all the farms in the county were fruit farms.[60]

As the value of the land increased throughout Orange County, investors and farmers with capital became an ever larger presence in San Juan, as elsewhere. William Chapman, for example, secured land in different parcels between the late 1890s and 1917, by which time he owned 350,000 acres in northeastern Orange County. Chapman introduced the large-scale production and marketing of the Valencia orange; unlike most other large landowners, however, he maintained his own packing house and label, and he established a labor camp for his workers rather than join the citrus cooperative (see below).[61] James Irvine was the single largest landowner in the county. He had settled in the region in the late nineteenth century, and, like Forster and Moulton in San Juan, he raised a diversity of products on his land. The Irvine ranch had livestock, and a significant portion of the ranch remained in low-risk crops such as grains, beans, and sugar beets, all produced by tenant farmers (who also farmed Irvine's lower-value and higher-risk crops). The ranch began citrus production in 1906 and had approximately 3,000 acres in citrus by 1940, even though most citrus farms were under 30 acres in size.

The new conditions governing land values and crop specialization, and the emergence of an industrial form of production, were nowhere better exemplified than in citrus farming. Citrus orchards were high-investment ventures: the ten-acre orange farm required an average investment of $15,810, whereas ten acres in most other crops required a mere $4,810.[62] Citrus production raised the per-acre value of land in Los Angeles, Orange, and San Bernardino counties to the highest in the state by 1910. Although citrus farms were small, averaging between ten and twenty acres, growers developed marketing mechanisms that made the industry "the most highly organized of all agricultural pursuits."[63]

In 1895 the citrus farmers of Orange and six other counties formed the Southern California Fruit Exchange, a marketing cooperative. Whereas oranges had previously been sold directly by the growers to buyers or commission merchants, by 1917 four-fifths of all the citrus fruit in California was sold through the exchange. The cooperative's advertising campaigns expanded the market and effectively made citrus, long considered a luxury commodity, part of the national diet.[64]

In effect, the exchange brought the small farm into the large corporate enterprise. In 1898 walnut growers in Orange County formed the Santa Ana Valley Walnut Growers Association, and a regional group was in place by 1905. By 1900 Orange County was producing 46 percent of the state's nut crop, and by 1930 it was responsible for 33 percent of the world market's English walnuts. When the cooperative first formed, it paid its members 6.5 cents per pound of walnuts. By 1910 that amount had more than doubled, to 14 cents per pound.[65] The major development in the packing and marketing processes for walnuts occurred after the formation of the state association in 1912, with the institution, in 1915, of a brand name: "Diamond Brand" walnuts had a uniform size, grade, and bleaching method. Mechanization increased as the market was stabilized by the work of the association; in 1925, machinery was implemented that allowed the establishment of a uniform cracking standard.[66]

The small farmer, the tenant, the manager, and the large farmer each had a distinct socioeconomic position, and while the small farm was numerically dominant in the county through the 1930s, the large farm accounted for the bulk of the county's agricultural products. In 1930, for example, 88 percent of the farms had less than forty-nine acres, and they accounted for only 19 percent of the acreage under cultivation. Forty-four percent of these farms were worked by the owner or part-owner, 54 percent by a manager or tenant farmer. In contrast, 70 percent of the fruit and nut farms were operated by their owners, generally by means of the cooperative management and marketing structure.[67]

The differences between large and small growers, and between the interests of large landowners and tenants, grew more pronounced with the introduction of high-value crops, which favored the interdependence of agriculture, industry, and finance. The result was a decline in the number of small farmers and in the practices of subsistence and dry farming everywhere in the county after 1910.[68] A relatively poor sector of farmers and tenants did manage to persist through the early 1930s. Their role in the economy, however, changed. Whereas in the early part of the century the small farmer developed the dried fruit industry and supplied local crops for large canning factories and smaller "mom and pop" packing plants, after 1920 small farmers often moved into jobs in town.[69] Many Mexican immigrants, Californios, and Indians from areas like Pala and Pauma settled in the farming towns of Santa Ana and Anaheim and in the small, new towns that grew as centers of the highly seasonal citrus, nut, and sugar beet crops. Between 1900 and 1910 Santa Ana, the urban center of the county, developed a population of Californio residents that was larger than San Juan's; these Californios resided largely in neighborhoods with recent Mexican immigrants, whose number exceeded the entire county's Californio population by 1910.

San Juan was fully integrated into the county's agricultural economy early on, but its demography remained relatively constant until the early 1930s. In 1910, San Juan's Californio and Indian populations together accounted for over 56 percent of the total population, while the Mexican population constituted a mere 4 percent.[70] Before 1910, land had been used chiefly for small and subsistence rural production. Thereafter, however, subdivision created lots that were too small for substantial farming. With the loss of their larger tracts of land, many long-established Californio and Indian residents came to reside around the town's center and on one side of the railroad tracks.

The continuity in San Juan's population into the 1930s was extremely important for the construction of a collective memory and identities within the new economy and society created by industrial agriculture.

In this community people knew each other well, both in terms of family background and often personally, from birth through old age. Long-time resident Paul Arbiso recalled how, around 1910, when the town had some five hundred residents, he could stand in the center of San Juan outside the poolroom, where there were no city lights, and merely "by looking at the fellows and how they walked, we knew who they were."[71] Even in 1930, the family names that had dominated town life from the late nineteenth century still identified the largest group of residents.

Californio and Indian Identities During the 1920s and 1930s

The communal familiarity that enabled Arbiso to recognize a man by the way he walked persisted among long-time San Juan residents, in part because of their shared oral and religious culture, with which they affirmed a commitment and responsibility to one another. Yet at the same time, the industrialization of agriculture and the rise of the wage labor economy connected San Juan and its residents ever more closely to a regional society in which the village played a relatively marginal role. Towns like Santa Ana, by contrast, where many of San Juan's own residents settled in search of year-round work, were growing into lively communities with central roles to play in the developing economy.

It was partly in the interests of creating a broader-based economy for the town that the priest St. John O'Sullivan decided to restore the mission in an effort to promote tourism. O'Sullivan, a victim of tuberculosis, was sent to San Juan for its warm climate with comparatively few parish responsibilities. After receiving herbal medicines and treatment from a Californiana, he recovered, and began the restoration project with the full support of the local population who had taken him in. Many of the tales and legends discussed in this chapter were in fact written down by O'Sullivan, who heard them as part of the routine telling of stories over dinner and in daily encounters. He recorded them in a set of notebooks he called his *libritos* and later translated them into English and published them with the assistance of Charles Saunders, a frequent visitor to San Juan during this period. The very process of restoring the mission—including the excavation and rebuilding of decayed objects—may have helped elicit and shape the memories that

O'Sullivan heard, for in one way or another most of the people in San Juan were brought into the project. So were artisans from Mexico and other small mission towns in California, many of whom lived with town residents during the period of restoration; these craftsmen worked at reconstructing and painting not only the mission buildings, but also the statues and other religious artifacts attached to the church. Once the mission opened for tourism, local residents took on the job of mission gatekeeper.[72]

Some historians have focused on the monumentalization of the California missions that took place in the early 1900s as forming part of an American effort to create a romanticized Spanish past. However, the meaning of the missions for Anglo-Americans is only one side of the story.[73] For the Californio and Indian town residents, the mission's new prominence fostered the articulation of versions of their history and identity that expressed deeply held interpretations of the past.[74] Yet these collective identities forged during the 1920s and 1930s were also part of the ongoing process of defining American national identity. Many ethnic groups who were not considered "white" and who therefore did not fit into the equation "American = white" articulated separate identities in an attempt to define their unique rights and legitimate place in American society. The voices and organizations of these groups formed part of a debate over the meaning of the term *American* that took place throughout local politics and culture. San Juan's experience is a modest yet representative version of the politics of ethnicity and collective identity that occurred elsewhere in the United States during these years.

The Club Hispano Californio and the Mission Indian Federation were the two most prominent organizations responsible for formulating a politics of ethnicity in San Juan. One important project of the Club Hispano Californio in this regard was its drive to rename the streets of the town. In 1933, in a bilingual petition sent to the county supervisors, club members argued that existing street names such as Occidental, Broadway, Commercial, Main, Water, River, and Garden "totally ignore the historic landmarks and well established ancient place-names of this locality."[75] Members instead proposed names that referred to colonial California, and in particular to local geography and history; suggestions included the names of families (hence, Yorba and Rios streets), the central irrigation ditch (hence, La Zanja), the original road through town (El Camino Real), the town center (La Plaza), the mission itself, and the cluster of former neophyte homes (Los Indios). Eighty persons signed the petition to change the street names, the majority of them being property owners on the streets in question. Virtually every name, regardless of its linguistic or national origin (only nineteen of the eighty signers had a non-Spanish surname), represented families that had been in the vicinity of San Juan since at least the late nineteenth century. This fact affirmed the overall stability of a significant sector of the town's families. When the county supervisors accepted the proposed street names, they stated that the existing (American) names had never been formally adopted but had gained currency simply "through usage and custom."[76] The renaming thus downplayed the significance of a time when the merchant-farmers dominated economic and political change within the town, favoring instead longer-held, if somewhat reconfigured, local notions of the meaning of place.

In 1934, one of the organizers of the Club Hispano Californio, Alfonso Yorba, drew a map that was similarly intended to represent the collective history of San Juan (see map 6). It was based, he said, on the recollections of Yorba's uncle and other residents of the town who had described to him the San Juan of their youth.[77] Strikingly, the configuration of the map represents an interpretation of history that is quite similar to that found in California documents drawn up after the emancipation of the neophytes and the secularization of the mission. Whereas each Californio home is clearly identified by owner, the map deliberately fails to name any of the Indians of the town; their residences are simply marked with the term *indios*, despite the fact that the names of Juaneños who resided in town or were from families long connected to the former mission town were well known locally. The designation *indios criados de Juan Avila* (Indian servants of Juan Avila), in the lower center of the map, is a particularly sharp rendering of this historical juxtaposition of identities, wherein *indios* remained virtually anonymous, while "Spanish Californians" were treated as individual persons with distinct names. The map is a fairly accurate rendering of the early 1880s in its placement of the mission at the town center. The mission orchards and vineyards still flourished, and townspeople also grew crops on pueblo land. Buildings were low in density.

Yorba's map and an article he wrote on the history of San Juan formed part of an effort by Californios to inscribe a collective memory of San Juan's past onto the town's landscape. In his article, instead of positing a Californio identity through its contrast with the *indio* (non)identity, Yorba focused on the cultural life and built structures of the town to define the Californio regional group.[78] In the San Juan of

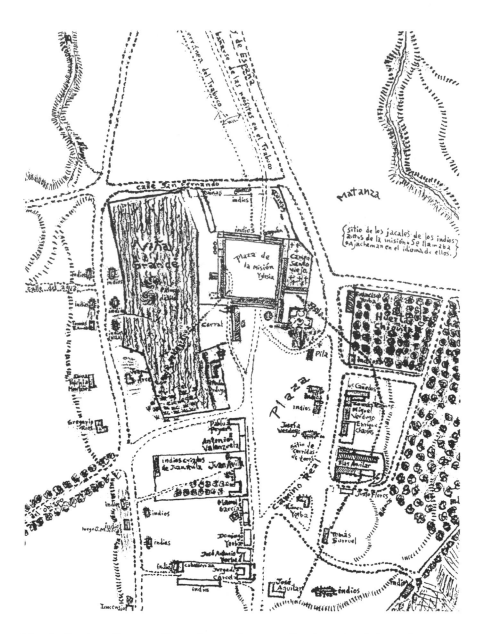

Map 6. Portion of a map of late-nineteenth-century San Juan, hand-drawn by
Alfonso Yorba, 1934. Compare this rendering of the mission and town center with
the assessor's version (map 5). Yorba presents a Californio view of history: Californio
residents are identified by name but *indios* remain anonymous. Courtesy Mission
San Juan Capistrano Archives.

the 1930s, he pointed out, Spanish was still the dominant language, and traditions of nicknames, games, songs, and music continued to be drawn from Mexican California. The adobes and the mission likewise enabled a collective life to persist in San Juan. Restored or in ruins, these buildings were symbols of a past that continued to shape the present. Yorba rebuked those who built "little wooden shacks" near their adobes and allowed the latter to fall into ruin. For him, this practice represented a turning away from the past, a trend that had begun after the introduction of the railroad in 1888, which in turn perpetuated the flourishing of new, and deleterious, economic and political forces in the region.

Yorba presented two versions of history, both of which were given some substance by the built and imagined historical space of San Juan; the members of the Club Hispano Californio also described their sense of and involvement in local history by renaming the streets of the town. In each case, long-held notions of ethnic identities were rearticulated: the *indio* was nameless, while the "Spanish Californian" was not only named but also clearly recognized as the possessor of property. At the same time, however, new notions of ethnicity were being brought into play. By the 1920s the term *Spanish Californian,* which had long connoted the privileges historically derived from the colonial position of the "Spaniard," embraced many persons of complex ethnic and racial backgrounds. Hence, persistent Spanish-language practices and customs identified with Spanish and Mexican California were sufficient to define "Spanish Californians." For Juaneños who spoke Spanish and had established close family connections with non-Indians, the historical distinctions between Californios and Indians did not form static boundaries. Many members of the Club Hispano Californio in fact also belonged to the Mission Indian Federation, the San Juan chapter of which was formed in 1924. Perhaps for many Mission Indian Federation members, the label *indio* on Yorba's map at least acknowledged their place in history, although it replicated the invisibility of Indian persons in colonial, Mexican, and U.S. documents.

In this period Indian identity was also being asserted by town residents who had previously claimed only "Spanish Californian" identity. Many members of the Indian Federation were one generation removed or more from the villages to the southeast. Their knowledge of Juaneño and other Indian dialects was fragmentary at best. Nevertheless, they joined other Indians in the region who were, in effect, constructing a public representation of their own history. Although Juaneños had not yet articulated a version of their past that would contest the favorable portrayal of the church's role in proselytizing their ancestors, their identity as mission Indians was beginning to bring them into new political alliances with a larger number of Indians. The photograph of delegates to the Mission Indian Federation convention of 1924 (see the frontispiece to this book) emphasizes the range of self-representations common among members of the federation. This variation is consistent with the emergence of new articulations of Indian consciousness and identity.[79]

Indian identity had been strongly asserted by some individuals in their personal lives, but the political expression of this identity came to the fore because of two developments. During the 1920s, when San Juan was building a high school and restructuring its elementary and secondary programs, Anglo-American residents of the town requested that Indian children be removed from the public schools and sent to the Sherman Indian school in Riverside County. Although it never was mandatory, many parents sent some or all of their children to this school for varying periods of their education; other Indian children remained in the San Juan public schools.[80] Then, in 1928, the California Indians Jurisdictional Act was passed, thanks to the efforts of the Mission Indian Federation and other groups to gain compensation for the lands California Indians had lost to the United States. More than four hundred individuals in Orange County alone registered to receive the benefits accruing to them through their status as California Indians.[81] Half of these lived in San Juan, the other half lived in Santa Ana, Anaheim, El Toro, Tustin, Orange, Fullerton, and Atwood. For some families, the years of denying Indian heritage because of society's prejudices resulted in ambivalent declarations: some parents registered only their children; other families remained divided, with some members claiming Indian status and others refusing to acknowledge any Indian ancestry.[82] Registration reflected a new consciousness about being Indian, and it initiated an era when Juaneños began to pursue the full set of federal benefits. From 1928 to the present, Juaneños received recognition as mission Indians, but not as a separate group; tribal status is still being sought.

Memory, Ethnicity and Community

The local memories of any community accumulate like the writing on a palimpsest, a parchment inscribed repeatedly, whereon the remnants of imperfectly erased earlier versions can still be seen underneath the newer writing. Memories of San Juan expressed in oral histories during and after the 1970s by men and women who recalled the town of their youth (from around 1900 through the 1930s) reflected deeply held ideas about that past, though filtered through the language and perspectives of the present and structured in part by the storytellers' relationship to the English-speaking interviewers and their questions. The history related by these men and women often includes elements of the history retold herein, though sometimes our interpretations diverge. In any case, the interviews suggest not only how memories help to forge group identity, but also how each group positioned itself within the town and how each group defined itself in relation to others.

Californios, still the largest segment of the population through the 1930s, when Spanish was the most commonly used language in town, for the most part spoke favorably about other national and ethnic groups in San Juan, which included Indian, Spanish, French, Irish, Portuguese, German, Mexican, Italian, and American residents. Californios sometimes identified relatives or spouses as having their origins in these other groups. Paul Arbiso, for example, referred to an "old Indian woman" who was his aunt through marriage to his uncle; Delfina Manriquez de Olivares mentioned the "old Indian woman" who helped her mother; and Gladys Pryor Landell spoke of "an old Indian named Diego" who lived down by the river and had worked in her parents' orchards.[83] All three also described other ethnic groups in a language that was, at least on the surface, free of antagonism. Delfina Olivares asserted, "There were maybe two or three American families and they used to go with us. We used to have fun and we used to mix together."[84] Paul Arbiso claimed, "When we went to school we didn't know nothing about talking English and those American boys over there, they didn't know how to talk Spanish. But they learned Spanish and we learned English. Out in the playground we spoke whatever we wanted."[85]

Gladys Pryor Landell presents one Californio perspective on San Juan that is clearly shaped by the predominance of Californios in the town's social sphere. Her father's family was from Philadelphia; he came west with his parents at the age of six and lived in Anaheim, where German was the common language, though he also learned Spanish. Her mother's family were Californios from the landowning Avila, Pryor, and Dominguez families. In her house Spanish was spoken, and the children did not learn English until they went to school.[86] Landell recalled a community in which no hostile distinctions were made according to ethnicity or nationality during the early years of the twentieth century.

For her, the town was simply a large extension of family. "I always thought everyone in Capistrano was related to me because we were taught to call them aunt and uncle. . . . You never called an older person by only their first name or their last name. It was always 'Tia' or 'Tio.' My father did the same, and everyone that came to the house always called my grandmother Tia Rosa. So naturally I thought we were all related, which many of us were distantly."[87] She also discussed the godparent relationships that created a community of fictive kin in her childhood. The godparents watched over, disciplined, and cared for their godchildren, always inquiring whether "they needed anything and wanted anything and always looked after them."[88] Status or economic differences among Californios were bridged by these social relations.

In contrast to Landell, whose position in San Juan society was obviously quite comfortable, Indians whose families had embraced their Indian identity before the 1920s, when many "Spanish Californians" began to acknowledge their own Indian ancestry, expressed some bitterness about the past. In their memories, "Spaniards," "Mexicans," and "Indians" were very clearly distinguished one from the other. They recalled the paternalism of the rich toward the poor, and the way sons and daughters were disowned because they married "Indians."[89] Evelyn Villegas, for example, talked of her father's disinheritance for marrying her mother, and how she and her brothers and sisters were rejected by her father's family even though their paternal grandmother was herself a mestiza, or of mixed origin. She said, "Your Spanish are very light, not all of them, but the majority are light complected people. In those days, . . . this is what I understand from my mother talking, they didn't want to be classed as Indians because the Indians were looked upon as low life in other words, you're just at the bottom of the totem pole there. And you say 'I'm Spanish' when you elevated yourself a little more." The tensions between Californios and Indians are exemplified in the villagers' views of the elderly Chola Martina (see figure 12).[90]

Reflections like these were built on stories told by grandparents and parents as well as on direct experience. For each generation, the public and political meaning of Indian identity changed. The generation of Indians who reached adulthood prior to 1920 often did not participate in the Indian Federation after its founding. They had grown up in an era when the religious community prevailed, and they maintained close relationships with Indian villages nearby. Evelyn Villegas's grandmother, for example, frequently cooked for the priest, and her life was ordered according to the religious calendar of the Catholic Church; but

Fig. 12. Chola Martina, San Juan, 1907. Martina was a *curandera* who healed with herbs. Her husband was a shoemaker. Some town residents spoke of her respectfully as Doña Martina; others remembered her as a *bruja,* or witch, who had the ability (that many Californios associated with Indian heritage) to cast spells and turn herself into a dog. Courtesy Southwest Museum, Los Angeles, photo no. N22092.

she also consulted the *curandero* and *curandera* and attended seasonal celebrations in Pala. Her antagonism toward institutions and persons who scorned Indians was clear in the stories she told her granddaughter: "The priest always had a lot of food to eat . . . after they ate the watermelon they'd throw the rinds at the Indians. That's what they got to eat." Her recollections, and her place within the community, contributed to shape her daughter's and granddaughter's defiant articulation of Indian identity. Evelyn Villegas's mother was a leader in the local chapter of the Mission Indian Federation, and Evelyn Villegas plays a leadership role in the Juaneño council of San Juan.[91]

The bell ringer José de Gracia Cruz likewise revealed his sense of the gulf that separated Indians from the dominant society in an interaction recorded by O'Sullivan in his *librito*. Speaking in an era when resistance was largely suppressed, Gracia Cruz relied on a language of double meaning to make his point. When asked by the priest O'Sullivan why he was not rich from his work as a sheepshearer, Gracia Cruz responded: "It is not good for an Indian to be rich, padre. There are not any rich Indians. It would not do, padre. A rich Indian is proud; he won't take orders from you or any American; but when all his money is gone . . . he is very humble." The irony escaped the priest, who heard in this statement only the words of a "child of the mission."[92]

In relating their early memories of San Juan, persons of European and Anglo-American origins accentuated the predominance of the Spanish language and the strong Californio and Indian presence in public life. Although they emphasized the close interaction of members of all national and ethnic groups during their youth, their language and descriptions nevertheless revealed a sense of unbridgeable difference based on social class and historical/racial pasts. These informants' awkward references to Californio and Indian ethnicity and to a social structure based unambivalently on ethnicity indicate one of the consequences of the changing economic milieu in San Juan in the early twentieth century. As more Californios and Indians entered the wage labor market in industrialized agriculture, they were drawn into a society that was constructing identities according to a polarized, English-language racial notion that focused, in this locale, on "whites" and "Mexicans." This notion, in turn, communicated the economic hegemony that shaped Anglo-Americans' particular historical identity. Yet the white/Mexican polarity did not define the social world of San Juan. As a result, ethnic references to Californios, Indians, and Mexicans were belabored and awkward for people whose families had migrated to San Juan in the nineteenth century. In their interviews for the Cal State Fullerton Oral History Collection, for example, Russell Cook and Ethel Rosenbaum Pease searched for ways to define the ethnicity of Californios and the relationship between the Californio and Indian populations.

Cook's memories of the town contrast sharply to Landell's town full of fictive relatives. His family arrived in San Juan in 1868 and purchased the Cañedo property in the late nineteenth century. Some of his relatives had also been squatters on the Yorba property in the 1870s. Yet he, like other descendants of migrants from this period, was careful to locate his family among the purchasers, rather than the squatters, of land-grant property, the latter historically being looked on with disfavor. Cook went to the San Juan Elementary School in the decade of the 1900s. "There were so many Indians and Spanish-speaking that I had to learn to talk Spanish so that I would know when to fight. [laughter] I mean, there was so many of them that there were no American games played. They were all Indian games."[93] Cook's remark about fighting was meant as a joke, but it betrays his acute sense of the potentially antagonistic differences that set him apart from other students. When questioned about the Indian population, he claimed that pure bloods had died out but that the Spanish-speaking population had "all got Indian blood in them more or less because of the mixing." The rest of San Juan's population, he said, "were all ranchers or farmers. The Spanish-speaking people worked on their ranches. . . . We had to rely upon their labor. So it made it very much a sort of a community affair. We had our Saturday night dances where we would all dance together, Spanish and all."[94] In his memory, Cook clearly distinguished perceived social groups by economic activity and equated Spanish speakers with a single mixed-blood race. In this, his definition diverged from Californio and Indian articulations of their identity, and it erased the Californio farmer from the record altogether.

Ethel Rosenbaum Pease was careful to state her lack of prejudice when talking about the Californios and Indians with whom she grew up. Born in 1892 in San Juan, as were her parents, she and her father had both been delivered by midwife Aguilar, a Californiana whose family had lived in San Juan for generations. Her memories of elementary school illustrate her construction of ethnicity: "I don't know how many of the children were of Spanish and Indian ancestry, which we call Mexican. I think when we were going, there were only about six or eight at the most who were not Mexican in the whole school. . . . Many of the children seldom went past the third or fourth grade and then they just quit. . . . Most of the parents were of Spanish extraction or mostly Indian and they just stayed home."[95]

Although Pease did not distinguish "Spanish" people from Indians when it came to behavior or social position, like Cook she drew a clear line between these populations and the "farmers." In discussing town fires, for example, she explained that "every farmer dropped what he was doing. . . . Even the Mexicans from Capistrano came. You'd see them coming by on their horses in a dead run with shovels. . . . These Mexicans didn't own anything, didn't farm or anything but they just did it."[96] Her memory that "Mexicans" did not farm or own anything is contrary to fact. In her construction of identity, however, they were defined against the collective group of persons of European and Anglo-American descent, whom she defines not in ethnic terms but in terms of occupation and status as property owners. Her family were successful homesteaders who farmed grain, cattle, walnuts, and, later, oranges. The workers, she recalls, were "local people . . . mostly they were Mexican people."[97]

Pease defined the Californio and Indian populations in the San Juan of her youth by using the twentieth-century notion of "Mexican," a racial identity equated with mixed blood, physical labor, and poverty. Such an understanding of San Juan's historic community is stated also by H. L. Remmers, a farmer who arrived in San Juan sometime during the 1930s and became one of a handful of large landowners nearby. Remmers did not have the experience of growing up in the town, nor did he have any close relationships with the town's Californio and Indian populations. Unlike Cook and Pease, therefore, Remmers did not search for ethnic terms in his interview. He defined San Juan's population with the straightforward simplicity characteristic of the Anglo-American newcomer of this era: "You see, what we had here were Mexican families that lived in Capistrano. They worked on the farms."[98]

This depiction of San Juan is that of a farmer whose position within an economically dominant Anglo-American community structured his interpretation of place. It was partly to combat this sort of characterization by giving meaning to ethnicity through historical identities that the members of the Club Hispano Californio petitioned to rename the streets after "historic place names" and "ancient landmarks" and thus inscribe their histories on town space. How Californios' and Indians' various articulations of their historical communities fit into the culture of Greater Mexico takes this story beyond San Juan, to an exploration of the ways in which ethnic and national identities were similarly being constructed and negotiated elsewhere in the American Southwest during the early twentieth century.

CHAPTER 4

Regional Culture

Colonial and Mexican regional history continued to be meaningful in the collective memory of residents of San Juan and persons of Juaneño and Californio background elsewhere in Orange County. This foundation for historical culture was strengthened after 1900 when immigration expanded the kinds of live performance offered. The ideas about history, society, race, and national identity presented in a vast array of theatrical genres and in cinema constituted a shared body of knowledge that connected local populations to a larger and international Spanish-language culture.

Plays and other live performances portrayed a world distinct from that embodied in English-language productions, one that proved invaluable for interpreting contemporary society. Entertainment was expanded and changed further with the development of the film industry. Silent movies complemented many a tent theater, popular circus, or high drama performance prior to 1930; after that date, although the movies became more widely available than live theater, actors, actresses, and family tent companies continued to circulate among the Spanish-speaking populations of the Southwest.

In this chapter my focus shifts from the local area of Orange County to examine the Spanish-language theater (defined in the broadest sense to incorporate multiple genres and types of performance, including film) that was, according to Nicolás Kanellos, "the most popular and culturally relevant artistic form" in Hispanic communities throughout the United States from 1880 through 1930. Large professional companies and smaller, traveling tent theater troupes and circuses performed all along the border and in such subregions as south Texas and the California central valley. The *carpas,* or tent theaters, would announce their performances by means of the *convite verbal,* an oral invitation delivered throughout the neighborhood by a clown or by local children from the barrios who would thereby gain free admission to the show. Entrance to these performances might be obtained with an egg, other goods, or a small sum.[1] Even following the rise and then dominance of the cinema during the 1930s, the worldview and sensibility fostered by the theater persisted, both in movies and in those companies that continued to travel from community to community to share their offerings.

Theater was integral to the process of building and defining an ethnic community in the Southwest during the crucial period when Mexican immigration dramatically expanded the region's population and migrant pathways established new social and geographical links between places like Orange County and distant towns and rural populations.[2] The infrastructure for these developments was laid in the late nineteenth century. The railroads that increasingly interconnected this cultural area were built partly by Mexicans and Americans of Mexican descent, and in the decade of the 1880s rail routes multiplied markedly. In 1881, for example, three railroads entered El Paso, Texas, connecting this long-established commercial stop on the Spanish trail to places on both sides of the border and, by 1884, directly to Mexico City.[3] The early 1880s saw the construction of a line through New Mexico and Arizona by the Atchison, Topeka, and Santa Fe Railroad, which connected these territories to the Gulf of California via the Sonoran railway. The Southern Pacific's "Sunset Line" was completed in 1881. Larger companies and the smaller *carpas* traveled this route and its many feeder lines to perform in small pueblos on both sides of the border and in the rural interiors and urban centers of each country. With the onset of the Mexican revolution of 1910, larger companies settled in cities, and notable theater centers developed. Laredo and San Antonio in Texas, Tucson and Los Angeles hosted touring companies from Mexico, Spain, and other countries in Latin America. Indeed, despite its eventual identity largely as ethnic theater in the United States, the international dimensions of this early flowering cannot be underplayed. By the 1910s, companies moved along the southwestern circuit bringing productions to San Antonio, Laredo, and Los Angeles that had originally been performed before audiences in Madrid, Buenos Aires, Mexico City, and New York.[4]

As the most popular artistic form, theater shaped a collective sense of history among Spanish-speaking populations that, though of diverse origins, came to reside together in long-established places like San Juan and in newer agricultural, mining, and railroad towns and cities. Theater audiences were conversant with representations of Spain, colonial Mexico, and other areas of Spain's New World empire. Well over half of the plays presented by the larger companies were written by Spanish dramatists. These playwrights, together with their counterparts in Mexico and elsewhere in Latin America, recreated sixteenth-century intrigues in the Spanish court and described life among the merchant and religious elites in colonial and postcolonial capitals from Havana to Mexico City to Manila. In a single evening of entertainment, the audience could see a melodrama in verse that reenacted political history in Mexico or critiqued New World slavery, and a modern social drama. The large, family audiences that frequented the theater were used to imagining past and present events in Spain and its former colonies, and to seeing plays that drew upon their religious imagination. In *La llorona* and *Las cuatro apariciónes de la Virgen de Guadalupe,* for example, audiences recognized well-known legends drawn from oral tradition and religious theater (see below). Oral tradition incorporated written cultural products and, in turn, contributed stories and themes, language and style, to written pieces. In their travels, actors and actresses encountered variations on old stories, tales, and formulaic elements of language; these they incorporated into their repertoire through improvisation of character or speech. Such innovations enabled the theater to speak to common elements of a shared historical and religious imagination.

The complexity of knowledge and ideas that defined the oral culture discussed in chapter 3 becomes evident through a study of the theater. Literacy rates for Orange County (see figure 11) suggest the significance of orality as a cultural practice among the Mexican-origin population who were unlettered in 1910.[5] The rise of literacy rates among Californios and Californianas from 1860 probably reflects trends elsewhere in the Southwest among regional peoples of Mexican descent. At the same time, the theater addressed regional audiences of Californios, Tejanos, and Tucsanenses who came from communities in which the older people were embedded in a folk culture centered primarily on orality and the traditions, legends, and historical references common to the culture of Greater Mexico. Despite the growing literacy of Californios and other regional groups in the Southwest, their sensibilities were also shaped by the formal elements of orality and by local cultures that developed out of the Spanish colonial experience. These shared dimensions of culture established the basis for growth of a southwest regional culture, despite variations in language, tradition, and history by state and locality within Mexico and the United States. Literate and unlettered adults of 1900 and 1910 were able to participate in a formal culture that incorporated the "high" arts within a popular setting. Audiences of all levels of erudition and social class attended productions together. The seating configuration, rather than the genre of entertainment or selection of repertoire, was what signaled social differentiation.

Formulaic elements and rhyme, serving as mimetic devices, are critical aspects of both oral cultures generally and the theater that arises in such cultures. The dominance of such formulas and rhyme in nineteenth-century theater pieces continued into the twentieth century in the works performed by Spanish-language troupes. A reliance on dialogue, long-drawn-out explanation, and such ploys of classical romanticism as the sinister villain, the perfect hero, and the formulaic plots of melodrama similarly addressed this aesthetic sensibility shaped by orality. A strong oral basis is suggested in the fact that through the 1910s the most popular dramas were written in verse, a form that helps to convey the plot to memory, or they were sung in the form of light comic opera, or *zarzuelas,* which relied on proverblike sayings and repetitive phrasing to draw audiences in. Although by the 1910s dramatic and vaudeville companies and the *carpas* were also performing modernist pieces, which departed from traditional forms by having minimal staging and an absence of formulaic dialogue, these companies did not discard their old repertoire. Rather, they continued to feature oratory, recitation, and the practice of *buen hablar,* a form that emphasized dexterity of speech and wordplay. Many of the 130 plays in one collection, *La Compañía Cómico-Dramática Villalongín,* were written by hand (perhaps as it was being dictated to an actor), copied from a text, or transmitted verbally, and dated. Published copies may well have been scarce at times (the plays in this collection dated from the 1840s through the early 1920s); the *apuntador* (prompter) who copied these plays thus performed the service of the *escrivan* in committing the words to writing. The possession of each text is clearly defined by handwritten notations placed throughout the text, or with the stamp of the performer. These markings of possession and also of stage direction suggest the vital relationship between the spoken and the written word that constitutes the performative dimension of theater.

In the Southwest, traveling theater joined highly localized cultures together in a broader regional culture, and there, as in Mexico, it helped shape national identities. In the United States in particular, popular theater began to give expression to the bilingual and bicultural sensibilities of the immigrant generation and their children. It contributed to building a common language of group identity and shared worldview. The following discussion of the theater rests on a conception of the United States as a country built on ethnic cultures of regional dimensions, connected through language and historical experience to cultures beyond national borders. The theater provides a graphic sense of the content of that historical consciousness and imagination, and some of the ways in which collective identity has been shaped.

An "Ethnic" Theater

Spanish-language circus, tent, religious, and dramatic theater was performed in California from the beginning of the colonial era. After 1848, steamships traveled regularly along the California coast, often bringing itinerant companies to perform in the older pueblos. Between 1860 and 1890, Mexican touring companies settled in Los Angeles and performed at newly established Spanish-language theaters and in the Opera House, sometimes presenting the work of local playwrights. Performances, announced in English-, French-, and Spanish-language newspapers, attracted an ethnically and socially diverse public, the varying status of which was reflected in seating arrangements (that is, by the price of a ticket).[6]

An evening's program would be very similar in structure to that found in professional theaters throughout the nation. Shakespeare and what would become the classic English-language stage repertoire were presented in a long evening of performance that might also include orators, orchestral music, jugglers, singers, minstrels, dancers, and acrobats. Yet whereas in English-language theater a split eventually occurred between "highbrow" and "lowbrow" offerings and audiences, such was not the case in Mexican theater.[7]

In Mexico, theaters in both the capital and the provinces (including the southwestern United States) continued to accommodate a broad sector of the population, and "high" culture remained standard fare for all classes.[8] Because this theater was developed for a Mexican national and immigrant audience that, despite increasing literacy, was still rooted in an oral tradition, it was accessible to lettered and unlettered, young and old people alike. The theater's long program bills thus carried a nineteenth-century tradition into the twentieth century. This enduring relationship between the legitimate theater and its broad-based audience is one feature that gave Spanish-language companies the classification of ethnic theater. New theatrical genres developed, but never in opposition to legitimate theater.

The social class distinctions that defined this audience of immigrants and native born were reflected in the hierarchy of seating within the larger theaters. In 1909, for example, seats in Teatro Calderón in San Antonio, Texas, ranged in price from 15 cents for the balcony to $1.00 for the *luneta,* or front circle; in the Teatro del Progreso in San Antonio, that range was slightly greater, from 10 cents for gallery seats to $1.50 for the *luneta.* In smaller houses, a single, general admission price might be charged. One production of *Tierra baja,* for example, had a ticket price of 30 cents, while *La almadía de Castro,* which was performed in two parts over successive nights, cost 10 cents per performance.[9]

To state the important differences between English- and Spanish-language theater is not to divorce the latter from central currents in American cultural life during the first three decades of the twentieth century. Other ethnic companies, especially those devoted to Yiddish theater and Italian opera, performed classic works in the original or translation, giving actors and actresses who later worked on the English-language national stage and in films their first break. Many English-language tent theaters had playbills similar to those common among traveling Spanish-language companies, with dramatic melodrama and a variety of other acts the standard fare. Tent theater, which built on traditions of medicine shows, Uncle Tom's Cabin troupes, acrobatics, and menagerie displays, was performed before English-speaking rural audiences throughout the nineteenth century, reaching its height of popularity in 1919. By then, the hundreds of touring tent theaters had begun writing their own plays, using smaller casts and fewer acts, and "making the dramas more relevant to small-town and rural life."[10]

English-language vaudeville also expanded its audience during these years. For the multiethnic troupe that performed on the vaudeville stage, performances were "egalitarian in a competitive way . . . the key criterion for success [being] the ability to put an act over."[11] Despite the emergence of highly centralized circuits and monopoly chains that dominated the forty or fifty theaters across the nation where big-time acts could be seen, there were about ten thousand other theaters or showplaces in the United States where vaudevillians could work. "The earnings of a small-time actor," one critic argued, "might be as much as $100 for a week, if he worked a full week, which compared very favorably with what he might have earned as an unskilled worker or even as a skilled craftsman."[12] While rooted in the immigrant and working-class backgrounds of its players, vaudeville spoke to a broad national audience, shaping over a generation of ethnic American identities.

Although the productions and performance styles of the Spanish-language stage crossed national boundaries and shared elements with other theater in the United States, the relationship between this theater and its audience was characteristic of ethnic theater in the way it shaped and affirmed community. Interaction was facilitated by the proximity of the *teatros* to downtown barrios—areas where Mexicans lived, worked, and shopped—and the frequency with which performances were mounted in neighborhood cultural centers, mutual aid societies, and churches. Audiences could be expected to attend with little prior notice. Broadsides for productions of Spanish-language legitimate theater in San Antonio, for example, announced "un gran función para hoy"—a performance to be held that same day. This broadside was written in a characteristically direct and personal style. The performance, it promised, reflected the delicacy and good taste of the modern, internationally acclaimed piece being offered, *Tierra baja,* which had been translated from Catalan into Castilian and other languages. The announcement thus appealed to the literary appetite of the anticipated audience, who were made aware of the performance's broad-based, contemporary appeal.[13]

This announcement was typical. Broadsides and playbills regularly assumed an avid audience available for hours of long entertainment. Employing a personal voice, they gave the illusion, at least, that a personal relationship existed between company and audience. Carlos Villalongín of the San Antonio–based Villalongín Company, for instance, addressed his announcement of the French drama *La abadía de Castro* to "las distinguidas familias que cariñosas acuden siempre á mi llamamiento" (the distinguished families who have always lovingly responded to my call). To affirm its value for the whole family, the company's publicity called the play "moral, sublime, and passionate." The full program also included orchestral music and silent film clips, shown during intermissions.[14] Similarly, a Spanish *zarzuela* company in 1909 announced six performances of comic light opera that constituted entertainment for the entire family. The playbill defined this company's productions as *altamente morales,* or highly moral, and emphasized the plays' high literary quality—a claim that underlines the points made above about the Spanish-language theater's presentation of "high culture" to a socially diverse audience.[15]

The name of the Los Angeles theater house known as California–El Teatro Digno de la Raza (California–Dignified Theater of the Race) reveals the personal relationship that theater companies attempted to establish with their public, again in a manner reminiscent of oral culture.[16] The name emphasizes that this is a "dignified" playhouse where legitimate theater, *teatro de revista* (a form of Mexican vaudeville), and variety acts were performed. The broadside for this particular evening was written in the voice of the actress Elisa García López, who stated that she dedicated the dramatic piece "con gran cariño a la colonia mexicana de esta ciudad" (with great affection to the Mexican colony of this city). In a warm, sentimental, highly personal invitation, she explained that her father was the author of the play and that he had died a few hours after finishing it. She would, she said, perform the play according to his last wishes. Thus the audience was invited into "her" family drama by means of the broadside: the melodramatic mood was established even before the performance began. After the play, García López recited prose and gave a speech; she was followed by a singer billed as the *Gardel mexicano* (after Carlos Gardel, the highly popular tango singer from Argentina, who was a cultural icon across the Americas), a dancer, and a couple with a variety act, who closed the show.[17]

The name California–El Teatro Digno de la Raza is also significant in that it reflects a notion of Mexican nationhood as articulated by the revolutionary generation of 1910. The term *raza* contests the racial nationalism that equated whiteness with citizenship, a concept then prevalent in the United States, Europe, and most of Latin America, by establishing the *mestizo* (mixed "race" of Spaniard and Indian) as the symbol of Mexican national identity.[18] A number of plays that were widely performed, especially around the time of national celebrations, illustrate in abbreviated form how the theater was involved in building a patriotic consciousness that often infused Mexican-American ethnic identity. Two well-known pieces that explain the origins of the Mexican War for Independence (1810; independence from Spain is celebrated on September 16) reveal two very different interpretations. *El grito de Dolores* was written in 1850 by the Cuban playwright Juan Miguel de Losada; *El Cura Hidalgo, o El glorioso grito de independencia* was written in 1910 by the Mexican playwright Constancio Suarez.[19] Each play was performed by the Villalongín company through 1920, though Losada's play was apparently edited to conform to early-twentieth-century patriotic ideas. A similar story line marks both plays: the priest Miguel Hidalgo y Costilla, from the town of Dolores, is presented as the leader of a local group of conspirators who are plotting to overthrow Spanish rule in Mexico. Learning that their plans have been revealed to Spanish authorities, they are forced to begin the revolt earlier than anticipated. Hidalgo gives the *grito*, or call for rebellion, from his church balcony, and the play ends with the revolt against the Spaniards in full swing.

Juan Miguel de Losada's 1850 play was written in long monologues of rhymed verse and focused on the drama of intrigue attendant on the betrayal of the rebels' plans. The promptbook was heavily edited to abbreviate this laborious form and to revise Losada's presentation of the independence struggle and the resulting nationalistic spirit. Losada had used the mode of heroic narrative so that he might compare Hidalgo favorably to the Spanish conquerors Cortés and Pizarro—a comparison that would be unthinkable for a Mexican playwright, especially by 1901, when Suarez wrote his piece. For Losada, Hidalgo was significant as a hero of Latin American independence, a cause for which he and other Cubans were fighting in 1850 (Cuba, Puerto Rico, and the Philippines did not gain independence until 1898). He therefore articulated an identity that embraced all the peoples of the Spanish Americas—"antes que todo soy americano" (above all I am American)—rather than the more narrow, national identity of Cuban or Mexican. The *apuntador* and director who worked from this promptbook crossed out references to *el águila americana* (the American eagle), replacing that symbol of national independence with the Mexican eagle. Arguments for independence that did not correspond to what was developing as "official memory" in Mexico were also cut—such as the phrase, spoken by a servant woman, "De unas maneras o de otras, al cabo, para nosotras habrá siempre despotismo" (in one way or another there will always be despotism for us—that is, women). This character's critique of gender inequity as part of the political ideology of the independence struggle is characteristic of Losada's embrace of universal rights and principles, as opposed to the specific, and generally more sexually and socially conservative, defense of the national group.

Suarez's 1901 play, in contrast, reflects a language of twentieth-century Mexican nationalism, including the notion of the *inspirada patriota*, or "inspired woman patriot." In his version, it is a letter from just such a woman, who has been arrested, that prompts Hidalgo to issue the call for independence and begin the war. Suarez also engages the religious imagination through the person of Hidalgo's niece, who prays to the Virgin of Guadalupe fervently, in a manner that would draw the audience itself into the act of prayer. Through this character, the play builds on the religiosity of an "imagined community" of Mexicans, a term used by Benedict Anderson to describe the phenomenon by which "members of even the smallest nation will never know most of their fellow-members . . . yet in the minds of each lives the image of their communion." During the past two centuries, Anderson argues, these imaginings have created nations "where they do not [in fact] exist."[20] Suarez assumes Mexican nationhood from the very first encounter with the Spanish. As Hidalgo states, "Lo que a mi me entristece en alto grado, es el estado humilante y servil que guarda nuestra patria, dominada hace tres siglos por España" (What saddens me to the extreme is the humiliated and servile state that our country is in, dominated for three centuries by Spain). For Suarez, Mexican nationhood rests squarely on an idealized Aztec past. Hidalgo refers to Mexicans as "hijos de Anáhuac," possessing "la ardorosa sangre de Cuauthémoc!"— sons of the place of Aztec origin, possessing the ardent blood of the last Aztec ruler, Cuauthémoc. This nationalist trend is augmented in the promptbook by a new ending that twice denounces the conquistadors and that glorifies the fight for equality and liberty.

The theater, in short, was an important medium for formulating ideas about national identity and history and bringing them into public discussion. In Mexico and the southwestern United States, plays were often used to tell the national story. And depending on where they were performed, those plays took on various meanings. *El 5 de Mayo*, for example, written in verse by Luciano Frías y Soto, concerns the origins of the national holiday that memorializes a battle fought between young Mexican republicans and the forces of Emperor Maximilian, who ruled Mexico's French-imposed empire between 1864 and 1867.[21] The day commemorates, in effect, the effort of patriot rebels to remove foreign rulers from Mexican soil, and in this sense it took on an added significance in the southwestern United States, which was looked on as Mexican territory that in 1848 was usurped by the United States. The promptbook suggests that *El 5 de Mayo* was performed each May, along with *Maximiliano I, emperador de México*, an exemplary piece of patriotic melodrama written by an anonymous playwright.[22] This play opens on a weak Napoleon speaking to his advisors about setting up an empire in Mexico. It then follows Napoleon to Austria, where he discusses with

Maximilian, a liberal noble interested in reform, the latter's appointment as emperor of Mexico. Most of this long drama, however, focuses on the story of republican resistance against Maximilian that brought Benito Juárez, Indian governor of Oaxaca, to power as the most impressive liberal president of nineteenth-century Mexico. In addition, the play stresses, resistance to the French was kept alive, to an important degree, by the actions of women patriots. The love stories that weave the play together are impressive for their complicated equation of romantic love, family love, and love of the patria.

Although the national story was often featured on the stage, dramatic offerings were not restricted to the narrow bounds of nationalist exposition. The *teatro de revista*, for instance, commented on the political life of the nation and brought the sacred, whether of patria or church, into the realm of irony and laughter. While plays with nationalist themes and melodramatic pieces generally conformed to what Jean Franco discusses as the new codification of gender roles after independence in Mexico, the range of theater pieces and genres that developed in the century following independence embraced multiple representations of women—including peasant and working women with diverse voices, attitudes, and behavior.[23] This diversity of representation is explained in part by the theater's structure. Women actresses held important positions in the family-based companies; they often directed these companies or established ones of their own. In the social world of the theater, women's independent judgment and actions were accepted. They often married more than once, for example. Families that enforced conservative gender roles for their daughters would not allow them to consider acting or singing as a career, yet these same families did not hesitate to attend performances that often included complex and contradictory gender behavior.

The theater's success was evident in the multiplication of Spanish-language theater houses in the United States between 1910 and 1930. Los Angeles, for example, supported five permanent houses with Spanish-language programs that changed daily. The California–El Teatro Digno de la Raza, mentioned above, was among fifteen other theaters that presented Spanish-language productions on a more irregular basis. Performances through the 1920s continued to feature many pieces of Spanish and Mexican origin, but during this decade playwrights of Mexican descent living in Los Angeles also began to add their plays to the repertoire, with stories based on local history and politics: land loss and

ethnic conflict, the Los Angeles of the immigrant, the massive deportations of Mexicans during the 1930s, and the problem of racial injustice
in the United States.[24] Men and women like Francisco Torres, who was
lynched in Santa Ana in 1891, were represented by these playwrights,
whose own experiences and close relationships to their immigrant audiences enabled them to address past and contemporary injustices with
power and insight. Thus the Southwest attained a new prominence
within the culture of Greater Mexico thanks to the efforts of these émi-
gré and Mexican-American dramatists.

   The movement of actors and theatrical companies across the international border effected a close interconnection between theater in
Mexico and the Southwest. The life of Lalo Astol typifies that of many
actors and actresses from Mexico who lived and worked for extended
periods of time in both countries. The son and grandson of traveling
actors, Astol was born in 1906 in Matamoros, Coahuila, Mexico, while
his mother was on tour with the family company. From 1915 through
the early 1920s he lived in Mexico City, where his mother and stepfather
directed the Teatro Hidalgo, one of the most prominent legitimate
theaters in the Mexican capital. During this period Teatro Hidalgo still
presented the standard "obras del teatro antiguo llamadas dramones,"
old-fashioned melodramas that often lasted up to seven hours. Astol
played both boy and girl parts in these productions with his brothers
and sisters.

   Actors who lived and worked in family-based theater companies
could find work relatively easily in cities on both sides of the border.
Late in the revolution of 1910, Astol's mother had formed a company
to take to the provinces, including the states of Michoacán, Guanajuato,
and beyond. Astol's brother later formed a touring company in Mexico
City targeted at the Southwest, and in 1921, at the age of fifteen, Astol
went to the United States with them. Lalo's purpose was to meet his
father, who was an actor in Laredo, Texas. Warmly greeted, he was
immediately invited to join the Compañía Teatral de Manuel Cotera;
he spent a season with them in San Antonio and toured other towns in
Texas, then returned to Mexico City during the 1920s following an
illness. Once recuperated, he continued to perform with his mother.
Later, he returned to Texas and joined the Compañía Azteca, which
took high drama and variety acts to the pueblos of south Texas.[25] His
career followed the traveling routes along the border to California, and
by the 1930s he was performing in Los Angeles.

When the audience for legitimate theater and variety declined, Astol began working in radio. His first programs were broadcast on an English-language station that included some Spanish programming. In 1947 he took a job in San Antonio, with the exclusively Spanish-language station started by Raúl Cortéz, and later he worked in television.[26] Actors with a background in legitimate theater brought to film and radio a solid knowledge of the historical production of culture. Through at least the 1940s, moreover, the interlocking of genres and media was common. Films were adapted for theatrical performance and vice versa, while the "old" repertoire of melodrama and modern pieces that Lalo had performed from 1910 through the 1930s continued to be offered long after the theater had lost its large audience.

Astol's career exemplifies the geographic extension of the theater across Greater Mexico and the versatility that actors developed performing large repertoires with small companies. These same characteristics define the history of the Compañía Cómico-Dramática Carlos Villalongín. Like many performers in nineteenth-century Mexico, Carlos Villalongín, born in 1872 in Chihuahua, began his career in the dramatic troupe of his father, touring northern Mexico and the southwestern United States. When his father died, the company disbanded and Carlos joined the provincial troupe of Encarnación Hernández, formed in 1849, which performed in the northern Mexican states of Coahuila, Chihuahua, and Nuevo León. After Encarnación's death in 1879, his widow, the actress Antonia Piñeda de Hernández, took over the direction of the troupe; she widened the company's geographic scope, targeting now the interior of Mexico, Mexico City, and sometimes the border areas. In 1900, the troupe played the newly constructed Opera House in San Antonio, Texas, to a packed opening-night audience. In 1904 Carlos Villalongín, by now married to Antonia Piñeda de Hernández's daughter, the actress Herlinda Hernández, took over directorship of the company. The two families of Hernández and Villalongín performed together as the Compañía Dramática Hernández-Villalongín until about 1910, when some members of the Hernández family broke off and the company was renamed La Compañía Cómico-Dramática Carlos Villalongín.[27] During the revolution the company settled in San Antonio, where they remained permanently based until their dissolution in the 1920s. From there they performed on both sides of the long Texas border and in northern Mexican cities; by 1915 they had extended their reach from Laredo, Texas, to Los Angeles, California.[28]

Toward a Collective Historical Consciousness

The plays performed by legitimate companies suggest a shared body of historical and contemporaneous references—ideas, images, and language that might have aided persons across generations to construe their world, invest it with meaning, and infuse it with emotion.[29] The plays provide a sense of the collective historical, religious, and social imagination of a broad audience. Each Spanish-language theater company had a large repertoire of plays that included melodramatic pieces by nineteenth-century authors, morality plays, dramatic essays, one-act tales, *juguetes cómicos* (comic one-to-three-act proverb-plays), *zarzuelas,* and burlesque pieces. Some works were performed repeatedly. Familiarity was a valuable asset, drawing the audience into the story line and enabling it to participate with the players in the construction of meaning.

Historical melodramas were the most common full-length plays presented to Spanish-speaking audiences in both Mexico and the United States from the mid-nineteenth century through the 1910s. The most popular pieces tended to be written by Spanish dramatists and set in Spain. Most plays were fashioned around the great myths and stories of tragedy and valor from Spain's literary Golden Age. The court, the monasteries, the nobility, and particular representations of the populace were familiar, as were the Spanish peninsular and New World cities depicted against the backdrop of conquest and empire.

One popular melodrama, Antonio Cortijo y Valdés's *El cardinal y el ministro,* takes place in 1712 Madrid.[30] Typical of nineteenth-century melodramas, the play is written in rhymed verse. The story begins with a problem: the cardinal, a foreigner who represents not only the power of Rome but also the influence of France and Italy, wants to become the archbishop of Toledo, of *nuestra España* (our Spain). The minister, Macanáz, seeks to protect the crown and the Iberian empire from the danger that this cardinal poses. Intending to warn the king, however, he is thwarted by the cardinal, who secures his arrest by writing a treasonous letter under the minister's name. The minister is taken prisoner; the cardinal becomes archbishop of Toledo. In the final scene, the minister is being sent into exile accompanied by his daughter. At the final moment, a letter arrives from the king; it acknowledges the conspiracy of the cardinal against both the crown and the minister, and gives

Macanáz authority to do what he will to the cardinal, who is, indeed, sent back to Rome by the minister.

This melodrama revolves around intrigue and deception. Ultimately, though, it is about the need to protect imperial sovereignty and Spanish identity—hence the nationalistic tone, which reappears as a dramatic element throughout. The audience thus confronts a version of eighteenth-century Spanish history that, however, crosses borders and time periods in its presentation of nationalist sentiment, a strong cultural and intellectual trend in nineteenth-century Mexico. The melodramatic quality of the play is maintained by the minister's daughter, whose love for her persecuted father is declared in long monologues that draw the audience into her despair. As she says, "es un tormento tal, que no es bastante un solo corazón para sentirlo" (it is too much torment for one heart to bear).[31] This love for her father is stronger than romantic love and reinforces the importance of family loyalty. It was in fact typical of these melodramas to have women express the deep love and devotion of parent or child, as well as to convey the feelings that bring the audience to sorrow, pain, joy, and pleasure.

Whereas Spanish playwrights depicted imperial Spain in their works, Mexican dramaturgists wrote plays that closely resembled peninsular style but represented colonial Mexico. Mariano Asorno's *San Felipe de Jesús, protomártir mexicano,* a four-act historical drama, is a good example.[32] The story takes place in the early seventeenth century, in the home of a wealthy family in Mexico City and in convents there and in Manila, ending in Japan. The plot incites both a historical and religious imagination. Felipe is a spoiled boy who has been sent by his father to a convent to become a good and dignified man capable of carrying on his father's name. By a ruse he escapes, leaving his cousin in his place, and ships off to the Philippines to become a rich merchant. As the audience is told, "que todo el que a Filipinas de comerciante se ha ido ha vuelto a los años con mucho oro en los bolsillos" (all who have gone to the Philippines as merchants have returned years later with a lot of gold in their pockets). Felipe is successful, grows to repent the disobedience of his youth, and joins a religious order in the Philippines. He willingly goes to Japan as a missionary, where he gives his life as a martyr in response to the choice posed by the emperor of Japan: "Queréis vivir felices en mi imperio o morir en la cruz?" (Do you want to live happily in my empire or die on the cross?). The dramatic emotion is carried by the characters of the maid and Felipe's mother, who suffer, are deeply sad, have premonitions, and seek hope through prayer. Here again is a play written in verse and rhyme, that has a straightforward moral, affirms a religious sensibility, and opens the historical world by representing the particular places of monastery and merchant household.

The most tenacious piece to survive the decline of nineteenth-century melodrama was *Don Juan Tenorio* by José Zorrilla y Moral, a romantic drama written in 1844 that became famous all over Latin America.[33] Founded on a folk tale, *Don Juan Tenorio,* through the use of metaphor, spoke to the sensibilities of an audience steeped in oral tradition. The action, set in Seville in the year 1544, takes place around the institutions of commerce and the church, then hard at work reshaping the New World. The plot involves the tension between good and evil, as embodied in the character of Don Juan Tenorio. When his actions are driven by love, they speak to the "higher principles" of his day: purity, beauty, truthfulness. Yet he is also driven by evil genius, which brings him to his death. He is allowed to repent, however, and his soul is redeemed at the end of the play. The archetypal power of this morality tale is exemplified by the fact that it was still playing before live audiences throughout the Southwest and Mexico over a century after it was written. By the late nineteenth century, moreover, it was performed throughout the cultural area of Greater Mexico to celebrate the Day of the Dead on November 1.

Mexican religious history was incorporated into the national theater by the late nineteenth century in such plays as *Las cuatro apariciónes de la Virgen de Guadalupe.* Forming part of a seasonal calendar of performances, these accessible plays strengthened the theater's relevance for a broad public. *Las cuatro apariciónes,* for example, a pageant of religious and national history, was performed by professionals and non-professionals throughout Mexico for the day of the Virgin of Guadalupe, December 12. This play reenacts the legendary appearance of the Virgin to Juan Diego, an Indian, in 1531 on Tepeyac, a small mountain where the Aztec goddess Quetzalcoatl/Tonantzin's temple drew people from great distances to worship. In four apparitions, a brown Virgin instructed Juan Diego to go to the bishop with the message that the Virgin of Guadalupe wanted a temple dedicated to her on that site. The bishop was hesitant and sent Juan Diego back for proof. In the last meeting she performed miracles that gave Juan Diego the proof he needed. The play ends with the words "Hoy la nación mexicana te proclama por patrona" (Today the Mexican nation proclaims you its patroness), underlining the role that this myth has played in the devel-

opment of Mexican national iconography, if not identity and consciousness per se.[34]

The incorporation of popular religious themes was crucial to establishing theater as the most culturally relevant artistic form.[35] José Joaquín Fernández de Lizardi's *La noche más venturosa,* for example, was
based on a shepherds' play, or *pastorela,* performed from the period of
Spanish conquest and well known throughout Greater Mexico.[36] *Los
pastores* was a nativity play the Jesuits had introduced during their evan-
gelization of Europe; Franciscans and Jesuits brought versions of these
plays to the New World to aid in the "spiritual conquest" of indigenous
peoples. The seven basic parts were the announcement of the birth of
Jesus Christ to the shepherds; their journey to find and worship him;
the attempts of Lucifer and his devils to stop the shepherds; the battle
between Archangel Gabriel and Lucifer, with the triumph of the archangel; the arrival of the shepherds at Bethlehem; their presentation of
gifts; and a closure with song and dance. Originally, popular versions
that played throughout Mexico had been intended to celebrate the birth
of Christ as an event in which good triumphed over evil. Yet because
the play was transmitted verbally, which allowed for improvisation and
variation, performances often took on bawdy secular or political meanings. As a consequence, its production was finally prohibited by the
Spanish government in 1769.[37] *La noche más venturosa* is a *pastorela* that
José Joaquín Fernández de Lizardi wrote down to be performed on the
professional stage as a symbol of national unity and triumph over colonial rule shortly after Mexico gained its independence from Spain in
1821. Although he was perhaps more interested in national identity than
religiosity, his appropriation of the religious folk tradition reinforced
that aspect of popular culture.

The legitimate theater often adopted plays with familiar story lines,
as Lizardi did with *los pastores,* with local variations being incorporated
into the translations. Nonprofessional performances of *los pastores,* for
instance, used local costumes, masks, and character types that expressed
syncretized indigenous and European imagery and ideas.[38] These vari-
ants were then brought to the Southwest by immigrants from Mexico,
with further relationships between culture, religion, and community
being added. In the Santa Ana barrio of Delhi, for example, a resident
related his version of the play to the neighborhood priest orally; the
priest then wrote it out into a script, but eliminated those parts he
considered irreverent or satirical. *Los pastores* was rehearsed in a pool
hall donated by a community member who had a prominent role in the

play. When performing the piece, the actors reinserted all the omitted passages and performed it the way they had in Mexico. The actors even sent to a pueblo in central Mexico for the masks used in the play.[39]

Delhi was but one of a number of Mexican communities in Orange County where immigrants performed *los pastores*. The center of such productions during the 1920s and 1930s was the barrio of Santa Fe, in Placentia. The group performed in Placentia, elsewhere in Orange County, and in certain barrios in Los Angeles County.[40] Regional themes and variations incorporated into these plays were then passed on through memory, a technique that encouraged both persistence and variety. This instance of popular theater illustrates the cultural connectedness of twentieth-century barrios such as Delhi with barrios and pueblos throughout the Southwest and Mexico, where *los pastores* was still performed and had been in some cases for centuries.

A final example of legitimate theater's incorporation of popular tradition is *La llorona*, a play by Francisco Neve, that presents one of three foundational legends of Greater Mexico. Neve's play is taken from an early-colonial version of the tale that is critical of the social stratification and gender relations of postconquest society in central Mexico. The main character, Luisa, a mestiza of humble, strongly indigenous background is betrayed by her lover and the father of her child. This man, the son of the conquistador Hernán Cortés, is a central figure within the Creole nobility; he betrays Luisa by marrying a woman of his own class. Driven insane by his duplicity, Luisa vengefully kills their son. She is prosecuted and executed, then appears as a ghostly figure who cries out in anguish during the night. Her apparition so terrifies her former lover that he dies, begging forgiveness.

Countless versions of *La llorona* (which means "the weeper") exist throughout Mexico and the Southwest, melding elements of European and indigenous cultural forms. Neve's version, which played to huge audiences on the professional stage, made stark references to the social injustices committed against Indians, and in particular Indian women and children, during the conquest and colonial times. Neve also created a strong and defiant character in Luisa. The coloration that Neve gave the legend seems to support José Limón's interpretation that it is chiefly the story of a woman who violates patriarchal norms. "Symbolically destroy[ing] the familial basis for patriarchy, . . . she kills because she is also living out the most extreme articulation of the everyday social and psychological contradictions created by those norms for Mexican women."[41]

The social criticism that was so much a part of oral tradition was enacted by the theater as well, and became increasingly overt in the melodrama and modern drama written from the 1890s on. The issue of race was one theme that, widespread in American melodrama by the latter part of the nineteenth century, easily found its way into the repertoire of Spanish-language legitimate theater. *El mulato,* for example, written by Alfredo Torroella and situated in 1870 in a factory town near Havana, presented an abolitionist view of Cuban slavery and the inequities of a color-based society.[42] Another play in this genre was *La cabaña de Tom, o Esclavitud de los negros* (Tom's Cabin, or Black Slavery), adapted in 1893 by Ramón Balladares y Saavedra from the influential American novel *Uncle Tom's Cabin* by Harriet Beecher Stowe.[43] Race melodrama criticized not only slavery and color injustice, but also the sexual exploitation of nonwhite women in the Americas.

Realist and modernist pieces were popular in Spain, Mexico, and the Southwest after 1900. For example, the play *El pan del pobre, o Los explotadores del trabajo* (The Bread of the Poor, or The Exploiters of Work) by peninsular authors Félix González Llana and José Francos Rodríguez, was first produced in Madrid in 1894. The action takes place in a pueblo on strike, with the characters including workers, women and children, factory guards, and soldiers. According to the promptbook, the play was performed extensively between 1911 and 1921.[44] Its popularity points to the solidarity frequently evidenced between the theater and a socially diverse but largely working-class audience.

Modernist plays were innovative in form, bringing everyday life on stage with direct language, sparse scenery, well-constructed dramatic plots, and penetrating psychological analysis. They introduced complicated or sophisticated inquiries in place of the formulaic structures of nineteenth-century plays, though the most popular pieces, such as Jacinto Benavente's *La malquerida,* remained highly melodramatic.

When Mexican playwrights working in the United States wrote about regional history, two major influences were at work: Spanish-language theater and Hollywood films. *Ramona,* for example, was adapted to the stage and film from Helen Hunt Jackson's enormously popular 1884 novel *Ramona: A Story.*[45] The Spanish-language version created by Los Angeles playwright Adalberto Elías González, titled *Los amores de Ramona,* broke all box office records in June 1927, drawing more than fifteen thousand people after only eight performances. That play soon found its way into repertoires all over the Southwest, and it was made into a film starring Dolores del Rio in 1928.[46] A later version,

Ramona: drama californiano, was adapted from the movie by Juan Padilla in 1930.[47]

Jackson wrote the novel as a defense of American Indian land rights and echoes the hostility toward Californios and Mexicans that was common during this period. The story line concerns the Californio family of Señora Moreno, a cruel matriarch. Ramona is a mestiza born illegitimately to a Scotsman and an Indian mother; she is adopted by Señora Moreno's sister, who dies, but not without having arranged for Ramona to be raised as a daughter by Señora Moreno, who, however, hates the beautiful and angelic mestiza. Ramona falls in love with the mission Indian Alessandro, a spokesperson for his village. The refinement of Alessandro is attributed to the missionaries, who are presented as wise and benevolent. Ramona and Alessandro's romance is the centerpiece of a story that portrays a countryside invaded by rough, anti-Indian American squatters. The elevated figures of the mission Indian and the missionary contrast sharply with Jackson's derogatory portrayal of the elite Californiana matriarch, Mexicans, and white squatters.[48]

Juan Padilla's adaptation from the film, in contrast, transformed Californio rancho society, with the glorified *hacienda* and its *hacendado* and *campesinos* (owner of the land and peasants) now posed as central figures. In this version, Señora Moreno owns property in both California and Mexico—an interesting touch, because it in fact reflected the situation of some landowning families in the nineteenth-century Southwest. Yet the play drops Jackson's focus on American Indian land rights and anti-Californio, anti-Mexican sentiment, building the story line instead around the Señora's hatred toward Ramona because of her illegitimate birth and the eventual resolution of this dilemma. In other words, by presenting a picture of old California that featured lavish haciendas rather than the simpler ranchos that actually existed, the play built a distinct historical paradigm; even so, it was one that at least addressed rural California history and made the area a subject for artistic exploration and representation.

Teatro de Revista and the *Carpa*

A new theater, the *teatro de revista* (theatrical revue), came to fruition with the Mexican revolution. This highly urban offshoot of vaudeville provided a commentary on contemporary politics, society, and culture through the use of language and humor that were highly irreverent, ironic, satiric, and iconoclastic. Offering a space in which audiences could "have access to modernity and become familiar with musical innovations whose place of origin was otherwise inaccessible to the gallery," the *teatro de revista* took up themes characteristic of vaudeville, but it did so "always in terms of appropriation, of Mexicanizing the foreign, of experimentation with one's own."[49] With this new form of theater, vaudeville became a national cultural production as actors appropriated foreign representations of the modern while they experimented with national themes. Brought to the United States during the 1910s, it influenced the content of much Spanish-language urban theater after 1920. *Teatro de revista* maintained the close relationship with the audience that had developed with legitimate theater. As a result of its popularity, performers trained in melodrama, *zarzuela,* serious drama, and comedy in small family-based dramatic companies found themselves doing variety acts by necessity during the 1920s.[50]

The *carpa,* or tent theater, was essentially a version of *teatro de revista* but performed with fewer resources and often in a rural or neighborhood setting for the whole family. The Mexican circus, or *circo-teatro,* had long presented acrobatics, clowning, and trapeze work along with theater pieces. These would be accompanied by puppetry, comedy acts, one-act farces, dramatic monologues, short comic operas, pantomime, dance, and other attractions, depending on the company's talents.[51] From the turn of the century until the late 1940s, the *carpas* represented a common form of variety entertainment throughout the Southwest. Raising tents on vacant lots, on level bits of dusty land in remote rural areas, and on the outskirts of barrios, *carperos* cultivated loyal audiences.

In *carpa* performances, *corridistas* sang folk ballads about traditional heroes and historical events. *Declamadores,* or orators, kept alive stylized forms of *buen hablar,* an oral-based tradition of elaborate speech, thus satisfying the public's respect for and pleasure in verbal dexterity and linguistic virtuosity. Although *carpistas* might speak with an overlay of literary respectability, they managed at the same time to subvert the socially respectable through their use of *picardía* (roguery) based on sexual and political allusions. In this way the *carpa* addressed the changing social reality effected by revolution and immigration.

A central figure in the *carpa* was the *pelado,* or feisty underdog, whose ironic commentary on society and politics was prominently featured in humorous sketches. The figure of the *pelado* took on the established order and played with the same themes of modernity that were worked out in the *teatro de revista*. Epitomizing *rascuachismo*, a term that defines "a way of confronting the world from the perspective of the downtrodden, the rebel, the outsider," by the 1920s the *pelado* had begun to draw on a hybrid mix of English, Spanish, and *barrio caló*, or slang, to express a bilingual, bicultural sensibility.[52]

Carpa and *variedad* (variety) shows in the Southwest helped to establish a new sense of identity for the immigrant generation, just as other "ethnic" theater had in previous decades. *Variedad* built on the *teatro de revista* as well as comic opera and operetta, and incorporated the *carpa*'s *pelado* as a comic figure whose bawdy humor colored critical commentary on politics and, in the United States, the situation of the immigrant. *Variedad* expressed the new spirit of a population both becoming increasingly urbanized and confronting new forms of entertainment: movies, radio, and phonograph records.

In the 1930s, as theater audiences began to turn to the movies for their amusement, performers joined the *carpas* to take their talents to small cities, barrios, and *colonias*. Demonstrating their solidarity with audiences made vulnerable by the depression and the forced repatriation to Mexico of tens of thousands, the *carpas* performed at benefits to raise money for mutual and legal aid and community relief.[53] In the massive San Joaquin cotton strike of 1933, which paralyzed production along a hundred-mile stretch, a Mexican circus installed itself in the largest camp of strikers and performed for them to keep their spirits up. As the performers moved through the San Joaquin Valley, in addition to entertaining the idled workers, they carried news of events, rallied support elsewhere, and raised funds for the cause.[54]

The *carpas* made regular appearances in Orange County. In 1935, for example, the Comité de Beneficencia Mexicana brought a *carpa* to Artesia barrio in Santa Ana for a number of days, with part of the proceeds going to the committee for relief work in the local community.[55] A few months later the Comité Oficial de Festejos Patrios brought a *carpa* to the same barrio for a six-day entertainment extravaganza; this time, part of the proceeds were used to raise funds for the Sixteenth of September Independence Day celebration.[56] One traveling company, the Gutiérrez Show, staged numerous performances immediately prior to the major citrus strike of 1936. Its sponsor was the local chapter of the Alianza Hispano-Americana, which worked with the other organizations mentioned above to generate support for the strikers. Fifty percent of the receipts from the Gutiérrez Show were used for Mexicans in need of relief.[57]

Mexican Cinema

Movies eclipsed the theater in popularity during the 1930s. As early as 1910 it was not uncommon to show films between performances of serious drama; a decade later this relationship was reversed, with *carpistas* and *revista* providing the intermission entertainment between film features. Even so, the vibrant relationship between audience and performers that had been cultivated by the stage was carried into audience expectations of and responses to the movies. Film stars made personal appearances at Spanish-language movie houses to sing songs and talk. Movie houses would also host live theater, inviting traveling and local companies to perform favorite and seasonal plays such as *Don Juan Tenorio*.[58] It should therefore come as no surprise that the repertoire of melodrama and high drama that helped shape audience tastes during the era of live theater was also successful on the screen.

In large cities, Spanish-language cinemas were established in theater districts, but in smaller cities, where such districts did not exist, attending the movies could be difficult. In Santa Ana, for example, established cinemas in the downtown area began to relegate "Mexicans" (meaning identifiable mestizos) to the balcony during the 1910s. Josefa Andrade recalled that her father came home one day and "swore he would never again go to such a theater," speaking of one of the four or five English-language movie houses where Mexicans were relegated to the balcony. "He said he wasn't an animal and only animals are segregated like that."[59] Individuals contested these policies, but their efforts did not change the structure of things until much later, when federal law and local political pressure produced by a growing civil rights consciousness during the late 1940s finally eroded the practice.[60]

It is true that the movies brought all ethnic groups into the same theater houses in small towns throughout the United States. Yet segregation clearly contradicted what some have cited as the movies' egalitarian promise. "Here was a revitalized frontier of freedom," writes Lary May, for example, "where Americans might sanction formerly forbidden pleasures through democratized consumption." After 1914, in May's opinion, the break with formality represented by classless seating and sexual mingling was only intensified by an architecture that mixed foreign and domestic, high and low culture together.[61] These reflections, however, neglect the experience of those who were not allowed to mix freely in the movie theaters.

Despite certain continuing inequities, the power of the cinema as a medium of mass culture and a promoter of change is undeniable. As Cathy Peiss effectively argues, moreover, the movies formed part of a commercialized leisure that evolved in close relationship with America's immigrant working class. The movies spoke to the immigrant, but rather than "Americanizing" people, film prompted the development of new ideas about what it meant to be American. The immigrant experience and stylized humor were presented on the screen side by side with new sexual norms. In the formula films of Cecil B. deMille, for example, sex, romance, money, and the enticing foreigner are intertwined to show that metamorphosis is possible through consumerism and sexual freedom. Peiss found that 40 percent of the working-class movie audiences were women, who came from every ethnic background.[62]

As part of the culture of consumption, film—on both sides of the border—was central to creating ideas about America and Mexico, "the American" and "the Mexican." Hollywood westerns systematically rendered offensive depictions of Mexican villains; films set in urban America depicted no Mexicans whatsoever; and films set south of the border presented all Mexicans as "greasers." With the exception of film stars such as Rita Moreno, Ramón Novarro, Dolores Del Rio, and Lupe Velez, Mexicans and other Latins were routinely portrayed as "bad guys," from the era of silent film into the 1930s. In an official letter of complaint written in 1919, the Mexican government warned that U.S. production companies might be restricted from filming in Mexico, and in 1922 movies featuring derogatory depictions of Mexicans were banned from Mexican cinema screens. In the mid-1930s Spain and other Latin American countries signed a reciprocal agreement with Mexico to ban all films that "attacked, slandered, defamed, insulted, or misrepresented peoples of Hispanic or Spanish origin."[63] Yet even despite such distortions, American films dominated the Mexican market by the early 1930s. Between June 1932 and July 1933, for example, 92 percent of the films shown in Mexico were produced in the United States, with Spanish soundtracks or subtitles added in Hollywood.[64]

In the nationalist atmosphere of the Lázaro Cárdenas administration (1934–1940), Mexico's own cinema industry turned toward the representation of Mexico's rural people and the Mexican revolution, and it embraced Mexican music. The movie that set the trend, *Allá en el ran-*

cho grande (1936) by Fernando de Fuentes, evoked a romanticized, mariachi-filled world of *haciendas, hacendados,* and *peones,* helped along by melodramatic romance and comic relief. Mexican films of the 1930s and 1940s tended to present the desire for mobility and wealth negatively, as *agringado* (Americanized). After 1940, during the conservative years that followed the Cárdenas era, formula plots exalted the family, peasantry, and working class and identified these groups as "lo mexicano," or the genuine Mexican. *Cine del pueblo* in fact idealized poverty, affirming its inevitable presence and transfiguring the poor into the emblem of the nation.[65]

Mexican immigrants' process of defining their identity during these years was strongly influenced by cultural productions created on both sides of the border. The derogatory language and images used to define Mexicans in the United States made contending definitions of *lo mexicano* that much more critical. Yet the popularity of English-language film continued.

The complexities of cultural life and cultural politics are apparent in the story of Luis Olivos, the owner of a Spanish-language theater in Santa Ana.[66] His is a story of cultural politics directed at dispelling the myths about Mexico and Mexican identity that his generation encountered at every turn in American society. Olivos was born in Santa Ana in 1918. His father had migrated to the United States from Mexico four years earlier to join his brothers, and his immediate family followed. Luis was raised on a ranch just outside town, graduated from high school in 1936, and did field work before securing a job as balcony usher at the Princess Theater.

He already loved the movies and had gone every Friday night to one of Santa Ana's five, always-packed movie theaters to see westerns. "I was a cowboy buff" who loved "western lore," he stated. But working the segregated balcony motivated him to seek a better situation, and after a little over a month Olivos met with the owner of the theater and suggested that a Mexican movie be screened the following week. The owner agreed. Soon Olivos was traveling an eighty-five-mile route throughout the county posting playbills to announce the weekly showings. "They call it in the business, 'beating the bushes.'" The Princess soon became known for its Mexican films, and a Mexican restaurant opened next door, serving food late into the night. Olivos eventually ran and then purchased the theater himself. After World War II, he bought the large Yost Theater in downtown Santa Ana, where he put on movies, stage shows, and plays.

Olivos states his intentions this way: "My first idea to run a movie house and have pictures with culture was to give the people a cultural look at what really Mexico is. . . . It's full of history. It's uplifting because it evolved from revolutions . . . monarchies and invasions, but . . . in school we were told that we were backward people. All we could see in the textbooks were Indians sitting on the sidewalk, big hats . . . that we weren't stable and we weren't to be trusted and that the Mexican was always the outlaw or the damaged. . . . We were the bandits. We were the dirty people. We were the uncouth people. We were this and that. We were the ones that beat up people."

Olivos's theater created an important site in Santa Ana for Spanish-language cultural productions. During the 1940s he began to rent radio time in Tijuana, Mexico, a few hours' drive away. He insisted that this publicity drew many immigrants to the city, having heard from a customer, "Know why we decided to come to Santa Ana? 'Cause when we going across the desert . . . we heard that in Santa Ana they're showing such and such a movie . . . and they're also presenting our artists." For Olivos, his theater gave the public something of their own, including the live interaction between audience and artist that had been the tradition in Spanish-language legitimate theater. Other lines of continuity with the theater were to be seen in Olivos's close connections to and feelings of affection for his public, like those nurtured by earlier performers and theater directors, and his insistence that the movies were for the whole family and the movie house was a place of decency.

The movies expanded the culture of Greater Mexico in the Southwest, furthering a tradition started by the theater. As actors and actresses traveled through the networks of camps, *colonias*, small pueblos, and urban barrios, they spoke to a shared colonial history, religious imagination, oral tradition, and the multiple cultural referents provided by a common language. In contributing to this regional culture, the theater, in all its performative dimensions from legitimate stage to *carpa*, drew on and added to an oral culture shaped by sophisticated verbosity and stylized elements that facilitated the commitment of plots and ideas to memory. Many of the theatrical pieces reflected religious tradition, iconography, and thinking, which they built into the expression of a Mexican patriotic sensibility and national identity, while the *carpa* and *teatro de variedad* addressed the new complexities of a bilingual and bicultural reality.

The construction of such an ethnic culture should be seen not as some sort of aberration within an otherwise homogeneous "American culture"; rather, the United States as a whole was in the process of being redefined. "Ethnic," "racial," and regional subcultures developed in relationship to changes that were taking place in American society and culture. This shift takes us beyond the discussion of culture to examine the "politics of space," or the way in which the political ordering of land and society molded images of nation and race.

CHAPTER 5

Racial and Ethnic Identities and the Politics of Space

Events in the American town of Santa Ana provide a detailed and nuanced understanding of the early-twentieth-century experience of Mexicans, Californios, and Indians. Founded in 1869 on the former Rancho Santiago de Santa Ana (see chapter 2), this town was where Modesta Avila went to report her defiance of the railroad, and, hence, of the new economic and legal order. Santa Ana was the business and financial center where decisions were made that transformed the countryside. It was also the heart of American society in Orange County.

English-speaking migrants of American birth and American parentage constituted the overwhelming majority of the population in Santa Ana, although after the town became the urban center of the county in 1888 it developed a more diverse population. Native whites of native parentage declined from 71 percent of the population in 1890 to 67 percent in 1930. Californios and Indians from San Juan moved to Santa Ana to secure year-round work and to join family members. By 1900 Santa Ana had a small population of Californio and Mexican residents who lived throughout the city in sparsely built neighborhoods. By 1910, their numbers were augmented by new immigrants from Mexico, and the city became segregated as a result of strong race prejudice against all dark-skinned people, regardless of what language they spoke.

The politics of spatial segregation led to the creation of the barrios, where a vibrant community life developed in the spaces of the neighborhood. Within the barrios a Mexican-American identity formed.

It constituted a collective identity sharply distinct from the one generally attributed to "Mexicans" by the dominant population and culture.

In Santa Ana, as in other American towns, spatial segregation defined and sustained a white racial identity in opposition to supposed characteristics of a "Mexican" race. The terms *white man, white farmer,* and *American schoolchildren* (a designation that excluded all nonwhite children) pervaded the language used by local government, administrators, and the English-speaking population in general. This language reflected regional and national trends. Its employment emphasized the consistent affirmation of the supposed dichotomy of "white" and "Mexican," without which the set of social relations sustaining white privilege—and hence the notion of a white "race"—would have become meaningless. In fact, "white" did not describe the biological or ethnic makeup of a group; rather, its meaning was always fixed in overt or implied relationship to constructed "racial" groups, the ascribed attributes of which were uprooted from the actual histories of the groups in question. The meanings of these constructed groups, in other words, were not based on the national identities that developed in Mexico, China, Japan, and elsewhere in the late nineteenth and early twentieth centuries, nor did they embrace the collective identities that developed in ethnic communities within the United States. Instead this politics of race was anchored solidly in language, and it was delineated in the social spaces of towns and cities, institutions, and workplaces.

The segregation of Mexicans was illegal in California. Mexicans and Mexican-Americans were considered white by law and so could not be segregated on the basis of race. Yet de facto segregation was maintained, through the actions of government officials, the voters who supported them, agricultural, industrial, and business interests, the residents of white Santa Ana neighborhoods, Parent-Teacher Association members—in short, all those who constituted the self-identified white public.

Racial antagonisms against people of Mexican descent had underlain the territorial conquest of the Southwest.[1] In fact, public support for the Mexican-American War of 1846 was the culmination of the transition from a belief in equality through "race improvement" (consistent with the Enlightenment belief in human progress) to the notion of "the innate superiority of the American Anglo-Saxon branch of the Caucasian race."[2] A purported "science" of racial difference had originated in Europe in the early nineteenth century and spread to the United

States, where it was transformed into a systematic justification for slavery and Indian removal. By 1840 American phrenologists writing for a broad public were disseminating their racial classifications and assumptions about the innate mental capacities of designated racial groups. Popular journals blended ideas on race from a variety of sources, including scientific treatises, monographs on history and philosophy, and novels and poems. But the catalyst for the overt adoption nationwide of racial Anglo-Saxonism was the meeting of Americans and Mexicans in the Southwest. After the war with Mexico only the most vigorous abolitionists defended Mexican rights, and even they generally agreed that "whites" were a superior race. As the abolitionist congressman Joshua Giddings of Ohio argued about Mexico, "It is true that their population is less intelligent than that of our free States; it is equally true that they are more rapidly improving their condition than are our slave States."[3] Giddings found Mexicans to be inherently inferior to Anglo-Saxon Americans in the free states, but more intelligent in their social policies, having abolished slavery in 1829.

Even as race ideas were shaping territorial conquest in the period 1850–1890, the meaning of race difference was being actively negotiated. For a few precious years, the politics of reconstruction challenged the ideas and laws that supported racial inequality. Yet violence against African-Americans and other actual or perceived nonwhite groups soon brought these negotiations over race difference to a halt. By the end of the nineteenth century a "scientific" nationalism had established the criteria by which to judge the achievements of large invented, and generally misconstrued, national groups. The idea of the Anglo-Saxon American came to subsume other branches of the Caucasian "race": "citizen" was now equated with "white."[4]

Race ideas obscured and misrepresented the collective histories, worldviews, and cultural practices of Mexicans and Mexican-Americans. Informed by the cultural systems of Greater Mexico and the ideas and iconography that developed among the Mexican-descent population, Mexican and regional Spanish-language culture offered interpretations of life and group identity distinct from those constructed in U.S. society. These ethnic interpretations had their foundation in history; work in agriculture and related industries, specifically ones with a highly seasonal organization of labor; and life in the neighborhood. The streets, alleys, backyards, shops, bakeries, restaurants, storefronts, and house lots where multiple dwellings were often built to accommodate large, extended families were spaces in which a close-knit community could be created. The relatively small barrios of Santa Ana, situated near fields, factories, and railroads, were populated in part by means of informal migration networks that linked family and kin; this connectivity, together with the small barrio size and the (often) shared nature of work and leisure, encouraged close interaction. The barrios were defined by a distinct politics of space that involved the appropriation of these places during a period when official land-use policies implied, and often enforced, an absence of rights to such.

Nineteenth-Century Racial Politics and Ideas

The manner in which self-defined white Americans constructed racial meaning prior to establishing a de facto segregated society after 1900 is illustrated in the lynching of Francisco Torres in Santa Ana in 1892. The event itself and the newspaper coverage of Torres's story are strongly revealing of racial attitudes in this town of American migrants. The purpose of both the lynching and the English-language reportage—which constructed clear racial identities of Mexicans, Indians, Californios, and whites, as well as interpreting the meaning of places like San Juan—was clear: each was an attempt to shape white racial hegemony. In a town where the increasing ethnic and social differences among residents were not yet inscribed on city space, and in a region where nuanced understandings of peoples from the former Mexican territory were still acknowledged, and diverse ethnic communities composed of Indians, Californios, Mexicans, Europeans, and a few Latin American and Chinese immigrants shared the social landscape with the majority Anglo-American population, the tide was about to turn.

Torres was lynched in jail during the early-morning hours of August 20, 1892, by a group of masked men. They entered the jail and asked another inmate if he was "the Mexican." "I told them I was a white man," the man stated, acknowledging the race attitudes that made Torres the object of this attack. When they found Torres, they pulled him from his cell and hanged him from a pole on the main street of town.[5]

The lynching had been anticipated. Torres was accused of killing the foreman on the ranch where he worked. The foreman had withheld $2.50 of Torres's $9.00 weekly wage to pay a county tax collector for a road poll tax that Torres reportedly owed. Torres, refusing to accept the deduction, the next morning demanded his full wage. A quarrel ensued; a short time later the foreman, McKelvey, was found dead. Torres disappeared. As soon as the news broke groups of men discussed hanging him, and the *San Francisco Chronicle* from upstate reported the story under the headline "Lynching Probable."[6]

The newspapers and rumors built Torres up as a dangerous bandit, using the incident to construct racial meaning. One newspaper, for example, argued that Torres was one of "a class of outlaws in Southern California most of whom are Mexicans [who] regard the world as their lawful prey." The press referred to the "good Mexicans" who cooperated in the investigation, and described the court interpreter as "one of our best Spanish citizens" (though Torres himself requested to have the man dismissed because of his antagonistic stance). This "Spanish citizen" was the son of a Californiana and a man named Carpenter, who had migrated from New York in the late Mexican period and who had committed suicide when he lost the rancho gained in part through his marriage. As is the case in the historic construction of race identity, the interpreter's mother's background defined his own for this English-speaking public. Unlike this "Spanish citizen," moreover, Torres was described as "a low type of the Mexican race, evidently more Indian than white."[7]

With such phrasing the newspapers drew on an ideology of race that had already been used to justify Indian removal and extermination policies. Torres's high proportion of Indian blood, they asserted, explained his purported violence.[8] "The sooner such savages are exterminated," one paper stated, "the better for decent civilization."[9] Most Mexicans, being racially and, hence, socially similar to Torres, were implicated too, for example in the sheriff's alleged suspicion that the descriptions of Torres given by his "Mexican associates" were unreliable. One article stated that Torres "was never observed close enough by white persons to obtain a very minute description from that quarter," implying a much greater physical distance than actually existed in this society.[10] A relationship between racial background and social menace was insinuated in the way the Californio and Indian communities through which Torres was chased were characterized: Mesa Grande, for instance, where Torres was finally apprehended, was described as a place "principally inhabited by Indians, half breeds, Mexicans and other . . . thieves and outlaws."[11]

Had Torres been jailed in Mesa Grande or a similar town, the outcome would have been different, as this population, some of which owned land, existed on a terrain of racial encounter and negotiation very unlike that found in Santa Ana. In townships inhabited primarily by Californios, Mexicans, and Indians, a fairer trial might have been provided. In fact, Torres was lynched even as the judge was deliberating moving the case to another court. The sign hung on Torres's dead body read "Change of Venue"—a vicious acknowledgment of the violent racial injustice that was always a possibility in the Western town.

Torres's capture and incarceration was a much-anticipated event because of what was at stake: the enactment of racial tensions in the public arena. Villagers waited at the train station in San Juan to see Torres as he traveled from San Diego to Santa Ana. In Santa Ana, where he was jailed, the city streets were thronged. Prominent in the crowds were Californios and Mexicans from all over the county, many of whom expressed strong sympathy for Torres when conversing with him through his jail cell window.[12] When the prisoner was brought before a crowd in front of the jail, a watermelon peddler offered Torres a melon from his wagon. Torres spoke to him and others in the crowd, but, one English-speaking journalist lamented, "all attempts to get other Mexicans to translate the remark proved without avail."[13]

This ethnic solidarity was also evident in the Spanish-language press, which echoed Torres's own plea of murder in self-defense. Contrary to what the English-language press reported, Torres seems not to have been at all villainous. He roomed with three Californio and Mexican laborers on the ranch where he worked, which was owned by Polish immigrants. He ate his meals with other workers at the home of the Monterolas, about a mile down the road, whom he paid Saturday nights for his week's board. His mother lived in Anaheim.[14] The newspaper *Las dos repúblicas* argued that Torres's guilt "perhaps consisted solely in his nationality" and insisted that the Mexican counsel in Los Angeles demand an investigation to find his murderers.[15] The counsel's request was dismissed by local authorities, however, who never sought to find the guilty parties—men who were rumored to include "prominent citizens" of Santa Ana.

The newspapers articulated ideas about the meaning of "white," "Mexican," and "Indian" that had gained stature in the United States between the 1836 Texas movement for independence from Mexico and the 1846 Mexican-American War. Despite anti-Mexican sentiment, the legal and property rights of citizens of Mexico had been guaranteed under the Treaty of Guadalupe Hidalgo. But the individual Mexican's racial status, as the Torres case makes clear, was not toward the upper end of the spectrum of the new race paradigm. Torres was made into a criminal figure by the fact that he was "more Indian than white." For the newspapers that supported the lynching, his racial status placed him outside the rights of citizenship that would otherwise have allowed him full access to legal representation as defendant.

The very process of classification emphasizes the contending understandings of race and ethnic identity in the 1890s, and the importance of place to sustain these understandings. Despite the many acts of violence that were justified by such ideologies of race, the racial status of "Mexicans" (that is, citizens of Mexican descent) remained potentially negotiable through the late nineteenth century because of their landownership, which facilitated the negotiation of status.

Torres was lynched at the beginning of a decade in which lynchings were at their height nationally, especially in the South and Southwest; these vicious acts formed part of a larger trend to end negotiation over the meaning of racial difference and equality.[16] For three decades, a time marked by the postwar Reconstruction and westward expansion, race relations and the meaning of racial difference had been fundamental political questions on the national scene. For Chinese in the West, negotiation of rights had been largely foreclosed by the Chinese Exclusion Act of 1882. The debates over exclusion focused on the rights of the white farmer as distinguished from the "coolies and other foreign serfs," and the rights of the white working man as defined by the California Workingmen's party during the 1870s.[17] Discriminatory legislation against the Chinese had been accepted by the California Supreme Court when an 1850 state law that barred Indians and African-Americans from testifying in courts was extended to the Chinese.[18] As Sucheng Chan points out, the assumption that the Chinese were passive victims who worked as cheap labor to enrich the state's agricultural and industrial interests has been reasserted in a historiography that has wholly ignored the substantial role Chinese farmers played in developing the state's agriculture both before and after exclusion.[19]

The nineteenth-century language of racial prejudice that established the dichotomy of white citizen/nonwhite alien or semicitizen was already shaping the California historiography during this period. It was in fact part of the process of defining the terms *Californio, Indian,* and *Mexican.* Herbert H. Bancroft, a historian and publisher who organized the first systematic recording of California's colonial and Mexican history, stated his ideas about race in a travel account he wrote in 1874 while conducting research in southern California.

Bancroft was not just any observer of California. His literary work-shop of the 1870s employed people from Latin America, the Caribbean, Europe, and the United States. He and his assistants performed thorough research in colonial and Mexican archives, copying and purchasing documents. In addition, two assistants recorded the narrative histories of some 150 Californios and California Indians (some of which were discussed earlier in this book). They produced the seven-volume *History of California* and the book *California Pastoral, 1769–1898*. Writing in the positivist tradition, Bancroft states: "My conception of the province of history is a clear and concise statement of facts bearing upon the welfare of the human race in regard to men and events, leaving the reader to make his own deductions and form his own opinions."[20] A man of his era, he believed that "the facts" spoke for themselves. His selection and interpretation of "facts," however, was steered by his assumption that history is about progress and the hierarchy of civilizations.

In his travel account, Bancroft writes of Californios as "native Californians (greasers)," with the parenthetical reference explained only insofar as he defined Californios: "The pure blood of old Castile, already somewhat mixed with that of the descendants of the people of Montezuma, was still further reduced by occasional unions of Mexicans and California Indians." Shortly thereafter he explains that in California "whiteness was the badge of respectability, and the white Anglo-American could take his choice from among the rich dusky daughters of Mexican descent . . . a too close scrutiny of the blood with which they allied themselves is not always palatable to the fathers of dark complexioned children, especially if the fathers are rich and respectable, and the sons and daughters educated and accomplished." For Bancroft, the authentic "whiteness" of the Anglo-American was superior to the "badge of respectability" claimed by the "white" Californio whose purity of blood had been "reduced" by racial mixture. Bancroft often details the features and color of people from the former Mexican territories, while leaving assumed the whiteness of Americans and Europeans, whom he never describes by color. The workers on the Couts ranch, for example, are described as "a multitude of every size and color," whereas Colonial Cave Couts, a southerner who had served in the U.S. army, been an Indian agent, and married into the landowning and elite Bandini family, is, together with Don Juan Forster, the Englishman discussed in chapter 3 who married into the well-off Pico family, are described simply as "the autocrats of the region." Bancroft took careful note of these men's

Californiana wives, however, describing Mrs. Forster thus: "Her features have rather an Indian cast though not unpleasing nor lacking intelligence," while Mrs. Bandini is "this pretty Mexico-California relic" (in but one of Bancroft's frequent references to Californianas as relics of the past). Californios, conversely, he describes as beaten men, living symbols of loss.[21] Both images have influenced the historiography—the image of the disoriented and destroyed former patriarch, for one, standing in sharp contrast to the stories I told in chapters 2 and 3.

Bancroft's description of pueblos like San Juan carries his notion that Spanish and Mexican society in California was a subordinate and now dead civilization, all traces of which would disappear with the advance of American society. Moreover, he assumes erroneously that the mission Indians had disappeared, a notion that not only shaped his interpretation of what he saw (and of what he did not see) but also continues to inform contemporary historiography. A clear example is his description of San Juan Capistrano, which begins: "driving through an adobe wall round to the backside of the adobe hotel (everything is adobe here even the people). . . ." Thus the architecture is equated with the people, and both are synonymous with decay. The villagers are described in one half-sentence: "After completing our observations" of the mission, he reports, "we spent the afternoon in writing up our books and taking notes on early California from dusky-imaged ancients, the results of which will be given in another place." His only reference to a historical Indian presence involves the "irregularly placed out-houses in which the Indians lived, some of them still standing and some in ruins." His ability to see the Indian population was clearly circumscribed by his interpretation of San Juan's former neophyte population, whom he describes later in the text as the "savage and semi-savage retainers" of Don Juan Forster when he lived at the mission "in a princely fashion" from 1846 to 1864.[22]

Bancroft's many assumptions inform his interpretation of Californio society in subsequent works as well. He turns to the "Black Legend," for example, which, generated in sixteenth-century England, emphasized the brutality of the Spanish (in contrast to the English) conquests in the Americas, and he did not acknowledge native American peoples as active agents in colonial society. His idea of the superiority of Anglo-American society led him to attempt to integrate this region into American national history through an overlay of multiple "facts" about Californio society that, however, leave it outside the great push of civilization, a concept that he venerated. Although his efforts to document this past led him to build the body of personal narratives from which emerge distinct voices describing California's past, Bancroft's own historical writing virtually eradicates those voices. Portions of these texts, Genaro Padilla observes, were set "into footnotes below the main narrative, revised and in many cases discounted."[23] As a result, I find it impossible to draw on the history that Bancroft wrote for information about California because he has selected and discussed the material without accounting for Californios, Californianas, and Indians as they understood and presented themselves. His assumptions of white and American superiority are tightly woven into his interpretation.

The Creation of a Segregated City

The society that fostered these ideas was mirrored by the American town of Santa Ana, where Torres was lynched. First plotted in 1869, Santa Ana was home to many of those who organized the farming economy, trade network, and industrial base that changed California's rural society. The small city, whose residents were overwhelmingly born in the United States for at least two generations back, replaced the ethnically diverse town of Anaheim as the urban center of Orange County when the county formed in 1888.[24] Through the 1890s the mixed population of farmers, skilled and unskilled workers, professionals, merchants, bankers, and industrialists lived scattered throughout the town rather than in socially stratified neighborhoods. Status was indicated not by location, but by the size of one's property and the nature of one's house. As in San Juan, chickens and other poultry, vegetables, and fruit trees were raised on town lots. City land served the subsistence needs of many of the town's working-class families, who were virtually self-sufficient in their production of edible goods. Up until around 1910, their children worked as laborers in the seasonal harvests, picking, pitting, and drying selected fruits; the wages they earned enabled them to purchase basic items.[25]

While Americans made up the majority of the population, English-speaking Canadians and a small number of Europeans, Californios, Mexicans, and Chinese also lived in Santa Ana.[26] Ethnic affinities characterized the individual households, which included immediate family as well as boarders and servants. The pattern of urban development seemed unrelated to ethnic allegiances, however. The railroad tracks on the east side of town created a juncture for the distribution of goods and nascent industry, and this was a place where working-class residents tended to live. But even near the tracks the class character of the neighborhood was tempered by the existence nearby of field crops, orchards, and the homes of merchant farmers. In the areas to the immediate south and northeast of Santa Ana's downtown, large landowners, professionals, merchants, and wealthy farmers built homes during the 1890s; even so, unpaved streets and the prevalence of rural production, of working farmers and tradesmen close by, produced a cityscape as yet unmarked by sharply differentiated neighborhoods.

The boardinghouse population, which was characterized by a regionally diverse group of native-born Americans, Europeans, Canadians, and an occasional Japanese family, illustrates the absence of class and ethnic differences in Santa Ana's urban geography at the turn of the century. These boardinghouses were located within the ten-block radius of downtown, often above shops and offices. Run by women heads of households, they provided an entrée into the town for single women and men, families with working adults, and migrants who arrived with capital to invest in farms, small factories, and real estate. One typical boardinghouse, at 510 N. Main Street, a block from the center of downtown, was run by a woman from Missouri, and she had four families of lodgers. The working adults included a capitalist from New York, a dealer in wood and coal from England, a seamstress from Indiana whose daughter was a dressmaker, and a housekeeper from Germany. The location and attributes of the rooms they rented—whether on an upper or lower floor; whether marked by warmth, airiness, ease of access, and good size—reflected the residents' relative social standing, just as the value of city lots and homes measured their owners' worth. The Richelieu and Rossmore hotels, too, had a good mix of renters, coming from across the United States and Europe and working in jobs as diverse as cigarmaker, capitalist, tailor, cabinetmaker, salesman, mining engineer, owner of the waterworks, and owner of a business college. These individuals represented the migration that would build the small town into a more highly differentiated cityscape in the next decade.

In 1905 the Pacific Electric Interurban Railway connected Santa Ana to Los Angeles, Santa Monica, and Watts, a change that encouraged the reordering and revaluation of urban property.[27] After this date land within the city limits was increasingly turned to residential use, and land values rose; this proved profitable for landowners who either ceased their farming operations or moved them to the city limits and beyond. Edwin Halesworth, for example, arrived from Cuba, Illinois, in 1876, purchased a large block of land in the northern corridor of town, and cultivated grapes, becoming a major producer and shipper of raisins. In 1906 he sold all his land except two lots. On those, he constructed a house for his family and another to sell. The rest of his former land was built in homes of standard bungalow style for middle- and working-class newcomers.[28]

New neighborhoods for a specifically middle-class population formed adjacent to the interurban railway tracks within an approximately five-block radius. At the same time industry, such as the Pacific Coast Soda Company, which employed fifty workers, began to locate on the western outskirts of town, where beans had previously been grown. By 1908 the Chamber of Commerce declared that Santa Ana had "passed the crucial village stage and has now entered the city list"; while an urban way of life is not yet featured in the boasting pamphlet, the material foundations for a differentiated urban geography had been established. Within less than a decade the city had paved three miles of streets and seventy-five miles of sidewalks, allowing for promenades through new uptown neighborhoods; extended gas and electrical services to most neighborhoods; and built a sewer system, a fire department, and a modern hospital.[29]

Two daily and two weekly newspapers published in Santa Ana by 1906 provide a record of how class differences in the walking city were bridged by an ideology of common access to property and respectability. Advertisers directed themselves to "gentlemen," "workingmen," and "ladies." H. C. Daves and Company, for example, sold "Correct Clothes for Gentlemen." T. Wingood's Dry Goods Store was "The Place Where They Treat the Workingman Right." The real estate agents Hickox and Barker asked readers: "Are You a Wage Earner? And Do You Pay Rent? Come and see . . . a home for you on the installment plan." Ads like these play on the general assumption that social stratification was an acknowledged difference bridgeable by consumption. What is not specified in these ads, but is understood, is the equation of the workingman and wage earner with white men. This equation was assumed in the state and national labor movement, and accepted by a broad spectrum of the population.[30]

The city space in Santa Ana was not socially differentiated in its aggregate structure, the significant exception being "Chinatown," a small area with as few as fourteen residents within two blocks of the new interurban railway depot and organized along the more chaotic pattern of the late-nineteenth-century town. In 1906, with the expansion of urban development downtown, Chinatown was declared a "public nuisance" by the city trustees, who ordered its buildings burnt to the ground. The Chinese (men who had been left stranded without wives and family by the Chinese Exclusion Act) were forced to seek other habitation, which the city trustees assumed would be located in what they called "the Chinese gardens in the suburbs," a large area where Chinese truck gardeners farmed on leased land.

The Chinese had made their home in Santa Ana for quite some time. In previous decades, they had lived scattered throughout the city and worked in a variety of jobs that included washing and brickmaking. The Chinese community appears to have been consolidated in a hierarchic structure by the turn of the century, when two Chinese merchants rented the town land on which the buildings of "Chinatown" were constructed. These merchants rented rooms to a total of twelve lodgers. The lodgers worked as clerks in the merchants' stores, farm and day laborers, vegetable peddlers, and cooks. The merchants may also have acted as intermediaries for the Chinese farmers who leased land in the area around Anaheim, and as labor contractors for the farm and day laborers. Chinese peddlers sold fresh produce door-to-door and were the town's most important source for fresh vegetables. This working community, with its cats, dogs, chickens, and other small animals, plus a horse, was perhaps an obvious target for the local press. Chinatown was described as "one big dwelling and a row of smaller shacks." One of the dirt-floored rooms in the row of "shacks" was described as "barely large enough for a miserable bunk." This dehumanizing language was similarly used to describe the Chinese men, who were referred to only as an amorphous group, never as individuals, in the newspaper coverage of the burning. In an outright effort to undercut even their commercial role in the city, journalists warned against buying any vegetables from the "yellow vendors," who were "wily enough to hide the loathsome signs [of disease] as long as possible."[31]

The burning fits within a long history of violence against Chinese residents throughout the West; in this case, it was generated by the city government's intention to promote standardized growth for a public consisting of "gentlemen, workingmen, and ladies."[32] Although the ostensible reason for the burning was the report of a case of leprosy to the health department, the press, the lawyer representing the woman who owned the property, and even the city trustees themselves suggested that this allegation of leprosy could not be substantiated. Before issuing the order to burn the buildings, therefore, the city trustees entered into a political understanding with the district attorney, who assured them that "no criminal action could be taken on the matter . . . as the complaint in such case would have to be issued by me." Even though the burning was not an example of the mob violence that had long plagued Chinese immigrants, it reflected an anti-Chinese sentiment that was strong in California's racial politics. Hence, the occasion took on the character of a great spectacle. The decision to burn the buildings was made in the early afternoon and was not announced to the public, but word spread quickly, and soon a crowd of a thousand had gathered to watch the early-evening burning. The alleged leper, Wong Woh Ye, had resided in the city for twenty years, yet the newspapers did not attempt to provide any information about him. Only the property owner and the Chinese counsel protested the burning.[33]

The trend toward differentiating city space according to the logic of standard urban growth, to move agriculture to the outskirts of town, and to build new and architecturally uniform neighborhoods was accompanied by demands on the part of city residents that "racial restrictions" be placed on residential property. Citizens who had previously defined their status by family reputation, civic involvement, and the appearance of their home now began to look to the Chamber of Commerce and city government to promote an urban order that would establish their social standing through affiliation with a desirable neighborhood.

As the city's population expanded from 8,500 in 1910 to 30,000 in 1930, new migrants came to constitute the majority of the population. The racial politics that they either confronted or participated in creating was foreshadowed in the pages of the 1910 manuscript census, a federal census conducted every decade, written out by hand; the census was arranged by household and recorded information on every person in a household. On the Orange County sheets of this document, the census enumerator stamped or wrote "MEXICAN" beside most Spanish surnames, whether their bearers were recent immigrants from Mexico or not. Frank O'Campo, for example, was born in California and settled in Santa Ana sometime in the late nineteenth century. He married twice, each time to women born in California; his second wife was a Juaneño woman who had been born and raised on a peanut farm near the city of Orange. At the time of both the 1900 and 1910 censuses, O'Campo lived on the east side of town in multiethnic, largely working-class neighborhoods near the railroad tracks. At each date he lived in a home that he owned, and he worked as a fish dealer peddling fish from a wagon throughout the city. Despite his California birth, length of stay in Santa Ana, the fact that English was the language spoken in his house, and that his now-deceased first wife was a Californiana, he and his children had "MEXICAN" stamped alongside their names in 1910. His son, Joe O'Campo, related the family story that around that same year the family awoke each morning to find cow dung slung on their house by neighbors who were trying to get the family to move out of the neighborhood. They eventually did move into one of the city's rapidly expanding barrios.[34]

Before the early-twentieth-century upswing in immigration, the county's Mexican population had decreased in size until it constituted only a small percentage of the Mexican-descent populations in San Juan, Yorba, Anaheim, Orange, and elsewhere. Between 1900 and 1910, however, this relationship began to change: the number of Mexican households in Orange County rose from 56 to 263, while the number of Californio households rose from 153 to 207. The increase in the Mexican population continued through the 1920s, so that by 1930 Orange County had the eighth largest Mexican population in California and the state's fourth largest number of Mexicans under eighteen years of age.[35] Recent immigrants from Mexico constituted 12 percent of Santa Ana's population in 1930, and 15 percent of Orange County's population.[36]

The "Mexicans" counted above for 1930 included Californios and California Indians with Spanish surnames. Yet that tabulation does not entirely misrepresent the identities that emerged over these years, in which "Mexican" came to mean more than national origin alone. As I argued earlier, ethnic and historical identities are grounded, to an important degree, in the physical place of community and the meaning given to that place. The historical distinctions that served to separate Californios from recent immigrants decreased markedly as they moved into the same barrios with these newcomers. Indeed, after 1910, with the exception of San Juan, Mexicans outnumbered Californios and Indians in all the county's mestizo and Spanish-Mexican–descent communities. Particular regional identities were thus superseded by other expressions of collective identity. Community came to be shaped by a shared experience of work and race prejudice, a shared (but not homogeneous) culture of Greater Mexico, and a common language—elements that embraced not only Mexicans but also Californios and Indians who lived in the barrios of the American towns.

Barrios were an integral part of the creation of social status and identity through the (re)ordering of city space. By 1916 Santa Ana had three large barrios: Artesia, Delhi, and Logan (see map 7). Artesia barrio was built on the west side of the town, in an area that had been swamp until it was partially drained for the construction of the Pacific Electric on Fourth Street in 1906.[37] Its first residents lived on the worst part of this land close to the city limits, among fields and orchards. Minnie A. Bray and others described this core area of the barrio when lodging a complaint regarding the "sanitation situation of the Mexican quarters" to the city council. "The premises," she stated, "are inhabited by Mexican families in disease breeding huts and tents of 30 or more in number on said plot of ground, without sewage, cease [sic] pools, or any provisions according to law."[38] Here small one-room dwellings and house-courts existed alongside tents and other substandard residences. An investigation of the area by the Chamber of Commerce recorded "no sewer connections in that particular part of town."[39]

The low cost of land within the heart of the barrio facilitated its purchase on a monthly credit system; from the early days of this barrio, therefore, some residents owned their lots and built homes with the help of family or kin. Lots and houses might also be sold or rented out. "The lower and cheaper land was bought by the Mexicans, and the better and more expensive land was bought by some white people and those Mexicans who could afford it," explained Helen Walker, a social worker, in 1928.[40] Note Walker's reference to "Mexicans" in contrast to "white people," reflecting the status of "Mexican" as a racial category by this time. Walker pointed to the fact that both groups could buy more expensive land when able, and that some Mexicans did. Meanwhile, because the core area of the barrio was damp and susceptible to flooding, over the years the white population slowly moved away and Artesia became the largest barrio in Santa Ana. Processing and packing plants pervaded the barrio, and fields and groves formed part of barrio space.

Delhi barrio (known originally as Glorietta), located at Santa Ana's southern city limits, was also built on farmland and swamp between 1910 and 1920, and grew quickly because of a sugar beet factory built nearby in 1910. The family of Señor Camarillo, who had been born in an Orange County *colonia* shortly before, moved to Delhi in 1910, among the first Mexicans to do so. The Camarillos were soon joined by many other families when a housing subdivision opened near the factory. By 1920 Delhi barrio had approximately one hundred Mexican home owners, whose property was generally valued at $25 each. Most families lived in their own homes, but the barrio also had house-courts and some houses were rented out. A few non-Mexicans bought or already had land they farmed in the environs of this addition; if they lived on their property, it tended to have a higher value than surrounding properties because of its location or size and the value of improvements. The least valued property among these owners was assessed at $55 for the lot and $50 for improvements.[41]

Delhi barrio remained highly rural, even after its incorporation into the city in 1928. Sr. Camarillo described the area around his house during his youth in the early 1920s thus: "Santiago Carranza lived across the street. On the other side there was a *rancho,* a *lechería* [dairy], and a water plant," and not far from the barrio, but connected to the rancho, was "another *pueblito* [little settlement]."[42] The children from the surrounding *colonias* and *pueblitos* attended the "Mexican school" that was subsequently built in the barrio.[43]

The sugar factory was recruiting Mexican laborers at the U.S.-Mexican border in El Paso by 1919; informed networks among Mexican workers across the West also passed the word when new factories opened. María Holguín was born in the state of Aguascalientes, Mexico, and her family finally settled in Delhi barrio in 1920. Her grandparents had come north to the United States in 1913 with their children and grandchildren, working at first in Montana. Her family settled in Delhi because "one of my grandparents' sons had gone to work in the sugar factory in Delhi. He had left his wife with his parents and then called for them all. . . . Many knew Delhi," Holguín stated, "because of the sugar factory. The factory got people from all over to come and work there."[44] Cecilio Reyes, born in San Luis Potosí, Mexico, was recruited at El Paso to work in the Los Alamitos and Delhi sugar fields; he arrived in the United States in 1922.[45]

The third barrio, Logan barrio, was formed in a working-class neighborhood near the tracks on Santa Ana's east side. In 1910 Californios and Mexican immigrants resided primarily on one street of this neighborhood, working largely as domestic, agricultural, and day laborers. Their absence from other trades and professions, together with their relative nonparticipation in business, is notable even in this working-class neighborhood, whose other residents worked in a larger variety of jobs.[46] By the 1920s many more Mexicans had moved to Logan, often

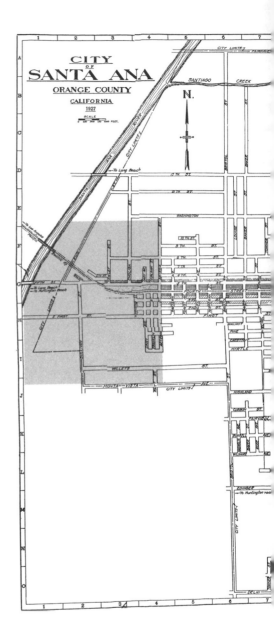

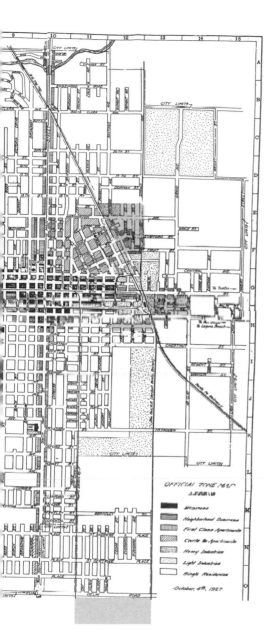

Map 7. The barrios of Santa Ana, zoning map, 1927. Most of the city is zoned for single-residence homes. The shaded barrios, in contrast, are on land zoned for industry, house-courts, and apartments. Logan barrio, to the northeast, is the largest of the three eastside barrios. The westside barrio of Artesia was built in part on swampy land. Delhi barrio, a portion of which is shown, lies to the south, next to a sugar factory. Courtesy Orange County Archives, Santa Ana, California.

drawn by work in the walnut groves that lay almost entirely within the barrio, and by the availability of low-cost lots and houses for purchase or rent. In addition to the walnut groves and increasingly dense areas of housing, packing and processing plants and a laundry defined this small barrio. The residents of Logan barrio maintained close connections through a church jointly built with residents from other eastside barrios and *colonias* near the railroad depot.

Urban barrios often formed around a particular place of work where property values were low, or where lots had been subdivided again and again for the profit of a land speculator, whereas outside the city limits employers and packing houses often supplied company housing in an effort to promote a stable work force.[47] In the larger area of Orange County, the historian Gilbert Gonzalez found that many *colonias* and barrios were established as citrus camps, where workers were initially tied to a single employer or packing house. Residential patterns ranged from company-built housing areas to communities in which workers laid out the streets, built their own homes, developed small businesses, and, as was also done in Santa Ana's barrios, engaged in the domestic production of clothing, livestock, and vegetables.[48]

Urban barrios were distinguished from other neighborhoods by several prominent features, which were related largely to the racial politics of employment. Women in the barrios, for instance, continued to produce clothes and subsistence foods for a longer period of time than other working-class residents in the city. Seasonal life and the temporal order of the barrio were defined by agricultural production; this marked, in turn, patterns of unemployment and migration. The built spaces of the barrios were less standardized than those elsewhere in the city, where new subdivisions for the middle and working classes tended to be built in the relatively inexpensive craftsman-style housing, often with family labor. Kits for these homes (generally one story and simple, featuring square rooms with elaborate woodwork and porches) could be purchased at prices affordable to workers, but not to those who labored primarily in fields and packing houses or as day laborers and domestic workers.[49]

Downtown: Urban Space and Ethnic/Racial Identities

Before we explore the ways in which barrio residents appropriated local space for community life, it is necessary to establish how public space *outside* the barrios was ordered and used, a process that in turn contributed to shaping ethnic identities. During this era of segregation, the "Mexican" and "white" populations interacted on downtown streets, in stores, and in parks, but they did so within the parameters of restricted "interiors." For example, the city prohibited Mexican-, African- and Asian-Americans from swimming in the public swimming pool except on the day before the pool was cleaned. Mexicans were required to sit in the balcony in movie theaters, and they were excluded from some restaurants by signs in the windows. Even so, some former residents of Santa Ana, like Jessie Mejía, who was born in Delhi barrio in 1918, spoke about the downtown of her youth favorably: "You could see everyone on Saturday nights right there."[50]

Santa Ana's downtown was the commercial, financial, government, and entertainment center of the county. Santa Ana residents shopped there daily for groceries, and those from more farflung areas shopped weekly or monthly on special trips. Recall Luis Olivos's eighty-five-mile route distributing flyers to announce the city's Spanish-language movies. From the 1890s on, Mexican peddlers like the one who offered Francisco Torres a watermelon plied their goods in the streets of central Santa Ana. In this downtown core by the 1920s, K. Estrada ran a fruit stand, C. Sánchez ran a tamale wagon, and J. Chávez ran a popcorn and peanut wagon. And in 1920, Ida Quívez ran a Mexican restaurant at a key location on Broadway—the only one among the Mexican shop, restaurant, and grocery store owners to cross the ethnic boundary of Main Street, though she did so by only one block.[51]

The Main Street divide emerged as the downtown developed and was not yet firmly established in 1910, when the children in figure 13 marched downtown. In 1916, the downtown core area extended for six blocks across Main Street: three blocks to the east, which became the "Mexican side," and three blocks to the west, which remained the "white side." In this core area residents of the town and county made their daily or weekly shopping trips, visited dentists, doctors, and lawyers, did their banking, attended the county's first city college or one of the professional schools, dined out, and went to the county's first movie theaters. In 1916 the 600 block of East Fourth Street, just east of Main, had cigar stores, druggists, insurance and real estate agents, a department store, professional buildings, a jeweler, fruit stores, barbers, a dairy shop, hardware stores, grocers, and bakers. Only one business on this core-area block had a Spanish name or owner. In the next two blocks of East Fourth Street, two Mexican restaurants, run by Mexican families for Mexican patrons, had already been established. By 1922 a

Fig. 13. Schoolchildren on parade, Santa Ana, 1910. Courtesy Seaver Center for Western History Research, Los Angeles County Museum of Natural History, photo no. H7931.

Mexican tailor, Juan Ramírez, had a shop in the 300 block of East Fourth, catering to a mixed clientele. On the next block east, La Estrella grocery store was serving the downtown's Mexican population. Farther along East Fourth Street one finds, in 1922, Mexican merchants running a drug store, a confectionery store and factory, groceries, restaurants, a boarding house, and a billiards room. Down six city blocks to the east of Main Street was a working-class district of rooming houses and small homes inhabited by working-class whites and a few Mexicans. Mexicans from smaller barrios that did not have their own commercial area shopped here daily. Another strong component of the area was the packing and processing plants near the East Fourth Street depot, around which clustered small canteens serving breakfasts, lunches, and dinners to the workers.

By the early 1930s, East Fourth Street had emerged as a well-defined Mexican commercial district. R. Rangel, a Santa Ana merchant who grew up in Delhi, affirmed this fact, saying that East Fourth Street was "an old Mexican shopping area; there was a lot of discrimination, so we knew where to shop."[52] Inexpensive department stores such as J. C. Penney and Montgomery Ward, discount stores like Gallenkamps and Thrifty Drugs, and the five-and-dime stores of J. J. Newberry and Kress predominated in the area of Fourth Street in the downtown's center, though in the 100 block there was also a bank, some dentists, and a conservatory of music that served the white public predominately. Mexican grocery stores and restaurants were fairly numerous by 1930, and the Princess Theater showed Mexican films from 1937 on. East Fourth Street ran toward the packing houses and railroad depot; West Fourth Street ran toward the county government offices, as well as the court-house, law library, and handsomely housed professional offices and banks . West Fourth also had the more expensive department stores and neighborhood shops, including a chocolate shop, tea shop, and barbers, butchers, bakers, and druggists.[53]

Segregation did not mean invisibility, regardless of the misrepresentation of Mexicans to justify policies of exclusion. At least annually, Mexican organizations joined together to mount celebrations marked by parades, dances, speeches, and other events that expressed a Mexican and Mexican-American identity quite unlike that insinuated in the harsh language used to sustain segregation. One of the most significant of these celebrations took place every September 16 to commemorate Mexican independence from Spain. In 1920, for example, the *grito de Dolores* (cry of Dolores), which marked the beginning of the independence movement in Mexico in 1810, was made in Birch Park, downtown Santa Ana—at dawn, rather than at midnight as in all the plazas of central Mexico. A parade, which was organized by local Mexican organizations, included bearers of an American and a Mexican flag, a Mexican band, two floats and decorated cars, and marchers dressed in holiday attire. In the afternoon, Mexican patriotic speeches were given, and an evening of entertainment concluded the celebration.[54]

By 1931, the parades and the spectacle of public celebration had grown more visible and complicated, in that the organizers had begun to draw in a larger number of city government officials and business-men. A queen was elected a few days prior to September 16, at a dance attended by over 3,210 persons; Sol Gonzales, a well-known merchant in Santa Ana, announced the winner, and she was crowned queen by the Mexican consul of Los Angeles, Rafael de la Colina, at the opening of the festivities in Birch Park. The full program of the celebration was announced ahead of time in the newspaper, with Mexicans and Amer-icans from throughout the county expected to attend. Evening events included patriotic speeches and musical entertainment. Floats entered in the parade the next day were sponsored by numerous car dealers, the creamery, and other local businesses. The afternoon speeches and games in Birch Park were followed by a huge public dance at the high school, to which everyone, the newspaper stated, was invited. In 1935, aug-menting these offerings, a Mexican orchestra played downtown all day, and young girls passed flowers out to passersby.[55] A Mexican aviator flew over the parade route, performing a program of air stunts. City and county officials were expected to give short speeches at the after-noon celebration. Over 1,500 Mexicans from throughout the county attended.[56]

Such celebrations are a consistent feature of immigrant America. Challenging exclusion from the national paradigm until they were in-corporated into it, they provided alternative versions of ethnic and pa-triotic identities for their own group. The urban festivities enacted in Mexican barrios and *colonias* throughout Orange County by 1920 con-trast sharply to the Sixteenth of September celebration hosted by Felipe Yorba in 1900.[57]

Like some Californios, Felipe Yorba was proud to assert his affinity with a Mexican national identity, in part to affirm Mexico's heritage of free and independent government, but also to counter the race/citizen dichotomy by which persons of Mexican descent were deprived of their civil rights. In that first year of the new century, over one thousand people attended Yorba's Independence Day barbecue in the town of Yorba, on the large acreage his family continued to hold. The American and Mexican flags hung on either side of a platform that had been constructed for the program, and the colors of the two republics were entwined about the speakers' podium. Judge R. P. Manriquez was the master of ceremonies, presenting the entire program in Spanish. Man-riquez read the Mexican Declaration of Independence and gave a long oration on the 1810 revolution and subsequent Mexican political history. Emphasizing that President Benito Juárez was a "pure Aztec," he noted his equivalence to George Washington as a national symbol (in fact, Juárez was not Aztec but Zapotec; yet by then Aztec had become a dominant symbol of nationhood). Manriquez elaborated on the triumph of the liberal constitution of 1857, and discussed Indian and mestizo heritage as a central component of nationalism.

The content of this speech did not differ greatly from that of those given during the 1930s. Different, however, are the location of the celebration, the public who attended, and the way the festivities and speech were covered by the English-language press—which was with great respect. This was not the case for celebrations dominated by the immigrant generation. The 1900 crowd represented the diverse origins of the county, with American and German town dwellers and farmers, Americans from Anaheim, and Californios and Mexicans from Yorba, San Juan, and the few other communities that then had a Spanish-Mexican–descent population. The entire crowd of one thousand was given a splendid dinner by Yorba, who thus displayed a kind of wealth not achievable by most Californios and the immigrant generation.

Racial Identities and the City Schools

The period in which individuals like Francisco Torres paid dearly—sometimes with their lives—for the race prejudice of the dominant population soon passed into one in which entire populations were defined as inferior racial groups through systematic policies of exclusion. By the 1920s such notions of inferiority were being justified by "scientific" studies. One of the most influential theoretical and practical measurements of group intelligence was developed in France beginning in 1890, when educators began to experiment with assessing differences between individuals of specified "national" and "racial" groups on the basis of "recall, moral judgment, and mental addition."[58] Standardized testing procedures were pioneered at Columbia University during the 1890s. It was primarily in the 1910s that the application of these procedures began to produce a body of "knowledge" about "white" and "nonwhite" races that defined white intellectual, moral, and emotional characteristics as superior to those of black, Mexican, and other ethnic groups. As one psychologist of racial difference argued in 1916, "We are at last beginning to get comparative mental measurements of the white and colored elements in the population of the United States." This author cited an experiment conducted by a (white) psychologist who was "accustomed to negroes" and therefore able to classify his subjects "into full blooded, three quarters, mulatto, and quadroon on the basis of color, hair, and features." While that researcher admitted a certain margin of error in this classification, he was able to reach "the clear result that, in the more intellectual tests, success increased with the proportions of white blood. . . . Full-blooded negroes secured [scores] about 64 percent . . . the quadroons . . . 96 percent" as high as whites.[59]

This new means of scientific classification was seized upon by educational reformers with the idea of enhancing the efficiency of schools and their role in shaping the social order. Typically, reformers argued that identifying innate racial capacities would enable the school to steer a child along paths of "self-realization and social service [for] which he is best adapted by reason of his mental, moral, social, and physical endowment."[60] Opposition to racial classification was voiced by a mere minority. One scientist, for example, argued that "whenever the attempt is made to talk about the abstract 'race' as if it existed in the actual world, we are faced by contradiction and halted by absurdities."[61] The overwhelming majority, however, adhered to the notion that either environmental or inherited characteristics define difference; in either case, the need for educational methods tailored to fit the perceived differences was affirmed.

In the Southwest, de facto school segregation began in Texas in the 1890s; by the 1920s most Mexican and native-born children such as Californios, Tejanos, and American Indians were placed in separate schools.[62] Santa Ana established its first segregated school in 1912. Designated for "Spanish children," it incorporated into a single category the children of recent immigrants as well as Californios. In Santa Ana as elsewhere in the Southwest, the school curriculum was similar to that used in Southern schools for African-Americans and in other parts of the country for southern and eastern European immigrants. The children learned "spoken and written English," including reading, writing, and spelling, and the "most simple and practical use of numbers." Girls and boys also received gender-based training: girls studied sewing and mending, while boys were taught "carpentry, repairing shoes, basketry, haircutting and blacksmithing." The curriculum emphasized "better habits of living." At the close of the school year the superintendent recommended that the program be continued, "to the end that we may, as far as possible, make of those children self-respecting, respectable and intelligent citizens."[63] The superintendent's objective was not to prepare students for admission to regular schools through English-language instruction, but to impart qualities of citizenship and intelligence that were, in his opinion, difficult to engender in "this class" of students.

Segregated classes in Santa Ana were initially held in temporary structures, old schools, the domestic science training building, or any available rooms.[64] By 1915 these facilities were located in four areas of the city and its outskirts, near or inside the emerging barrios, and the schools educated the children through the third grade.[65] In 1918, however, representatives of the (white) Lincoln Parent-Teacher Association (PTA), representing Logan neighborhood, appeared in force at a school board meeting to protest the presence of Mexican children, "whether in the main school building" or in a "Mexican make-shift school upon the Lincoln grounds." Apparently the school board had already promised the PTA that it would arrange the physical removal of Mexican children. The proximity of their children to Mexican children, the parents now argued, constituted a "rank injustice to our school, our teachers and our children"; segregation, they stated, was necessary on "moral, physical and educational" grounds, thus echoing prevailing ideas that moral judgment and mental ability were related and could be measured. The school board approved a resolution in support of the PTA and appeased the parents by passing a further resolution to "segregate the sub-normal pupils in the grammar schools."[66]

Six months later the board sought a more elaborate classification system that could not be legally disputed by Californio and Mexican parents whose children were being segregated. In January 1919, the school board invited the city attorney to discuss the legal ramifications of the systematic segregation citywide of all children of Mexican national descent. At this same meeting, the Mexican Pro-Patria Club presented a petition to the school board which demanded that all children subject to segregation be returned to "their respective schools."[67] The protesters included the parents of children who had been attending regular city schools and club members who supported their civil rights. Any discussion of the petition that took place was not recorded. Instead, the minutes noted the remarks of the district attorney to justify school board policy. He stated: "It is entirely proper and legal to classify [students] according to the regularity of attendance, ability to understand the English language and their aptness to advance in the grades to which they shall be assigned." To circumvent a lawsuit in a state that legally segregated Chinese and American Indian but not Mexican or African-American children, he added that this classification was to be carried out "regardless of race or color": in other words, it could be taken to embrace all "sub-normal" students.[68] "Mexican" students were subsequently placed in "Mexican schools" on the basis of perceived racial characteristics alone. Joe O'Campo, who attended the Fremont Mexican School, stated that the school authorities were "blatant about it being a Mexican school. And, if they saw that you were dark skinned then ZAP, you'd be thrown in that school."[69]

By September 1919 four permanent Mexican schools had been built in or near the barrios to the west, east, and south of town.[70] In addition to whatever formal and theoretical justification for segregation prevailed, local politics also expressed the notion that whites had the right to a particular education by virtue of their being identified wholly and exclusively as "Americans" or "citizens." This political view simultaneously suggests how notions of whiteness had to be constantly reaffirmed by the deliberate spatial ordering of society, an ordering that was tied not only to a social segregation but also to a related economy of monetary worth. The notions of "white" and "citizen," essential to the construction of difference, were defining property values.

These values are apparent in the language of prejudice used not only by the school board but also by the Chamber of Commerce Advisory Committee and even by the teachers in the Mexican schools, who employed it in their deliberations over the location and quality of Mexican schools in 1928 and 1929; because the Mexican population had grown substantially, schools in each barrio needed to be enlarged. "White schools," "American school children," and "the Mexicans" were common terms in these debates. The constructed notions of race and nationality that were reflected in this language found their way not just into the curriculum, but also into decisions regarding school buildings and the selection and salaries of teachers.

The first question addressed in the yearlong deliberations about new Mexican schools was their appropriate cost. The school superintendent, always cautious for legal reasons, stated that although "fine buildings" for Mexican schools were a good idea, "the population among the Mexicans has proven so migratory that permanent buildings have not been advisable." This misrepresentation of Santa Ana's Mexican population was bolstered by the school board's business manager, Mr. G., who argued against costly buildings because of the "type of work being carried on" in the Mexican schools, which required "a different type of building arrangement than the white schools." Mr. G., in short, did not want to spend a large sum "on a Mexican school, especially when we do not have proper facilities for the American school children."[71] New rooms for Artesia and Delhi Mexican schools were estimated to require an outlay of $2,500, whereas rooms for the white schools required an estimated $8,000.[72]

Teachers in the Mexican schools were paid a minimal salary. In 1921, for example, the head teachers at five schools each received $2,000 annually, but at the Fifth Street (Mexican) School the head teacher received only $1,800, and at both Logan and Santa Fe (Mexican) schools the head teachers received a mere $1,675.[73] A politics of gender that discriminated against hiring married women teachers because their husbands could support them intersected with racial politics to provide lower pay to Mexican school teachers. In 1923 the school board decided to hire married women teachers to teach at the Mexican schools alone. The majority of these teachers were white and, because they were married, had trouble getting work elsewhere.[74]

The geographic location of Mexican schools reflected the political economy of an urban structure designed to affirm notions of whiteness through segregation. By 1928 "race restrictions" were in place in all of Santa Ana's residential neighborhoods. The Chamber of Commerce Advisory Committee argued strongly that all new Mexican schools should be placed within the barrios, as "any effort to locate a Mexican school outside the district itself will meet with decided and instant opposition."[75] Artesia Mexican School was already located outside the boundaries of Artesia barrio; a school board member argued that if the board approved a second Mexican school in that neighborhood outside the barrio, "all the voters in that district would do all in their power to defeat any school bonds." In fact, "over 200 white residents of the district" brought a petition to a January 1929 meeting affirming their "decided opposition" and demanding that the proposed school be moved "further west and north or south of the present site."[76] The board then entertained the idea of moving all Mexican children to a proposed "Mexican center" in Delhi barrio, just outside the city limits. Logan barrio's Mexican school was by now also far too small. The idea of placing this school outside the barrio on undeveloped land was countered by the argument that "the next residential development of the city" would be to the east of Logan barrio and that this property "should not be marred by a Mexican school site" in the vicinity.[77]

The logic of property ownership and value was continually used against the Mexican families who, even when property owners, lived in neighborhoods where the city had not extended sewage and flood channels or paved the streets. Instead of improving infrastructure within the barrios, urban planners sought to contain or displace the Mexican population. At the end of the yearlong deliberations of 1928–1929, it was decided that Artesia's Mexican school should be built with fourteen classrooms near, though not within, the barrio because flood conditions within the barrio proper made such a large building too precarious. Logan Mexican School was "kept in the center of the Mexican district," and homes in the surrounding neighborhood were condemned to allow its expansion. For city planners and the board, this displacement of families by condemning property anticipated a demographic shift in the eastern portion of the city. The school was intended as a "temporary school" because, the Chamber of Commerce Advisory Committee stated, "the Mexican will likely be crowded out soon."[78]

One teacher alone in the Mexican schools joined her voice with those of the parents. She canvassed residents in Artesia barrio to learn of parents' objections to busing their children to the proposed "Mexican center" in Delhi. Also utilizing the logic of property rights, she stated that "from one-third to one-half of the Mexicans own their homes" in Artesia barrio; what's more, she said, these home owners opposed their children's removal to south of the city.[79] In contrast, the majority of the teachers in the Mexican schools voiced an opposite opinion, arguing instead for a spatial politics that would remove the children from the influence of their neighborhoods. One teacher, Mrs. W., objected to the establishment or expansion of Mexican schools inside the boundaries of the "Mexican settlements" because "adults lounged around the buildings during the day as well as at night." The teachers who worked in the barrios were annoyed, she stated, by "Mexicans hanging around the grounds which was not good."[80] To this objection, an advisory committee member responded quite bluntly: "Mexicans would hang around any public place as they do around the city park, and going across the track would not eliminate that feature."[81]

The attitudes expressed in these debates were lodged in the memories of children who received their education in the Mexican schools. Joe O'Campo, born in Santa Ana in 1922, attended Fremont Mexican School. When asked about the curriculum, O'Campo said that it consisted of "woodshops" and "language"—if, he added, "prohibiting [us] from speaking Spanish was teaching English." "That was [the extent of] it," he stated emphatically. O'Campo's description suggests the extent to which school policy shaped subjective experience. His sardonic remark indicates clearly the negative attitudes that Mexican students endured, as embodied in the school's emphasis on manual training and its coercive use of language to enforce a particular culture and worldview.

The internal order of the Mexican school was meant to shape the meaning of difference. School policy, moreover, discouraged Mexican children from pursuing their education beyond elementary school. In the Artesia (Fremont) Mexican School, O'Campo recalls, explaining how school authorities deliberately prolonged a Mexican student's grammar school years, students went "to kindergarten and then primary-first and then secondary-first and then the following year to the primary-second and so on and so on."[82] The relatively advanced age at which students graduated from Fremont (which O'Campo noted to be two or three years different from other students) left them either ready to work, out of their obligation to the family economy, or "embarrassed" to go on to the advanced grades. O'Campo reported being one of only three from his class who continued their education at the junior high school level. These reflections give added meaning to an otherwise innocuous note in the school board minutes: "It was necessary to transfer thirty elementary school students from Fremont and other Mexican schools to the facilities at Willard Jr. High."[83] The occasional pressure brought to bear against the school authorities prompted them to transfer older children to the junior high. "Overageness" was a common trait among students of Mexican, African-American, and certain other ethnic backgrounds. In San Bernardino County in 1928, for example, approximately 79 percent of the Mexican students were overage for their grade, as opposed to only 33 percent of the white students.[84] This difference reflected school policy rather than scholastic competence or innate ability.

Josefina Andrade, born in the Logan neighborhood in 1932 and schooled in the late 1930s and early 1940s in the Logan Mexican School, also remembers a school schedule and curriculum that emphasized the attitudes of the administrators. Logan School, she stated, was in session for only half the day, the teachers, Andrade recalled, having been sent to Logan on a part-time basis from neighboring white schools; the students worked the other part of the day in agriculture to help their parents. The school records suggest, however, that Logan School had the half-day schedule only for the duration of the approximately three-week walnut harvest in the fall. All the more valuable, then, is Andrade's recollection because it suggests how official policy structured her memory of childhood: Logan School seemed to her to have been organized in a piecemeal fashion, without committed, regular teachers or a curriculum and class schedule that compensated for school time children lost when they were at work. Andrade, like O'Campo, emphasized the prohibition against the use of Spanish, the punishment being getting one's mouth washed out with soap. Both Andrade and O'Campo went to high school, but Andrade dropped out when family circumstances required her to work.[85] Although her generation had a somewhat higher rate of graduation from high school than did O'Campo's, the long-established pattern of the pre–World War II years, when approximately one to three Mexican students graduated from high school annually, was still common.

Child and Family Labor
in Industrial Agriculture

The consequences of not finishing high school among the population at large were formidable. A 1940 study on employment in Orange County reported that anyone who did not receive a high school education or equivalent training would be relegated to working in agriculture or an unskilled occupation. Although most jobs in the county were in these areas, the average starting hourly pay was only 25–34 cents an hour, while more skilled jobs earned 35–44 cents; the agricultural wage, moreover, did not rise significantly, even after a lifetime spent in the fields and associated packing plants.[86]

Mexican children were not the only ones to work in agriculture nationally; rather, their employment and preparation by the schools for work in agriculture fit a national pattern. Work in industrialized agriculture structured the world of native-born and immigrant workers alike in many areas of the United States. Wherever cotton, tobacco, sugar beets, berries or cranberries, orchard crops, or large-scale truck farming entered into industrial production, migration had a significant impact. The family-based system of agricultural labor was widespread in fourteen states of the union during the 1920s, and the rate of child labor was high. From 1920 to 1924, a series of studies of child labor in agriculture was conducted, covering approximately 13,500 children; it was found that they worked in such diverse places as the sugar beet–growing sections of Colorado and Michigan, the cotton-growing counties of Texas, the truck and fruit farming areas of southern New Jersey, Maryland, Virginia, Illinois, Washington, and Oregon, the wheat and potato regions of North Dakota, and the tobacco-growing districts of Kentucky, South Carolina, Virginia, Massachusetts, and Connecticut. Other studies show children as migratory cannery workers in New York, Delaware, and Maryland. Children and adults would go from the city to the countryside to harvest the tobacco crop, and women and children worked long hours in the nearby cigar and tobacco factories.[87] In Georgia children shelled pecans in factories where they worked alongside their mothers. In one factory employing four hundred, about one-quarter of the workers were children. A Southern teacher who taught adult education classes complained that many children attended night school because during the day they worked beside their mothers in factories on piece work. "This is one reason," she said, "why the illiteracy is so high in Georgia."[88] Similarly, a Mrs. Smith, who was a principal in Roswell, New Mexico, wrote the Children's Bureau, in the Federal Department of Labor, to report that "many of our school children are kept out of school months to pick cotton for home folks, also for remuneration."[89] While some of these examples derive from the Depression years, other studies from the 1910s and 1920s show that child labor was a common fact in earlier decades as well. In 1919, for example, a considerable number of persons who worked in the oyster and shrimp canning industry on the Gulf Coast migrated seasonally from Baltimore and New York, causing their children to miss school for long stretches.[90] Sugar beet field work, which was particularly tedious and painful, was performed largely by immigrants (child and adult workers) from Europe and Mexico. The Mexican workers, however, in some cases at least, received the worst housing.[91]

This, in essence, was America's industrialized agriculture. Men, women, and children worked in monotonous and tiring tasks for longer hours than did laborers in factories, and under just as much pressure. By 1930, sixty-seven thousand child wage earners aged ten to fifteen and another four hundred thousand "unpaid family workers" (meaning wives and children) were working in April, which was only the start of the season for work in commercial agriculture.[92] Although certain crops brought the whole family into the harvest, some, such as oranges, were harvested primarily by men and boys, while other family members went to work in canning, packing, and allied sectors. Because family and community were closely tied to the agricultural production schedules, family time, in a sense, became an outgrowth of industrial time.[93]

Orange County's agricultural industry thus has to be understood in the context of rural and urban development nationwide. For here and elsewhere, low wages and the pattern of seasonal employment created a family economy in which multiple wage earners were needed if the family was to survive. Many students by their early teens had to quit school to supplement the family income. The interests of the industry, rather than of barrio students, were foremost in the minds of school officials as they made decisions. Theirs was a collaborative effort to restrict some children's access to an education that might lead to other and better work.

In 1934, for example, Mexican parents from Delhi barrio petitioned the school board to start school in August and suspend it during the month of September "in order that children may help their parents during the walnut season." In response, a school board member conferred with the principals of the Mexican schools, who "did not recommend that this change be made. . . . Mexican schools," explained the board member, already "are in session on a minimum school day or half-day" during the walnut season. The school principals argued that change was not advisable, despite the fact that walnut picking generally required families to move away from the area, or if not, it certainly disrupted the daily rhythms needed for schoolwork to get done. At the meeting at which the issue was discussed, one board member requested that "the petitioners' names be checked."[94] This suggestion had ominous overtones, for 1934 was a period of massive deportation and repatriation of Mexican nationals, and a time characterized by much worker harassment in response to a virtual mass strike in southern California agriculture that had begun in 1933.[95] The power relations starkly visible in this interaction—a petition, its denial, and implied surveillance and punishment—reveal the cornerstone of this overall policy of educational segregation: its fundamental motive was to ensure a steady supply of labor for agriculture.

The connection between the politics of segregated education and industrial agriculture is further revealed by the school policy shift that took place after a mass strike paralyzed production of the orange crop in 1936. This strike was one of many that signaled the dawning of an era when local labor and civil rights activists, inspired by Mexican worker activism through the Southwest, joined together in a regional labor movement (see below). In September 1937, in response to these threatening changes, the school board met in closed session to establish school boundary lines. Segregation policies were now leveled at specific neighborhoods, which made the possibility of legal challenge even more remote.[96]

Another Politics of Space: The Barrio

The recollections of Mexicans who grew up in this era (1920 through 1940) emphasize that the barrio was a place where the convergence of past and present, ideas and experience, work and religion, contributed to shape collective identities. The barrios have a central place in poetry, in literature, in older people's memories, and in the expressions of youth culture—where the *cholo* and *pachuco* have appropriated the barrio in their lexicon and symbolic systems.[97] To examine the articulation of Mexican identity during this era through the politics of space is to understand how the barrios developed and how their spaces were appropriated for community life.

As we have seen, the barrios in Santa Ana had begun to take form by 1910. Most immigrants settled in a barrio only after having lived in a number of *colonias,* labor camps, or other barrios.[98] Josefina Ramírez, from Santa Anita barrio (outside the city limits of Santa Ana, just across the river from Artesia barrio), exemplifies this migratory life. She first immigrated with her mother and uncles to Texas, where they lived in a railroad camp together with other Mexican-, African-, and Anglo-American families. She then came with her mother and sisters to California, where in Casa Blanca (Riverside County) she met and married Ramón Ramírez. The couple moved to a rancho in Buena Park, where they worked "regando betabel" (irrigating beet fields); then to Colonia Independencia in Westminster, Orange County; then on to "un otro rancho" (another ranch); and finally they returned to Colonia Independencia. At that point they had children, and rather than continue changing locations, Josefina's husband "iba a trabajar en las naranjas hasta Riverside y luego venía—iba y venía" (would go to work in the orange groves in Riverside and then return home—he would go and return). When he found more permanent work in orange groves in Tustin, Orange County, in the late 1920s, the family moved to Santa Anita, where they bought a lot onto which they moved a house in the mid-1930s.[99]

These migration patterns shaped the social ordering of the entire Southwest. Family and fictive kin were joined across this broad region as each sector of the family moved to a given place and persons from the same town or region in Mexico migrated across the network thus formed. The ties that linked Southwestern barrios both to one another and to localities in Mexico further defined the region after 1900, enabling potential immigrants and people already on the migratory path to acquire a broader knowledge of the United States than they could have gained in one place alone. This knowledge was also informed by the nature of other kin's experiences in widely separated communities, experiences that were also incorporated into and passed on via the formal cultural productions created in this region. Bonds among family, friends, and neighbors were not weakened by seasonal migrations. Many families worked each year in particular crops, often traveled in the company of extended kin, and returned to their barrios when they could work locally. An urban subculture, embracing Mexican and Mexican-American identities, developed in similar fashion in barrios across this larger region: that is, it arose partly because of the physical movement of individuals and families.[100]

Seasonal employment defined the temporal dimension of the barrios. It set the tempo of community life, of people's movement on the streets. These work rhythms distinguished the barrio from the rationalized eight-to-five schedule of the year-round service, trade, and professional jobs that dominated neighborhood life elsewhere in the city.

These daily and seasonal rhythms are strong in the memories of those who lived in the barrio. Josefina Andrade, for example, recalls that her father would come home at the end of the season with "a big bag of beans, flour, fat, a large sack of oranges he placed near the kitchen door, and canned goods, bought with the season's pay." The family would have "chickens and other things around the house for that nonwork period of winter."[101]

Seasonal employment also meant working in a variety of generally unskilled jobs, the only ones available to Mexicans. During the winter months, un- and underemployment among Mexican agricultural workers was chronic. Manufacturing jobs (most of which were agriculture-related) also tended to be highly seasonal. In 1919, for example, only 63 percent of the men and 10 percent of the women who worked in manufacturing jobs in Santa Ana had year-round employment.[102] Income varied among barrio families according to the number of gainfully employed family members and the degree to which the principal wage earner was able to find steady work.[103] Employment began at an early age. One man who lived in Logan barrio remembers starting to work at age eight. Although his early employment and that of his mother were precipitated by the death of his father, his story was not uncommon. "Hey you name it, I did it. I started picking sugar beets in Talbert. Just a kid then. . . . My mother went to work after our father died. She got a job as a maid in some apartments in that Grand Central Market area downtown."[104]

The way the barrio was laid out actually helped families to overcome these low-wage economies by providing room for additional living space or a small business. The irregular pattern of already-built homes allowed for a certain amount of expansion. Wherever lots were large enough, dwellings were built in the rear to accommodate larger families, married children, relatives, and sometimes renters or boarders. In Logan barrio in 1923, 7 percent of the houses were built to the rear of others; by 1933, that number had risen to 16 percent, and by 1941, to 21 percent, the highest density achieved. The barrios themselves expanded in size and density over time as white residents on adjacent streets moved to other neighborhoods, and nonstandard structures, such as small buildings in alleys, rear dwellings, and house-courts (one-to-two-room residences built around a central courtyard that contained all the plumbing) were erected (see appendix 5).

The social relationships embedded in the physical world of "houses, rooms, stairways, streets, sheds and alleyways" contributed to the use of the neighborhood as community space, thus infusing it with further meaning.[105] The communal space of the streets was augmented by neighborhood businesses. An observer in 1928, for example, noted that Logan barrio had regular grocery stores that served as general stores and "specialty stores and shops, located in the homes of the entrepreneurs. There is a 'nextamalia,' where Americans as well as Mexicans go to buy tamales, enchiladas, or tortillas; a candy shop down an alley where delicious 'dulce calabazas' may be bought; a potter sells handmade ollas, bean jugs and jars, made in his own yard."[106]

In Logan the busy commercial main street was also the most densely populated. The Ruíz and Martínez General Store stood in the center of the barrio, together with a Mexican-owned barbershop and a white-owned grocery store. By 1933 the Logan Mexican School, a second grocery store and barbershop, a billiard room, and a tamales shop (most of which were owned by barrio residents) served as meeting points for the neighborhood and for people from other Santa Ana barrios. The core streets of Logan and Stafford were paved in 1928 on the request and at the expense of their residents. At the street dance held to celebrate the event, a "Mexican orchestra" played into the night and "people (Mexican mostly) came from far and near to join in the fun."[107]

The paving of the street was the result of strong community ties, in which commerce played an important role. In addition to spearheading similar efforts aimed at urban improvement, the *comerciantes* formed committees to negotiate for urban amenities, provided aid in times of labor strife, mediated between civic bodies and barrio residents, sponsored celebrations and cultural events, and engaged in benevolent work. Examples of their work abound.[108] They were in turn enthusiastically supported by barrio residents.

In Artesia barrio, some residents operated small service businesses out of their homes—such as the soft drink and cigar stand run by E. Pérez—or ran pushcarts in the streets, as Pedro Gonzales did.[109] The city council considered numerous requests for licenses to operate such businesses in the 1930s, evidence of the viability of small commerce.[110] Restaurants, barbershops, bakeries, tortilla factories, pool halls, grocery stores, other enterprises, and workshops were run out of homes. Artesia barrio also had a formal commercial core where merchants, artisans, and a few professionals operated.

Each barrio had particular qualities that defined it as a neighborhood. Delhi barrio, for example, which originated outside the city limits near the sugar factory that was built in 1910, had a significant population of home owners by 1920, and virtually all its residents were from Mexico. By 1928 the barrio had a post office, a few grocery stores, several barbershops, a number of small restaurants, a dance hall, several pool halls, and a Catholic church. The most densely populated part of the barrio were those blocks on or surrounding Central Street near the church and the union hall.

Catholic churches were extremely important places in the barrios, and the money for their construction was often gathered by barrio residents themselves. The presence of priests and churches meant that the religious calendar celebrated in Mexico was superimposed on the seasonal rhythm of agricultural production in the United States, thus adding a further nuance to the organization of barrio time. The priest of the Delhi church, José Origel, had come from Mexico in 1927, a refugee of the Cristero revolts.[111] He was a conservative who cast a watchful eye over the community, intent on reinforcing the traditions and customs that residents had brought from Mexico. In 1922, the people of Logan (which had no church of its own), Artesia, and other eastside barrios formed the first Spanish-speaking Catholic parish in Santa Ana. They raised money to build a small, beautiful church on East Third Street. Artesia barrio also secured a parish, Our Lady of Pilar, sometime in the 1930s. Until the congregation raised enough money to build a larger church, people sat in their cars or on the church grounds to listen as the mass was broadcast from the first little chapel.[112] The formal places of church and church hall were supplemented in most homes by altars, which allowed for daily reverence and cultivated a particular kind of memory, one conveyed through sacred images.

The community life of the barrios fostered certain collective interests and identities; work engendered other expressions of identity. Indeed, an agricultural worker's entrance into labor meant becoming skilled in fast-paced production in field, orchard, and packing house. As barrio populations became more established, a pattern of specialization in particular jobs and particular crops occurred. As Lucas Lucio, a representative of citrus workers in 1935, began his testimony to a U.S. Senate subcommittee: "In the first place, the orange pickers are a skilled group and many of them have been working for ten or fifteen years or more at the business of picking oranges, and for the same packing houses."[113]

Specialization made sense because the work and the way labor was contracted differed for each crop. By 1917, for example, orange picking was done "more and more . . . by a gang of skilled pickers under the direction of the packing house."[114] A foreman, who was often Mexican, would organize the crew, usually picking them up in the barrio and returning them at the end of the day. He would also determine who would work where in the grove. Because trees had different bearing capacities, this selection could affect the pickers adversely. To know and be on the foreman's best side was important to workers, whose low hourly wage was derived from or supplemented by piecework in which a predetermined number of cents was paid per box of oranges picked.

The highly tedious job of harvesting beets also required tremendous field skill, strength, and endurance, since the hand labor requirements for the crop remained "almost unaffected by technological improvement from the inception of beet growing until 1940."[115] The beet crop had two labor peaks, one in the spring, when thinning was done (on hands and knees), the other in the fall, when the beets were pulled from the ground, their tops were cut off with a long, hooked knife, and they were tossed into a pile. Significantly, the two sugar factories near Delhi barrio paid more for factory work than for field work; moreover, it was mostly white workers who got signed on for factory operations, with Mexicans being employed at the factory only to haul the beets.

Walnuts were generally picked by the whole family. One observer described the season in 1928 like this: "In trucks or wagons, buggies or Fords, entire Mexican families go out into the orchards and camp right there until the picking time is over. The children pick, the uncles and aunts pick, the mother and sisters pick, while the father and the big brothers shake the trees."[116] In this operation, families were often allotted a given acreage to work.

The skills that workers developed in these crops strongly influenced their sense of collective identity as laborers. During strikes workers attempted to get those skills acknowledged, but they also acted according to a very deliberate logic because of their respect for those skills. One contemporary study explained that logic thus: "The Mexican agricultural worker thinks of himself as a specialist in some certain crop such as citrus fruits, celery, or melons. There are occasional interruptions of employment because of weather conditions, but even when such interruptions occur, Mexican laborers do not compensate for reduced earnings by working Saturdays and Sundays. They usually work about ten hours daily from Monday through Friday. Only in extreme instances can they be prevailed upon to work Saturday mornings."[117]

Whereas men tended to define themselves as skilled workers, women generally articulated their role as workers through their relationship to their families—as mothers, wives, and blood and fictive kin. Many women, however, developed astute skills in paid work of various types. Around World War I, for example, Mexican women began to secure jobs previously held by non-Mexican women workers in the numerous packing and processing plants that were being built near the barrios. They first acquired the least skilled jobs available, but whether the work they performed was grading, sorting, packing, or recording the quantity and quality of fruit, vegetables, and nuts, it required skill, speed, and care.[118] In the orange-packing plants, machines did the brushing and washing and eventually took over much of the grading process by 1917, but the perishable fruit still needed to be hand-wrapped in tissue paper and packed in boxes. In walnuts, although the packing process began to be mechanized around 1912, cracking, a tedious and difficult job, was not mechanized until the mid-1920s.[119]

Wives were rarely employed on a permanent basis in the fields and factories, however.[120] Daughters thus often took jobs outside the home to supplement the wages of the principal male wage earner, a pattern found among other immigrant groups in America when the male head of household's steady employment was precarious.[121] In one study of

Mexican women's employment in Los Angeles and Orange counties conducted in 1927 and 1928, the majority of those interviewed stated that they worked because of the men's irregular work and the combined effect of low wages, high rents, and large families to support.[122]

Lucy Romero, for example, had extensive experience in canneries, orange picking, vegetable cultivation, and domestic work. In vegetables, she said, "We did everything like a man," hoeing the ground and sowing and transplanting peppers, cucumbers, and tomatoes. For her, the male worker was the point of comparison by which she measured and defined the work task. And although she took pride in the work she and other women did in the fields in work groups, she placed the responsibility for the family income squarely on her husband. Indeed, although Romero sometimes worked field jobs during the day, she preferred night shifts in the walnut packing plants during the four months of that crop's production; that way she could be home cooking, sewing, and taking care of the children during their waking hours.[123] Like many Mexican women of her generation, she worked with the consciousness of a mother—that is, for her children's benefit.[124] Whenever possible, however, women with children worked in paid labor only out of necessity. Serefina Andrade, for example, stayed home and saw to household needs while her husband and sons worked in the fields and factories and her older daughters worked in the packing houses and laundries.[125]

The prevalence of women in wage work lent a particular order to the use of space in the barrio. Jovita Hernández described her neighborhood, where residential patterns—such as houses built in a square pattern rather than in a row—facilitated child care. When the mothers were away at work, one of the grandmothers would watch all the children from the four contiguous houses. When family wasn't available, neighbors would watch out for one another's children.[126]

The ties between neighbors were strengthened by a work structure that brought persons into jobs through the family and fictive kinship networks that defined most barrios. Orange picking incorporated this structure into the formal organization of the picking crews. The beet industry relied for workers on the neighborhoods built around the fields and beet factories. Walnut processing drew on the entire county for workers. Vegetable production relied largely on word of mouth and often employed women during the picking season.

Lucy Romero told a story in which this sense of community solidarity plays a role. She was working with a group of women in a vegetable field. The boss asked her to keep the crew going while he stepped out for a while. When he left she told everyone, "'All right, let's take a break.' And we stopped and rested, laughed and told stories, moved about. Then I said, 'Let's get back and work so hard he won't know we stopped.' The boss was pleased when he returned; he had no idea that we had rested."[127] This memory affirmed not only the women's close bonds, but also the fact that her subversion of the boss's authority was possible only because she knew their capacity to work fast and efficiently; remembering the incident produced great pleasure for Mrs. Romero in her old age. Her workplace experience and her consciousness of women's capacity to do grueling labor for pay formed an important part of her identity, even though she relied on her husband to support the family and made the male worker the point of comparison to define the difficulty of a task. Throughout her story, however, paid work is partnered with her obligations at home: home, community, and workplace are solidly linked.

Identity and the Meaning of Place: The 1936 Strike

The connections between home, community, and workplace are clearly reflected in the organization and nature of the labor movement as it developed during these years. The first unions among Mexican workers in Orange County were conceived in the barrios. Among them was the Confederación Uniónes Obreras Mexicanas (CUOM), which had a large presence in Santa Ana and elsewhere in the county. The fifteen Orange County locals (out of twenty-four in southern California as a whole) in fact accounted for a significant proportion of the approximately 2,500 CUOM members in 1928; the next year Orange County was home to eight of the union's eleven remaining locals, four of which were in Santa Ana alone. CUOM locals promoted a "strong cultural campaign" to build schools and libraries, "exclusively Mexican hospitals," orphanages, and almshouses; in addition, the central leadership asked each local to establish a defense committee in their barrio to protect the legal rights of Mexicans. The CUOM stopped functioning in 1933, but the social programs it had designed remained on the agenda of *mutualistas* (Mexican mutual aid societies) thereafter.[128]

The large number of CUOM locals in Orange County suggests that the organizational links necessary to launch the massive strike wave that paralyzed crop production in California between 1933 and 1936 were in place early on.[129] Many of these strikes spread from Los Angeles and Riverside counties into Orange County; others were initiated in Orange County. In 1935, for example, Orange County vegetable workers staged a major walkout, and orange pickers were ready to strike if their union demands were not recognized prior to the start of the 1936 picking season.

Mexican immigrants of this era have been understood as a generation shaped by their participation in and experience of the Mexican revolution of 1910 and its antecedents.[130] This consciousness was accorded a central role in the recorded memories of labor organizer Dorothy Healey, who stated: "What stands out in my memory, first of all, is the fact that Mexican women were playing leading roles. You were still dealing . . . with that generation that had come from Mexico after the struggles of revolutionaries in Mexico."[131] As we saw in chapter 4, the revolution contributed to the development of Mexican national identity on both sides of the border. But as significant as that event was to some, the collective experiences that shaped life in the United States were, to others, equally important. For many of this generation, it was the barrios that made it possible to survive difficult economic and social conditions, through the forging of community.

The 1936 citrus strike illustrates the political nature of the barrio and the way in which this space fostered collective identities. The protest grew out of the momentum created by the mass strikes in agriculture from 1933 on. In early 1936, the Confederación Uniónes Campesinos Obreros Mexicanos allied with the Agricultural Industrial Workers Labor Union and the Filipino Labor Union to form the Federation of Agricultural Workers of America. In March this group sent a petition to the citrus packing houses outlining three central demands: union recognition; the establishment of a uniform family wage for the male citrus worker, regardless of race or ethnicity; and a new structure to define labor-management relations.[132] Instead of negotiating, the industry responded by forming its own organization, the Associated Farmers, to control labor and coerce striking workers.[133] On June 11, 2,500 orange pickers struck, and not an orange was picked in northern Orange County that day. The strike was concerted and included workers from Santa Ana, Santa Anita, Orange, Fullerton, Placentia, La Habra, Villa Park, San Juan Capistrano, El Toro, and Atwood.[134]

Nightly strike meetings were held within the barrios, with representatives from each barrio—not from the workplace, significantly—forming the general strike committee that decided how to play out the strike. Meanwhile, the workers were being represented by delegates elected from their barrios, the Mexican consul in Los Angeles, and union officials. The overall solidarity of Mexicans countywide was evident not only in the dedicated participation of women, men, and children in strike committee discussions and the distribution of food and other supplies to striking families, but also in the visual spectacle of protest. Truckloads of women "hecklers" rode through the county harassing the strikebreakers and police, and people along the roads called out to the caravans of arrested workers, "Hurrah for the strikers! Don't give in!" as the strikers waved back.[135]

Attacks on the barrio were now launched, reflecting the way in which race politics fortified coercive labor structures. Vigilantes attacked participants in the nightly strike meetings in each barrio, sometimes using tear gas. On July 7 during a meeting of 115 Mexican men, women, and children in Placentia, "one hundred ranchers drove up . . . each . . . armed with a new axe handle." In Anaheim and El Modena, simultaneous strike meetings were broken up. In one barrio truckloads of masked men drove up to the meeting place and threw bombs into the hall, destroying an adjoining storefront. On the single evening of July 10, vigilantes smashed the windows of a meeting place in Anaheim while the meeting was in progress, disrupted a large meeting in La Habra, and broke up a smaller one in Placentia, where they hurled twenty tear gas bombs into the room and wielded clubs against those who ran out. Barrio residents said they could not sleep because the tear gas filled their homes. The sheriff had already issued a "shoot to kill" order against the strikers, thus implicitly giving license to vigilante activity. Meanwhile, white women and children took to the orchards to pick oranges in defiance of the strikers, and white college students from Los Angeles helped staff the roadside barricades.[136]

The decision to end the strike was finally reached on July 25. None of the central demands were met, though the growers did make some concessions. Yet the articulation, through this and other strikes, of the complex identities of two generations of immigrant and native-born southern Californians continued to reveal new directions for collective action and politics. The labor and civil rights struggles that began in the 1930s and 1940s thus slowly forced an end to behavior that affirmed the notions of "white," "American," and "Mexican," notions so strongly and disturbingly characteristic of this era.[137]

Conclusion

Two conquests of the rural society around San Juan Capistrano, one originating in Spanish colonial times and the other the result of war, the United States' territorial expansion, and the simultaneous capitalist transformation of the countryside, produced new landscapes but were unable to obliterate memory of the past. Pablo Tac left a record of Luiseño and Quechnajulchom identities. Modesta Avila symbolically protested Californios' loss of land and wealth. Luis Olivos discovered in Mexico, and in Mexican films, a sense of his own history that had been misrepresented in the schools he attended in Santa Ana during his youth. Each acted from a particular understanding of the past that drove him or her to challenge the prevailing structures of domination. The pain of conquests and race politics is recorded in each of their lives: ultimately, all three suffered early death or met tremendous defeat even as they attempted to contest these structures.[1]

The tension between the destruction of Indian societies and their endurance was repeated in this local history numerous times. And expression of this tension, and a critique of the way Indians are studied as artifacts, is made by James Luna, a Luiseño/Diegeño artist. One of Luna's installations, entitled "The Creation and Destruction of an Indian Reservation," communicated a pervasive sense of emptiness and void with a barbed-wire fence, a few personal artifacts, a sign, and a video monitor replaying the performance of the opening night's destruction continuously, near the remains. This piece was about La Jolla Reservation, one of the villages I mentioned earlier, to the southeast of

San Juan. In "The Artifact Piece," Luna lay down on a planklike exhibit box, thus making his own inanimate body, along with such artifacts as his divorce papers and diplomas, a part of the display.[2] Both pieces criticize the treatment of Indian history by scholars who write as if they were dissecting dead cultures and dead peoples. At the same time, they use humor to challenge the audience to reflect on their own perceptions of history.

Despite this tension between destruction and survival, San Juan's population of Indians and Californios was a persistent and ethnically diverse community. Landownership of even small lots was central to the continuation of this historical community, and the struggles to farm and maintain subsistence economies brought the actions of Californianas into the foreground. Their particular expression of land rights was grounded in colonial and Mexican law, but the way those rights were interpreted in the American period served to sustain a world of work and a cultural life that affirmed deep bonds of community. Remembered for its spiritual roots in the oral tradition of the late nineteenth century, San Juan remained a close-knit society where the sensibilities of older traditions shaped knowledge and influenced the appropriation of new ideas by subsequent generations. This history of San Juan went unacknowledged in the memories of its English-speaking population, who perceived themselves as part of a collectivity of farmers and remembered the seemingly interchangeable "Mexicans" and "Indians" only as workers. For them, the persistent meaning of this regional past had no bearing on the present.

The populations dubbed as "Mexican" in the racialized climate of the early twentieth century were not all born in Mexico, but most shared at least part of the culture of Greater Mexico, which thrived in communities whose people had originated somewhere in the former Spanish colonies. Within American towns, Californios, Indians, and Mexican immigrants created a community life that was marked by a close relationship between workplace and barrio. Families and neighbors worked together in the fields, orchards, and packing plants. The barrio was defined temporally by the overlay of seasonal work, religion, and family time. Its physical space was appropriated for community life in multiple ways. In addition, the growing interconnectedness of the Southwest was fostered by migration pathways and articulated through the emergence of new expressions of Mexican national consciousness.

Spanish-language culture as it was conveyed by professional theater, the *carpa,* the *tanda de variedad,* and Mexican films contested U.S.

cultural representations of "the Mexican." Immigrants drew on this transnational development of language, images, and content to define "lo mexicano" over time and to interpret the bilingual and bicultural reality in which they lived. Long-held ideas and oral traditions represented in the repertoire of legitimate theater were augmented by new representations of Mexican national identity, which informed a twentieth-century Southwestern historical experience that originated in the popular culture not only of the United States but also of Mexico. This close interrelationship between Mexico and the Southwest explains, in part, what Amalia Mesa-Bains defines as the "resiliency of Chicano culture and art," which in turn derives from the experience of "communities that live between tradition and innovation."[3]

The race politics that pervaded Southwestern society after 1900 constitutes a critical dimension of U.S. national history. Part of my intention in this book has been to emphasize the manner in which ideas about "the Mexican" contributed to the formulation of a "white" and "American" identity. The meanings that the "white" citizen and city official assigned to "race" were central to their understanding of who they were. Only after World War II did Mexicans in Orange County begin to win formal challenges against the "facts" that whites used to define and justify notions of racial difference. The turning point was a civil rights suit against segregated schools, which was won in 1945; this victory initiated locally a process of negotiating the meaning of race that began to be felt nationwide only after 1954.[4]

The intellectual foundation that informed the era of segregation was not challenged in any significant or systematic way until the 1940s, when psychologists and social theorists began to study the psychological and emotional bases of prejudice itself. Unlike their predecessors, they used extensive testing to measure and define the racist, the anti-Semite, and the authoritarian personality. These scholars referred to "ethnic" groups rather than national or racial groups in their attempt to describe cultures (or social systems, institutions, traditions, language). They conceived of "ethnocentrism" as an ideological belief system pertaining to groups and group relations.[5] Their work took prejudice, rather than difference, as the social malady that needed to be understood and changed. This book is inspired by that project and tradition.

A Note on Quantitative Method: The Federal Manuscript Census, 1860–1910

The quantitative dimension of this study was developed from the federal manuscript censuses for 1860 through 1910 (excluding the 1890 census, which was destroyed in a fire). These censuses are long forms filled in by the census enumerator who went from door to door to get his answers. The enumerator always recorded the name, birthplace, age, gender, and occupation of each person living in a dwelling. These dwellings were recorded by census number and organized by household, with the head of the household listed first and the information about other household members listed underneath, generally in order of descending age and relationship to the household head. I also organized the material in my data base by households. I found it instructive to note the order in which the enumerator recorded his information, because it often suggested broader structures of rural and town society.

The data bases included information on all 293 households in San Juan and Santa Ana townships in 1860, and 538 households in 1870. By 1880, the number of households in the two townships had increased to 1,214. For that year, I input data on all 176 of the households headed by a person with a Spanish surname, as well as the entire population of San Juan Village (which appeared separate from San Juan Township only in the 1880 census), and randomly selected 30 percent (or 324) of the non-Spanish-surnamed households. The same random selection process was used for the 1900 and 1910 censuses as well; in 1900 I included the whole area of Orange County, which was formed in 1889. In 1900, 4,688 households were enumerated in the manuscript census. For the data base I randomly selected between 8 and 10 percent of the non-Spanish-surnamed households, and all the Spanish-surnamed households (a total of 241). In 1910, the population had grown to include 8,554 households. I selected from 5 to 20 percent of the non-Spanish-surnamed households, and all the Spanish-surnamed households (574). These percentages were chosen to achieve a statistically significant number of households for each urban and rural area (see below).

Through the data base category "Ethnicity" I placed individuals together according to their particular backgrounds and larger historical experiences. I've used the terms *Californio, Mexican, Indian, European, Anglo-American,* and *Other Ethnic.* The detailed exploration of the emergence of the regional term *Californio,* and the term's changing social and cultural meaning, accounts for a significant portion of this study, as does analysis of the meaning of Indian, Mexican, and, to a much lesser extent, white identity. The book does not explore the histories of other groups in any depth.

In practical terms, Californios were Spanish-surnamed individuals born in California with at least one Spanish-surnamed parent also born in California. Mexicans were born in Mexico but not in the area that became the U.S. Southwest. Indians were identified by having "I" marked beside their name in the column for race. In 1860 they almost invariably lacked a surname. By 1870 and until 1900, Indians who still lived in San Juan and other Californio communities had adopted a Spanish surname and were not generally identified as Indians again until the 1910 census. European immigrants were so classified because they were born on the European continent. In my data base area, they originated primarily in the German principalities (or, after unification, Germany), Prussia, Poland, and occasionally France and other Western European nations. Anglo-Americans were identified by their birth in the United States, their English (or Anglicized) last names, and their racial status. The African-American population was very small between 1860 and 1910 and so was included in the "Other Ethnic" category, along with Chinese and Japanese (who were virtually absent in my random samples from 1880, 1900, and 1910, although each group constituted a small but historically significant population in Orange County); Canadians and the occasional Australian, Jamaican, and Icelander also appear in this category. African-Mexicans were entered according to their birthplace, as either Californio or Mexican.

The "ethnicity" of the entire household was taken into account only in a rough way. If a household had persons from different ethnic origins, it was listed as being of "mixed ethnicity." This designation applied to the children of the household only if they were twenty-one years of age or older. A household with five California-born Spanish-surnamed adults and one Mexican-born adult, for example, was considered to be of "mixed ethnicity." Likewise, a household with two Mexican parents and two grown children who had been born in California was also considered to be of "mixed ethnicity" because the children's historical past was related both to the California historical experience and to the historical experience of the parents. This category of "mixed ethnicity" provided useful information about households and communities up to 1880. Thereafter, however, social and demographic change rendered it less informative, and it was not included in subsequent data bases.

The data on land and personal property available in the 1860 and 1870 censuses was listed beside all individuals who possessed such holdings, so it was tabulated by "ethnicity." Hence, the tables on property and wealth (in contrast to the tables on occupation and literacy) are inclusive, rather than reflecting only the head of household and oldest woman in the household (when not its head).

The data base for each household contained information on the oldest female in each household, unless the head of household was the oldest woman, in which case the next oldest was also listed in the category "oldest female." For 1860 and 1870 the demographic characteristics of the "oldest female" were analyzed as if she were the wife or mate of the head of household; after 1880, the relationship between head of household and other members of the household was listed in the censuses and so could be entered into the data base. Beginning in 1860 the information for the oldest female included her age, birthplace, ethnicity, literacy, occupation, and property. In 1870, information on the "foreign" or "native" birth of her mother and father was listed as well, and from 1880 forward the actual birthplaces of her parents were given. In 1900 and 1910 five additional categories of information became available: the number of children born to her, the number of her children still living, the data on her immigration (where applicable), and whether she spoke English. I thus included a significant amount of revealing information about the oldest female in each household.

The data base contained similar information on the heads of household: age, gender, birthplace, ethnicity, literacy, occupation, and property. In 1870 the native or foreign birth status of the parents of the head of household, and from 1880 on the parents' actual birthplaces were also included. In 1900 I added more data about the head of household: date of immigration, English-speaking or not, owner or tenant, dwelling place free or mortgaged.

The data base also contained information on the entire household: size; number of family and nonfamily members who worked; the occupations of other household members; whether the household was of mixed ethnicity (1860 to 1880); whether others in the household (besides the head and the oldest female) were literate; and whether the children attended school (this information was not always available). For 1900 and 1910 I entered the occupations of family and nonfamily members of the households by gender.

Occupations

What follows is a list of the occupational categories that I used to group the multiple jobs listed in the censuses. Under each main category are listed all of the pertinent job titles as they were entered in the census. One can trace economic and social change by following the additions of jobs by decade. In the list for 1860–1880, the categories without a date first appeared on the 1860 census; categories that were added in the 1870 and 1880 censuses are so identified. All job titles are assigned a date for clarity. So much economic change took place by 1900 that separate lists are used for 1900 and 1910.

1860–1880

agriculturalist (category added in 1880)
1880: apiarist, vinegrower, winegrower, viniculturalist

artisan
1860: blacksmith, bricklayer, butcher, cigarmaker, carpenter, cooper, hostler, hatter, painter, pianoforte maker, plasterer, saddler, shoemaker, silversmith, soapmaker, stonemason, tailor, tinsmith, watchmaker, wheelwright
1870: baker, brewer, barber, miller, paperhanger, scrape maker, silver plater, wagon maker, upholsterer
1880: adobe mason, dressmaker, harnessmaker, house painter, lithographer, milliner, printer, seamstress

business
1860: shopkeeper, barkeeper, restaurant keeper
1870: stable keeper, hotel keeper, saloon keeper

1880: liquor saloon keeper

business agent
1860: cattle trader
1870: broker
1880: hay dealer, real estate agent

communication and urban services (category added in 1880)
1880: bartender, constable, fireman, justice of the peace, postmaster, undertaker, telegraph operator, waiter, restaurant worker, notary public

cook
1880: cook in restaurant

employee
1860: clerk
1870: bookkeeper, keeper of records, merchandising clerk, searcher of records

farm laborer
1880: farmhand

farm overseer (after 1880, foreman)
1880: foreman, ranchman, mining superintendent

farmer

farmer and stockraiser/vaquero
1870: stockfarmer

gardener (category added in 1880; prior to that time listed under "other")

housekeeper

keeper of boarders (category added in 1880)

laborer
1880: livery stable worker

merchant
1880: lumber merchant and grocer, grain merchant, fruit store owner, retail liquor dealer, general merchandiser, book store owner, hay and liquor dealer

miner
1880: gold miner

other
1860: peddler, priest, gardener (changed to a discrete category in 1880)

1870: clergyman, fisherman, mariner, musician, freighter
1880: meat peddler, photographer, drayman

professional (category added in 1870)
1870: physician, surveyor, druggist
1880: lawyer, dentist

ranchero or stock raiser
1870: sheep raiser
1880: wool grower

servant

shepherd, herdsman
1870: herder
1880: sheepherder, sheepshearer

teacher, common school worker
1880: music teacher

teamster

transportation worker (category added in 1880)
1880: harbor pilot, stage driver, railroad engineer, railroad agent, railroad brakeman, mariner and sailor

vaquero

washing
1880: washing and wash house operator, washerwoman, laundryman, laundress

Substantial growth of urban areas and changes in agricultural production in the last decade of the nineteenth century required that we adjust some of the occupational categories in the 1900 and 1910 data bases. The new categories are the result of a significant reordering of work processes and work lives in an industrial economy. Hence the prominence of sales/clerical work, of skilled, semiskilled, and unskilled labor, and of the semiprofessional and professional. Even when categories remain intact, many contain new job designations. The categories listed in the data base for 1900 and 1910 that remained the same as for the period before 1900 are listed first in the list below, followed by categories that were introduced in 1900–1910. All job titles were used in 1900 unless specifically noted as belonging to 1910.

1900–1910

Categories carried over from earlier censuses

agriculture: vinegrower, winegrower, orange grower, fruit grower, orchardist, fruit grower and nurseryman, apiarist, budder

business: agricultural implements dealer, merchant of artist supplies, bicycle dealer, brewer, confectionery storekeeper, contractor/ builder, department store dealer, dry goods storekeeper, feed store- keeper, furniture storekeeper, grocer, hardware storekeeper, hotel keeper, landlord/apartment owner, leather goods dealer, liquor storekeeper, livery keeper, manufacturer, merchant, merchant of Chinese goods, millinery store proprietor, music dealer, peddler/ huckster, piano dealer, real estate office/agent, restaurateur, saloon keeper, trader/dealer, vintner, wood/coal dealer

1910: pool room proprietor, "broker/own shop," real estate office operator, fish dealer

day laborer

farm laborer: farmhand

farmer: small farmer, farmer and fruit grower, farmer and wool grower, farmer and vaquero

housekeeper

keeper of boarders, lodging house proprietor, keeper of lodgers, boarding house keeper

manager/foreman (hotel, farm, mill, general store, sugar factory, oil co., section foreman, motor car co.)

professional: banker; capitalist; chemist; chief of police; clergyman, minister, preacher; dentist; editor; engineer (mechanical, electrical, civil); geologist; governmental official, commissioner; judge; law- yer; pharmacist, druggist; physician; publisher; school principal/ directress; schoolteacher; veterinarian

rancher

Categories added in 1900

sales/clerical: agent, bank teller, bookkeeper, cashier/checker, clerk/ salesperson, collector/solicitor, fish salesperson, insurance agent, mail carrier, newspaper solicitor, notary public, railroad agent

(Southern Pacific), secretary, stenographer, telephone operator, timekeeper, traveling salesman, stationer

semiprofessional: abstractor, accountant, artist, auditor, author/ writer, aviator, chiropractor, conductor, court reporter, dispatcher, draftsman, health officer, inspector, interior decorator, interpreter, inventor, investigator, lecturer, librarian, manager/foreman (packing house, ranch, gold mine, street car co.), messenger, music teacher, musician, newspaper reporter/correspondent, nurse, optometrist/optician, park warden, photographer, postal inspector, postmaster, sea captain, sculptor, sexton, speculator, superintendent, surveyor, taxidermist, technician (medical, dental), undertaker

1910: manager of a hotel, farm, mill, general store, sugar factory, oil co., motor car co.; section foreman

semiskilled labor: apprentice, barber/hairdresser, bartender, bill posterist, bottler, boxmaker, brakeman, butler, butter maker, cable splicer, chainman, conductor, cook, creamery worker, deputy sheriff/constable, drayman/hack driver, elevator operator, factory operative/worker, fisherman, foundryman, horseshoer, lineman, longshoreman, lumberjack/lumberyard employee, marble worker, meatcutter, metalworker, milkman, miner/placer miner, molder, night watchman, nurseryman/nursery farmer, pantryman, pattern maker, pipefitter/pipemaker, policeman, pruner, rattan worker, sander, sailor/soldier, sawmill planer, seamstress, service station worker, shepherd, stevedore/steward, switchman, tamale maker, teamster, telephone repairman, tool dresser, towerman, trucker/ driver, waiter/waitress, warehouseman, well driller/borer, *zanjero* (ditch digger)

1910: creamery man, delivery man, fumigator, gauger, marshall, sheepshearer, stickerman/planing mill worker

skilled labor: baker, bicycle repairman, blacksmith, boat builder, boilermaker, brewer, bricklayer, butcher, cabinetmaker, carpenter, carpet layer/weaver, carriage maker/painter, cement finisher, cigarmaker, compositor/printer, cooper, coppersmith, dressmaker, engineer (stationary and locomotive, wharf, oil well, city water works), electrician, floor layer, forest ranger, glassblower, glazier, gunsmith, harnessmaker, hatter/milliner, horse trainer/horseman, jeweler, jockey, lathe machinist, leather craftsman, linotype operator, lithographer/printer, locksmith, machinist, mechanic, mid-

wife, miller, painter/house painter, paperhanger, piano tuner, plasterer, plumber, potter, roofer, saddler, sausage maker, sawyer,
sheetmetal worker, shipsmith, shoemaker, silversmith, stonecutter,
stonemason, tailor, tanner, telegraph operator, tile setter, tinsmith,
upholsterer, vaquero, watchmaker, welder, wheelwright, wood-
carver

1910: roofer/shingler, shoemaker/cobbler

unskilled labor: boardinghouse worker, boiler washer, bootblack,
   busboy, cannery worker, carwasher, companion, concrete worker,
   dishwasher, domestic/maid, fruit packer/canner, fruit picker, gardener, gatekeeper, handyman, helper, hod carrier, hostler, hotel
   worker, housekeeper/house servant, house mover, hunter, janitor,
   kitchen helper, laborer (not farm laborer), laundry worker/laun-
   dress, millhand, newspaper carrier, oil worker/pumper, porter, railroad laborer, restaurant worker, scavenger, section-gang worker,
   servant, street sweeper, window cleaner, woodchopper, yardman

1910: baggage handler, caretaker, factory hand, roustabout/oil field
   worker, woodcutter

Note to the Paperback Edition

With the exception of the 1860 manuscript census, the undercount of
Indian people is severe and makes it impossible to include a statistically
significant Indian population in most of my quantitative analysis. I have
included the Indian population of 1860 in Appendixes 2 and 3 and in
Table 2, but the respective figures for later years in those tables, and the
absence of a statistical analysis of the Indian population elsewhere in my
text, is due to the undercount. Some Indians are undoubtedly counted
among Californios and Mexicans, but I am unable to identify them as
such unless Indian status is established by an "I" in the manuscript censuses "race" column. I interpreted ethnicity according to the criteria
listed on page 214. Indian work patterns, modes of subsistence, exchange, reciprocity, and household structures are rarely, and poorly, reflected in census data. The census material is a valuable indicator of social organization and change, but by no means provides a total picture.

Property Value by Group, Santa Ana and San Juan, 1860 and 1870

		Santa Ana Township			San Juan Township		
		No. of Households	Land	Other Assets	No. of Households	Land	Other Assets
Californio	1860	33	$66,700	$66,700	40	$38,350	$75,250
	1870	58	39,500	15,895	34	23,400	15,420
Mexican	1860	70	7,000	13,475	31	3,550	5,575
	1870	77	3,290	10,785	25	1,975	1,950
Indian	1860	19	1,000	750	34	1,300	600
	1870	0	0	0	2	200	100
European	1860	33	38,700	14,300	8	3,500	9,150
	1870	126	289,075	137,565	21	13,300	15,925
Anglo-American	1860	4	0	300	1	1,100	8,500
	1870	147	168,831	106,160	28	45,700	22,000
Other	1860	10	0	1,800	3	400	200
	1870	17	5,750	2,450	3	0	0
Total	1860	169	113,400	97,325	117	48,200	99,275
	1870	425	506,446	272,855	113	84,575	55,395

SOURCE: Federal Manuscript Censuses, 1860 and 1870.
See Note, p. 221

Household Composition by Group, Santa Ana and San Juan, 1860–1880

	Total No. of Households	Avg. Age of Head of Household	Avg. Household Size	Avg. No. of Family Members Working	Avg. No. of Other Household Members Working	% of Households with Members from Diverse Ethnic and Regional Origins
			1860			
Californio	73	38.0	6.3	1.3	1.4	40.8
Mexican	101	35.5	4.3	1.1	1.6	46.7
Indian	53	45.0	4.5	0.8	1.0	12.0
European	41	34.9	4.2	1.0	2.4	65.0
Anglo-American	5	31.0	4.4	1.0	1.2	100.0
Other	13	39.9	4.7	0.9	3.6	80.0
			1870			
Californio	92	36.5	4.4	1.0	0.5	12.9
Mexican	102	40.9	3.7	1.1	0.6	45.7
Indian	2	—	—	—	—	—
European	147	38.4	3.0	1.0	1.9	37.9

(continued)

	Total No. of Households	Avg. Age of Head of Household	Avg. Household Size	Avg. No. of Family Members Working	Avg. No. of Other Household Members Working	% of Households with Members from Diverse Ethnic and Regional Origins
			1870 (continued)			
Anglo-American	175	37.7	3.4	1.1	1.2	18.3
Chinese	11	28.0	1.1	0.8	0.5	0.0
Japanese	1	—	—	—	—	—
Central/South American	8	37.8	2.5	1.1	0.0	0.0
			1880			
Californio	102	41.8	5.7	1.3	1.2	19.0
Mexican	68	43.8	4.7	1.2	0.7	46.2
Indian	7	38.5	5.4	1.4	0.7	0.0
European	90	42.6	3.9	1.1	1.8	50.0
Anglo-American	214	42.7	4.6	1.8	1.7	15.5
Canadian	8	44.0	5.7	1.6	2.6	33.3
Chinese	12	30.5	3.2	1.0	2.7	13.7
Spanish-surnamed from Southwest	3	41.6	5.6	1.6	2.6	33.3
Latin American	3	57.3	6.0	1.0	NA	33.3

SOURCE: Federal Manuscript Censuses, 1860, 1870, 1880.
See Note, p. 221

Employment by Select Occupation and Group, Orange County, 1900–1910

	% of Californios		% of Mexicans		% of Europeans		% of Anglo-Americans	
	1900 (N=153)	1910 (N=207)	1900 (N=56)	1910 (N−263)	1900 (N=91)	1910 (N=96)	1900 (N=272)	1910 (N=410)
Farmer	20	22	20	4	56	55	49	39
Business	3	3	—	4	3	5	6	9
Unskilled	63	66	74	88	18	21	14	12
Professional	—	—	—	—	7	2	6	7
Sales/clerical	1	—	—	—	1	1	6	11
Semiskilled	10	6	3	3	2	4	11	12
Skilled	3	3	3	1	9	12	7	9
Other	—	—	—	—	4	—	1	1

SOURCE: Federal Manuscript Censuses, 1900 and 1910.
See Note, p. 221

Indices of Barrio Formation
in Santa Ana: Logan, Artesia,
and Delhi Barrios, 1916–1947

	No. of Dwellings	Spanish-surnamed as % of Households	% Owner-occupied	Spanish-surnamed as % of Owner-occupied	% Rear Dwellings
			Logan		
1916	101	40	—	—	—
1923	151	57	—	—	7
1933	209	65	29	47	16
1941	215	75	35	61	21
1947	210	84	44	87	14
			Artesia		
1916	48	18	—	—	—
1923	156	37	—	—	6
1933	460	51	29	44	4
1941	471	64	36	52	6
1947	489	68	53	62	5
			Delhi		
1941	204	94	45	92	11
1947	221	92	59	94	10

SOURCES: *Santa Ana City Directory, 1916* (Santa Ana: Santa Ana Directory Co., 1916); *Orange County Directory, 1923* (Long Beach: Western Directory Co., 1923); *Orange County Directory, 1933* (Long Beach: Western Directory Co., 1933); *Orange County Directory, 1941* (Long Beach: Western Directory Co., 1941); *Southern Orange County Directory, 1947* (Santa Ana: Western Directory Co., 1947).

Notes

Introduction

1. People v. Modesta Avila, Criminal Case No. 6, Superior Court of Orange County, October 15, 1889.

2. Recently various researchers have turned to personal narrative and similar sources to lend dimension to social and historical events and processes. I am thinking here especially of Natalie Davis's use of "pardon tales" to explore how sixteenth-century men and women narrated, and thus constructed, their lives (*Fiction in the Archives: Pardon Tales and Their Tellers in Sixteenth-Century France* [Stanford: Stanford University Press, 1987]); of Cathy Peiss's use of the personal writings of one young woman in a manner that promises new perspectives on race relations and sexual norms in New England's working class (paper delivered at the Organization of American Historians, Atlanta, 1994); and of Christine Stansell's use of court records to depict gender relations (*City of Women: Sex and Class in New York, 1789–1860* [New York: Knopf, 1986]).

3. More recently, Juaneños have been attempting to gain recognition as a tribe and to affirm their particular interests and historical role. Some have retaken the name Acâgchemem as a result.

4. Edward W. Soja, *Postmodern Geographies: The Reassertion of Space in Critical Social Theory* (London: Verso, 1989), p. 31.

5. Ibid., p. 6.

6. See "Questions on Geography" in Michel Foucault, *Power/Knowledge: Selected Interviews and Other Writings, 1972–1977* (New York: Pantheon Books, 1980), pp. 63–77.

7. I am particularly influenced by Américo Paredes's notion of the culture of Greater Mexico; see his collected essays in *Folklore and Culture on the Texas-Mexican Border,* ed. Richard Bauman (Austin: Center for Mexican American Studies, University of Texas, 1993). The Borderlands historiographic tradition

sprang from the work of Herbert Bolton and remained an influential school through the 1950s; see Bolton's important initial essay, "The Mission as a Frontier Institution in the Spanish-American Colonies," *American Historical Review* 23 (1917): 42–67, which remains characteristic of his approach. Gloria Anzaldúa explores the more contemporary meaning of borderlands in Anzaldua, *Borderlands/La Frontera* (San Francisco: Spinsters/aunt lute, 1987).

8. I refer here to the work done by historians associated with the journal *Annales: Economies, sociétés, civilisations,* founded by Marc Bloch and Lucien Febvre in Paris in 1929. Marc Bloch's own work in rural history remains important; see especially *French Rural History: An Essay on Its Basic Characteristics,* trans. Janet Sondheimer (1931; Berkeley and Los Angeles: University of California Press, 1966). More recent work includes Emmanuel Le Roy Ladurie, *The Peasants of Languedoc,* trans. John Day (1966; Urbana: University of Illinois Press, 1974); and Fernand Braudel, *The Mediterranean and the Mediterranean World in the Age of Philip II,* trans. Siân Reynolds, 2 vols. (1966; New York: Harper & Row, 1972). These historians began to use the word *espace* shortly after World War II to refer to the research on a given place done by an interdisciplinary team of scholars. A historian often directed the research endeavor.

9. Jean-Jacques Courtine and Claudine Haroche, *L'Histoire du visage: Exprimer et taire ses émotions, XVIe–début XIXe siècle* (Paris: Editions Rivages, 1988); and the series "Les Lieux de mémoire," directed by Pierre Nora; see especially Nora, ed., *La Nation,* 2 vols. (Paris: Gallimard, 1986).

10. Albert Camarillo, *Chicanos in a Changing Society: From Mexican Pueblos to American Barrios in Santa Barbara and Southern California, 1848–1930* (Cambridge, Mass.: Harvard University Press, 1979), p. 53.

11. For scholarly treatments see, for example, Richard Griswold del Castillo, *The Los Angeles Barrio, 1850–1890* (Berkeley and Los Angeles: University of California Press, 1979); Ricardo Romo, *East Los Angeles: History of a Barrio* (Austin: University of Texas Press, 1983); Antonio Ríos-Bustamante and Pedro Castillo, *An Illustrated History of Mexican Los Angeles, 1781–1985* (Los Angeles: Chicano Studies Research Center, University of California, Los Angeles, 1986); Mario García, *Desert Immigrants: The Mexicans of El Paso, 1880–1920* (New Haven: Yale University Press, 1981); and George J. Sánchez, *Becoming Mexican American: Ethnicity, Culture, and Identity in Chicano Los Angeles, 1900–1945* (New York: Oxford University Press, 1993). Among the many writers who treat the barrio in their work is Sandra Cisneros; see, for example, her *House on Mango Street* (Houston: Arte Público Press, 1985). A recent art exhibit that focused on Latino street life was "Urban Revisions: Current Projects for the Public Realm," Museum of Contemporary Art, Los Angeles, May 15–June 24, 1994; discussed, with illustrations, in Richard M. Carp, ed., *Saber es poder/Interventions Urban Revisions: Current Projects for the Public Realm* (Venice, Calif.: Gemini Graphics, 1994).

12. For more on this urban struggle, see Lisbeth Haas, "Grass-Roots Protest and the Politics of Planning: Santa Ana, 1976–88" in *Postsuburban California,* ed. Rob Kling, Spencer Olin and Mark Poster (Berkeley and Los Angeles, University of California Press, 1991), pp. 254–280.

13. Stuart Hall, "Cultural Identity and Diaspora," in *Identity: Community,*

Culture, Difference, ed. Jonathan Rutherford (London: Lawrence & Wishart, 1990), p. 225.

14. Joan W. Scott, *Gender and the Politics of History* (New York: Columbia University Press, 1988), p. 6.

15. See Benedict Anderson, *Imagined Communities: Reflections on the Origin and Spread of Nationalism* (London: Verso, 1991), esp. pp. 1–7.

16. G. Sánchez, *Becoming Mexican American,* pp. 7–8, 10–11.

17. Paul Gilroy, *There Ain't No Black in the Union Jack: The Cultural Politics of Race and Nation* (Chicago: University of Chicago Press, 1987), p. 38.

18. David Roediger, *The Wages of Whiteness: Race and the Making of the American Working Class* (New York: Verso, 1991), p. 7. See also Barbara Fields, "Ideology and Race in American History," in *Region, Race, and Reconstruction: Essays in Honor of C. Vann Woodward,* ed. J. Morgan Kousser and James M. McPherson (New York: Oxford University Press, 1982); and Alexander Saxton, *The Indispensable Enemy: Labor and the Anti-Chinese Movement in California* (Berkeley and Los Angeles: University of California Press, 1971).

19. Ramón Gutiérrez, *When Jesus Came, the Corn Mothers Went Away: Marriage, Sexuality, and Power in New Mexico, 1500–1846* (Stanford: Stanford University Press, 1991).

20. For a succinct rendering of these questions and the historiography, see Eric Foner, *Nothing But Freedom: Emancipation and Its Legacy* (Baton Rouge: Louisiana State University Press, 1983).

21. Douglas Monroy, *Thrown Among Strangers: The Making of Mexican Culture in Frontier California* (Berkeley and Los Angeles: University of California Press, 1990); Camarillo, *Chicanos in a Changing Society;* and idem, *Chicanos in California: A History of Mexican Americans in California* (San Francisco: Boyd & Fraser, 1984).

22. David Montejano, *Anglos and Mexicans in the Making of Texas, 1836–1986* (Austin: University of Texas Press, 1987). For critiques of work that employs static race paradigms, see Tomás Almaguer, "Ideological Distortions in Recent Chicano Historiography: The Internal Model and Chicano Historical Interpretation," *Aztlán* 18, no. 1 (1987); and David Gutiérrez, "The Third Generation: Recent Trends in Chicano/Mexican American Historiography," *Mexican Studies/Estudios Mexicanos* 5, no. 1 (Summer 1989).

23. Gutiérrez, *When Jesus Came;* Sarah Deutsch, *No Separate Refuge: Culture, Class, and Gender on an Anglo-Hispanic Frontier in the American Southwest, 1880–1940* (New York: Oxford University Press, 1987); Antonia Castañeda, "Presidarias y pobladoras: Spanish-Mexican Women in Frontier Monterey, Alta California, 1770–1821" (Ph.D. diss., Stanford University, 1990); and Deena Gonzalez, "La Tules of Image and Reality: Euro-American Attitudes and Legend Formation on a Spanish-Mexican Frontier," in *Building with Our Hands: New Directions in Chicana Studies,* ed. Adela de la Torre and Beatríz Pesquera (Berkeley and Los Angeles: University of California Press, 1993), pp. 75–90.

24. See the comparative study of Los Angeles, Tucson, Santa Fe, and San Antonio in Richard Griswold del Castillo, *La Familia: Chicano Families in the Urban Southwest, 1848 to the Present* (Notre Dame, Ind.: University of Notre Dame Press, 1984).

25. See Paredes, *Folklore and Culture,* pp. 129–142, for one of his earliest essays, "The Mexican Corrido: Its Rise and Fall" (1958).

26. See how Tomás Ybarra-Frausto relates cultural productions to the popular imagination in "I Can Still Hear the Applause: La Farándula Chicana—Carpas y Tandas de Variedad," in *Hispanic Theater in the United States,* ed. Nicolás Kanellos (Houston: Arte Público Press, 1984), pp. 45–61; and Nicolás Kanellos, *A History of Hispanic Theater in the United States: Origins to 1940* (Austin: University of Texas Press, 1990).

27. Stuart Ewen and Elizabeth Ewen, *Channels of Desire: Mass Images and the Shaping of American Consciousness* (New York: McGraw Hill, 1982): 82. For the original quote see Viola Paradise, "The Jewish Girl in Chicago," *Survey* 30 (1913): 701.

Chapter 1

1. See Henry Reichlen and Paule Reichlen, "Le Manuscrit Boscana de la Bibliothèque Nationale de Paris: Relation sur les Indiens Acâgchemem de la Mission de San Juan Capistrano, Californie," *Journal de la Société des Américanistes* 60 (1971): 267–268.

2. On strategies of conquest, see R. Gutiérrez, *When Jesus Came,* esp. pp. 39–94.

3. Fr. Zephyrin Engelhardt, O.F.M., *San Juan Capistrano Mission* (Los Angeles: Standard Printing Co., 1922), p. 13.

4. Raymond White, *Luiseño Social Organization,* University of California Publications in American Archaeology and Ethnology, vol. 48, no. 2 (Berkeley: University of California Press, 1963), pp. 91–194. On villages, see Reichlen and Reichlen, "Le Manuscrit Boscana," pp. 269–270.

5. See Doug Monroy's discussion of this process in *Thrown Among Strangers,* p. 48.

6. On early contact, see Antonia Castañeda, "Sexual Violence in the Politics and Policies of Conquest: Amerindian Women and the Spanish Conquest of Alta California," in de la Torre and Pesquera, *Building with Our Hands.* On the change in Indian reception of the Spaniards and on revolts, see George Harwood Phillips, *Chiefs and Challengers: Indian Resistance and Cooperation in Southern California* (Berkeley and Los Angeles: University of California Press, 1975), pp. 22–26; idem, *Indians and Intruders in Central California, 1769–1849* (Norman: University of Oklahoma Press, 1993), pp. 32–64; and Edward Castillo, "The Assassination of Padre Andres Quintana," *California History* 68, no. 3 (Fall 1989): 116–152.

7. The original Spanish manuscript is published in Carlo Tagliavini, "L'evangelizzazione e i costumi degli Indi Luiseños secondo la narrazione di un chierico indigeno," in *XXIII International Congress of Americanists* (Easton, Pa.: Eschenbach Printing Co., 1905), pp. 633–648. An English translation appears in Minna Hewes and Gordon Hewes, "Indian Life and Customs at Mission San Luis Rey: A Record of California Indian Life Written by Pablo Tac, an Indian

Neophyte," *The Americas* 9 (1952): 87–106. In what follows, quotations from Tac's treatise are my translations of Tagliavini, "L'evangelizzazione."

8. See, for example, Miguel Leon-Portilla, ed., *The Broken Spears: The Aztec Account of the Conquest of Mexico* (Boston: Beacon Press, 1962); Rolena Adorno, "New Perspectives in Colonial Spanish American Literary Studies," *Journal of the Southwest* 32, no. 2 (Summer 1990): 173–191; Serge Gruzinski, *The Conquest of Mexico: The Incorporation of Indian Societies into the Western World, 16th–18th Centuries,* trans. Eileen Corrigan (Cambridge: Polity Press, 1993); and James Lockhart, *Nahuas and Spaniards: Postconquest Central Mexican History and Philology* (Stanford: Stanford University Press, 1991).

9. Tagliavini, "L'evangelizzazione," pp. 638–640; parentheses are Tac's.

10. White, *Luiseño Social Organization,* pp. 91, 104–110.

11. Robert Heizer, ed., *Handbook of North American Indians,* vol. 8: *California* (Washington, D.C.: Smithsonian Institute Press, 1978): 550–55.

12. White, *Luiseño Social Organization,* pp. 171–178.

13. Heizer, *Handbook,* vol. 8: *California,* pp. 550–555; Raymond White, "The Luiseño Theory of 'Knowledge,'" *American Anthropologist* 59 (1957): 1–19.

14. *Alcaldes* also represented powerful rebel figures. A significant number left mission territory and, as fugitives, instructed and led Indians in farflung areas against the Spaniards. See Phillips, *Indians and Intruders.*

15. Tagliavini, "L'evangelizzazione," p. 643.

16. Ibid., p. 642.

17. Ibid., pp. 638, 642–643.

18. *Baptismal Register,* San Juan Capistrano Mission Archives.

19. Engelhardt, *San Juan Capistrano,* pp. 7–8.

20. See Phillips, *Chiefs and Challengers,* p. 24; and White, "Luiseño Theory of 'Knowledge,'" pp. 1–8.

21. *Baptismal Register;* see, for example, the first entries made between December 19, 1776, and January 4, 1777.

22. *Baptismal Register;* see, for example, the entries made between October 22, 1778, and February 5, 1779.

23. Engelhardt, *San Juan Capistrano,* p. 182.

24. See *Baptismal Register,* entry nos. 1249–1342, for a representative sample of these trends.

25. Apolinaria Lorenzano, "Memorias de la Beata," 1878, MS C-D 116, p. 7, Bancroft Collection, Bancroft Library, University of California, Berkeley.

26. The mission was supplied with goods from missions in Baja California and from Mission San Gabriel. San Juan Capistrano became one of the most productive of Alta California's missions, cultivating grapes, corn, wheat, legumes, vegetables, and cattle and other livestock. See Robert Archibald, *The Economic Aspects of the California Missions* (Washington, D.C.: Academy of American Franciscan History, 1978), pp. 164–165; and R. Louis Gentilcore, "Missions and Mission Lands of Alta California," *Annals of the Association of American Geographers* 51 (March 1961): 46–72.

27. This photo was taken by George Wharton James, whose work included *Old Missions and Mission Indians of California* and the *Tourist Guidebook to*

Southern California, both published in 1895, when California's incorporation into Western Americana was at its height.

28. Eulalia Pérez, "Una vieja y sus recuerdos," MS C-D 139, p. 15, Bancroft Collection.

29. Ibid., p. 9; Lorenzano, "Memorias," pp. 9–13; Julio César, "Cosas de indios de California," 1878, MS C-D 109, p. 69, Bancroft Collection. On the extensive production and early travel and trade that initiated California's entrance into the world economy, see Erwin Gustav Gudde, trans. and ed., "Edward Vischer's First Visit to California," *California Historical Society Quarterly* 19, no. 3 (1940): 193–216; Gentilcore, "Missions and Mission Lands," p. 69; and David Hornbeck, *California Patterns: A Geographical and Historical Atlas* (Palo Alto, Calif.: Mayfield, 1983).

30. Pérez, "Una vieja," pp. 8–10.

31. Reichlen and Reichlen, "Le Manuscrit Boscana," p. 260.

32. M. R. Harrington, *Chinigchinich* (Banning, Calif.: Malki Museum Press, 1978), pp. 72–73; and for literary commentary on this manuscript, see Francisco A. Lomelí, "Fray Gerónimo Boscana's 'Chinigchinich': An Early California Text in Search of a Context," in *Reconstructing a Chicano/a Literary Heritage: Hispanic Colonial Literature of the Southwest,* ed. María Herrera-Sobek (Tucson: University of Arizona Press, 1993), pp. 118–139.

33. Pérez, "Una vieja," p. 13.

34. Francis Guest, "Cultural Perspectives on California Mission Life," *Southern California Quarterly* 61, no. 1 (1983): 14–19.

35. Felipa Osuña de Marrón, "Recuerdos del pasado," 1878, C-D 120, p. 4, Bancroft Collection.

36. Miguel León-Portilla, *Endangered Cultures,* trans. Julie Goodson-Lawes (Dallas: Southern Methodist University Press, 1990), p. 10.

37. Reichlen and Reichlen, "Le Manuscrit Boscana," pp. 266–267.

38. Magnus Mörner, *Race Mixture in the History of Latin America* (Boston: Little, Brown, 1967), p. 60; Angel Rosenblat, *La población indígena y el mestizaje en América,* 2 vols. (Buenos Aires, 1954), 1:180.

39. On how people negotiated the meaning of their status and shaped their lives within the context of legal restrictions, see David G. Sweet and Gary B. Nash, eds., *Struggle and Survival in Colonial America* (Berkeley and Los Angeles: University of California Press, 1981). For more on *casta* identity, see León Nicolás, *Las castas en México colonial* (Mexico City, 1924); José Pérez de Barradas, *Los mestizos de América* (Madrid: Espasa-Calpe, 1976); and on *castas* in Baja California, see Doyce Nunis, Jr., *The Drawings of Ignacio Tirsch: A Jesuit Missionary in Baja California* (Los Angeles: Dawson's Book Shop, 1972).

40. Jack Forbes, "Black Pioneers: The Spanish-speaking Afroamericans of the Southwest," in *Minorities in California History,* ed. George Frakes and Curtis Solberg (New York: Random House, 1971), p. 25.

41. See Gonzalo Aguirre Beltrán, *La población negra de México, 1519–1810* (Mexico City: Ediciones Fuente Cultural, 1946). See also the files of the lawyer Gregory Yale, who represented Juan de Dios Sepúlveda, a colonist of African descent, in the 1850s in California; C-B 461, Bancroft Collection.

42. R. Gutiérrez, *When Jesus Came,* p. 190.

43: Jack D. Forbes, *Black Africans and Native Americans: Color, Race, and Caste in the Evolution of Red-Black Peoples* (New York: Basil Blackwell, 1988), p. 2; Rosenblat, *La población indígena* 2:136–138; Ralph Vigil, "The Hispanic Heritage and the Borderlands," *Journal of San Diego History* 19 (1973): 33.

44. Pérez, "Una vieja," p. 1.

45. César, "Cosas de indios," p. 1.

46. Guest, "Cultural Perspectives," pp. 47–51.

47. Ramón Gutiérrez discusses the development of polarized identities through conquest in "Unraveling America's Hispanic Past: Internal Stratification and Class Boundaries," *Aztlán* 17, no. 1 (Spring 1986): 79–101.

48. Maynard Geiger, O.F.M., "Mission San Gabriel in 1814," *Southern California Quarterly* 53, no. 3 (1971): 237–238.

49. John Francis Bannon, *The Spanish Borderlands Frontier, 1512–1821* (New York: Holt, Rinehart & Winston, 1970), pp. 61–79.

50. Forbes, "Black Pioneers," p. 23.

51. Ibid., p. 22.

52. See David Weber, *The Mexican Frontier, 1821–1846: The American Southwest Under Mexico* (Albuquerque: Univ. of New Mexico Press, 1982), pp. 158–78.

53. Theodore H. Hittell, *History of California*, vol. 2 (San Francisco: N. J. Stone & Co., 1897), pp. 93–95; C. Alan Hutchinson, *Frontier Settlements in Mexican California: The Híjar-Padrés Colony and Its Origins, 1769–1835* (New Haven: Yale University Press, 1969), pp. 131–132; Fr. Zephyrin Engelhardt, O.F.M., *The Missions and Missionaries of California*, vol. 3 (San Francisco: James Barry Co., 1912), pp. 379–402.

54. Hutchinson, *Frontier Settlements*, p. 153.

55. Ibid., pp. 167–171; and C. Alan Hutchinson, ed., *A Manifesto to the Mexican Republic* (Berkeley and Los Angeles: University of California Press, 1978): 3.

56. Land Grant Case 347 S.D., p. 52. (Note that land grant cases are to be found in several repositories, in manuscript form and as copies of manuscripts. I used the Bancroft Library collection in my research.)

57. Ibid., pp. 48 50.

58. David Weber, *Mexican Frontier*, p. 66. See also his chapter on comparative emancipation in the Southwest.

59. The narratives of ordinary and elite Californios suggest that they accepted the conclusions of the *Manifesto*. Hutchinson (*Manifesto,* pp. 15–16) lists, for example, Juan B. Alvarado, Mariano G. Vallejo, José Fernández, Antonio María Osío, José de Jesús Vallejo, Vicente P. Gómez, and Manuel Castro.

60. Bishop Joseph S. Alemany, *Mission San Juan Capistrano*, Land Grant Case 388 S.D., pp. 32, 109.

61. Hutchinson, *Manifesto*, p. 96.

62. Ignacio Sepúlveda, "Historical Memoranda," July 9, 1874, C-E 65:14, p. 2, Bancroft Collection. See also Doña Teresa de la Guerra de Hartnell, "Narrativa de la distinguida matrona californiana," March 12, 1875, C-E 67, p. 2, Bancroft Collection.

63. Sepúlveda, "Historical Memoranda," pp. 2–3, 6.

64. Hutchinson, *Manifesto*, pp. 76–77.

65. Ibid., p. 77: "Son dueños de la tierra que cultivan, y de los intereses que adquieren con su trabajo."

66. Land Grant Case 347 S.D., pp. 58–60. The narratives frequently recount the sacking of the missions by the administrators; see, for example, César, "Cosas de indios," p. 3; María Inocenta Pico de Avila, "Cosas de California," 1878, C-D 34, p. 17, Bancroft Collection.

67. See Leon Litwack, *Been in the Storm So Long: The Aftermath of Slavery* (New York: Alfred A. Knopf, 1979); and Willie Lee Nichols Rose, *Rehearsal for Reconstruction: The Port Royal Experiment* (Indianapolis: Bobbs-Merrill, 1964), for examples of slaves claiming land they had previously cultivated. Also see Ira Berlin et al., eds., *The Destruction of Slavery*, vol. 1 of Freedom, a Documentary History of Emancipation: 1861–1867 (New York: Cambridge University Press, 1985); Foner, *Nothing but Freedom*, p. 2; and idem, *Reconstruction: America's Unfinished Revolution, 1866–1877* (New York: Harper & Row, 1988), for the role of the state in emancipation.

68. Engelhardt, *San Juan Capistrano*, p. 85.

69. See Phillips, *Chiefs and Challengers*, p. 37.

70. Hutchinson, *Frontier Settlements*, p. 129. See Hewes and Hewes, "Indian Life and Customs," pp. 87–106.

71. Engelhardt, *San Juan Capistrano*, p. 112.

72. Phillips, *Chiefs and Challengers*, p. 40.

73. Engelhardt, *San Juan Capistrano*, p. 131.

74. For the petition, see Land Grant Case 89 S.D., 1852.

75. J. N. Bowman, "Prominent Women of Provincial California," *Southern California Quarterly* 39, no. 2 (1957): 161; María Juana de los Angeles, Land Grant Case 281 S.D., 1852.

76. Terry E. Stephenson, "Forster vs. Pico," *Southern California Quarterly* 18, no. 1 (1936): 25.

77. Hutchinson, *Frontier Settlements*, pp. 227–228.

78. César, "Cosas de indios," p. 4.

79. Engelhardt, *San Juan Capistrano*, pp. 121–122.

80. See W. W. Robinson, "The Indians of Los Angeles as Revealed by the Los Angeles City Archives," *Southern California Quarterly* 20 (December 1938): 161.

81. David Weber, *Mexican Frontier*, p. 208.

82. Howard Lamar, "From Bondage to Contract: Ethnic Labor in the American West, 1600–1890," in *The Countryside in the Age of Capitalist Transformation: Essays in the Social History of Rural America*, ed. Steven Hahn and Jonathan Prude (Chapel Hill: University of North Carolina Press, 1985), pp. 293–326, 300.

83. Sherburne Cook, ed., *The Conflict Between the California Indian and White Civilization* (Berkeley and Los Angeles: University of California Press, 1976), pp. 302–308.

84. Monroy, *Thrown Among Strangers*, pp. 127–129, 134.

85. Leonard Pitt, *The Decline of the Californios: A Social History of the Spanish-speaking Californians, 1846–1890* (Berkeley and Los Angeles: University of California Press, 1966), pp. 9–10. See also Robert Glass Cleland, *The Cattle*

on a Thousand Hills: Southern California, 1850–1880, 2d ed. (San Marino, Calif.: Huntington Library, 1951), p. 30.

86. See Phillips, *Chiefs and Challengers,* pp. 5–13; and see Edward Castillo, "An Indian Account of the Decline and Collapse of Mexicanos' Hegemony over the Missionized Indians of California," *American Indian Quarterly* 13, no. 4 (Fall 1989): 391–408.

87. Gregg Layne, "The First Census of the Los Angeles District: *Padrón de la Ciudad de Los Angeles y su jurisdicción año 1836,*" *Southern California Quarterly* 18, no. 3 (1936): 81–99; orig. census pp. 1–63.

Chapter 2

1. For a good description of the logic behind and legal structure of a *pueblo,* see Monroy, *Thrown Among Strangers,* pp. 104–106; and Ríos-Bustamante and Castillo, *Illustrated History of Mexican Los Angeles,* pp. 25–38.

2. Land Grant Case 130 S.D., 1852, pp. 5–6, 15. .

3. Layne, "First Census," census pp. 38–40, 59–60.

4. Land Grant Case 89 S.D., 1852, p. 52.

5. Ibid., pp. 55–57.

6. Layne, "First Census," census pp. 40–41, 61.

7. Terry Stephenson, *Don Bernardo Yorba* (Los Angeles: Glen Dawson, 1941), p. 27.

8. Bruce Conde, "Santa Ana of the Yorbas," *Southern California Quarterly* 21, no. 1 (1939): 78.

9. M. R. Harrington, trans., "Will of Don Tomas Yorba Year of 1845," *Southern California Quarterly* 33, no. 1 (1951): 25–38.

10. Richard Henry Dana, *Two Years Before the Mast and Twenty-four Years After* (New York: P. F. Collier & Son, 1909), p. 81.

11. On the emergence of Lynn and Lowell, Massachusetts, for example, see Alan Dawley, *Class and Community: The Industrial Revolution in Lynn* (Cambridge, Mass.: Harvard University Press, 1976); and Thomas Dublin, *Women at Work: The Transformation of Work and Community in Lowell, Massachusetts, 1826–1860* (New York: Columbia University Press, 1979).

12. Dana, *Two Years Before the Mast,* p. 284.

13. Ibid., pp. 81–82.

14. As I will later argue, the negative images of Californianas contributed to shape their experience of conquest. On those stereotypes, see Antonia Castañeda, "The Political Economy of Nineteenth-Century Stereotypes of Californianas," in *Between Borders: Essays on Mexicana/Chicana History,* ed. Adelaida R. Del Castillo (Encino, Calif.: Floricanto Press, 1990), 213–236.

15. Terry E. Stephenson, "Tomás Yorba, His Wife Vicenta, and His Account Book," *Southern California Quarterly* 23, nos. 3–4 (1941): 127–156. Stephenson reproduces large parts of the extant account book, which he found on loan to Bowers Museum in 1940–1941.

16. See Sidney W. Mintz, *Sweetness and Power: The Place of Sugar in Modern History* (New York: Viking, 1985), for an excellent account of the history of this

product. In England, the consumption of sugar among the laboring classes exceeded its consumption by the wealthy in 1850 (p. 143). In California, however, sugar remained a product used almost exclusively by the elite, who bought it in bulk. See also Christine Stansell, *City of Women: Sex and Class in New York, 1789–1860* (New York: Alfred A. Knopf, 1986), for a comparative sense of the labor and social worlds in which these goods were produced on the East Coast.

17. Harrington, "Will of Don Tomas Yorba," pp. 30–33.

18. Stephenson, "Tomás Yorba," pp. 138, 144, 148, 150.

19. Engelhardt, *San Juan Capistrano,* pp. 140–146; Bancroft, *History of California,* 7 vols. (San Francisco: History Co., 1884–1889), 4:625, 2:305–306.

20. The Taroje family later lost the property to Blas Aguilar, a longtime Californio resident of San Juan; the photo is thus titled "Adobe of Blas Aguilar," an example of the all-too-frequent erasure of Indian history in documents from the Mexican and American periods.

21. Duplicate Tax Assessment List of Los Angeles County, Fiscal Years 1857, 1858, Orange County Archives, Santa Ana, California.

22. Engelhardt, *San Juan Capistrano Mission,* p. 157.

23. William Spicer uses the term *cycles of conquest* in his comprehensive study of the policies of conquest and their effect on Indian peoples across the U.S.-Mexico border; see *Cycles of Conquest: The Impact of Spain, Mexico, and the United States on the Indians of the Southwest, 1533–1960* (Tucson: University of Arizona Press, 1962). Patricia Nelson Limerick presents a view of conquest as a relentless historical process; see *The Legacy of Conquest: The Unbroken Past of the American West* (New York: W. W. Norton, 1987).

24. Albert Hurtado, *Indian Survival on the California Frontier* (New Haven: New Haven University Press, 1988), p. 1.

25. Richard Griswold del Castillo, *The Treaty of Guadalupe Hidalgo: A Legacy of Conflict* (Norman: University of Oklahoma Press, 1990), pp. 189–190, and article X, p. 95. Griswold del Castillo has an excellent discussion of U.S. and Mexican debates over the treaty and of the treaty's significance. Disturnell's *Map of Mexico,* published in 1847, was appended to the treaty. Almost the entire area of the Southwest (except New Mexico) is marked "Apacheria," underscoring the significance of the Apaches' and Navajos' historical presence and claims to the region.

26. Griswold del Castillo, *Treaty of Guadalupe Hidalgo,* pp. 190–91.

27. Robert A. Trennert, Jr., *Alternative to Extinction: Federal Indian Policy and the Beginnings of the Reservation System, 1846–51* (Philadelphia: Temple University Press, 1975), pp. 97–98. Trennert presents an important analysis of how the government likewise attempted to forge peace with hispanicized and "so-called wild tribes" in Texas and New Mexico (pp. 61–130). On Indian populations divided by the border, see Oscar J. Martínez, *Troublesome Border* (Tucson: University of Arizona Press, 1988), pp. 53–79.

28. Robert F. Heizer, ed., "Report of Special Agent John G. Ames on the Condition of the Mission Indians, 1873," in *Federal Concern About the Conditions of California Indians, 1853 to 1913: Eight Documents* (Socorro, N.M.: Ballena Press, 1979), p. 65.

29. Albert Hurtado, "Controlling California's Indian Labor Force: Federal

Administration of California Indian Affairs During the Mexican War," *Historical Society of Southern California Quarterly* 61, no. 3 (Fall 1979): 228; George H. Phillips, "Indians in Los Angeles, 1781–1875: Economic Integration, Social Disintegration," *Pacific Historical Review* 49, no. 3 (August 1980): 427–445.

30. Gold was first discovered by John Sutter, a federal Indian subagent who had settled in California prior to 1846, on land that he leased from the Yalisumni Nisenan Indians. See Hurtado, *Indian Survival,* pp. 100–124; and Phillips, *Indians and Intruders,* pp. 135–156.

31. Robert F. Heizer, ed., *The Eighteen Unratified Treaties of 1851–1852 Between the California Indians and the United States Government* (Berkeley: Archaeological Research Facility, 1972), pp. 56–57.

32. Each treaty used a distinct or specific language, though this particular phrase appeared in virtually every treaty; see ibid., pp. 41, 44, 47, 50, 54, 62.

33. Heizer, "Report of Special Agent Ames," p. 54.

34. Robert Cowan lists three ranchos granted to the "Christian Indians of San Miguel" in San Luis Obispo County in 1844. All claims were rejected by the land commission, as was the 1841 claim of one league to Indians of San Rafael. See Cowan, *Ranchos of California* (Fresno: Academy Library Guild, 1956), pp. 35, 27, 50, 102. Other claims listed in the federal land claims index include that of "Simeon, Indian, San Gabriel Tract" (*Federal Land Records* [National Archives, Washington, D.C.], p. 554) and "Filipe, neophyte, Buena Vista" (*Federal Land Records,* p. 456). These claims, too, were rejected.

35. Florence Connolly Shipek, *Pushed into the Rocks: Southern California Indian Land Tenure, 1769–1986* (Lincoln: University of Nebraska Press, 1987), p. 32.

36. See Heizer, "Report of Special Agent Ames," p. 67. For documents about Indian land claims and their relationship to the Treaty of Guadalupe Hidalgo, see idem, *The California Indians Versus the United States* (Socorro, N.M.: Ballena Press, 1978), esp. pp. 127–129. On early policy, see James J. Rawls, *Indians of California: The Changing Image* (Norman: University of Oklahoma Press, 1984), especially pp. 137–170.

37. Heizer, "Report of Special Agent Ames," p. 55.

38. Shipek, *Pushed into the Rocks,* pp. 35–39.

39. This and subsequent statistical references are derived from the Federal Manuscript Census of 1860, unless otherwise specified.

40. Engelhardt, *San Juan Capistrano,* p. 205.

41. Herbert Harvey, "The Luiseño: An Analysis of Change in Patterns of Land Tenure and Social Structure," in *American Indian Ethnohistory: California Indians,* vol. 2 (New York: Garland, 1974), pp. 188–89. Temecula was often the site of Luiseño creation stories: it was from there that people dispersed after the death of their leader, Ouiot. The village of Temecula was granted an area within the boundaries of the contiguous Rancho Temecula; granted to Pablo Apis, chief of the Temecula group of Luiseños, by Governor Pio Pico on May 7, 1845, and patented in 1873 (ibid., p. 19). The anthropologist Raymond White conducted field research at Pauma and Rincon in 1947; see White, "Two Surviving Luiseño Indian Ceremonies," *American Anthropologist* 55 (1953): 569–578.

42. Again, unless otherwise specified, this and all subsequent statistical ref-

erences are derived from the Federal Manuscript Censuses of 1860, 1870, and 1880 and provide information on the entire area identified on map 2.

43. Lucile E. Dickson, "The Founding and Early History of Anaheim, California," *Southern California Quarterly* 2 (1918–1920): 26–37.

44. These processes are described for communities from Santa Barbara southward to San Diego in Camarillo, *Chicanos in a Changing Society* and *Chicanos in California*. Also see Mario García, "The Californios of San Diego and the Politics of Accommodation, 1846–1860," *Aztlán* 6, no. 1 (1975). On town building in San Diego in the 1850s and Mexican participation in this process, see idem, "Merchants and Dons: San Diego's Attempt at Modernization, 1850–1860," in *Mexicans in California After the U.S. Conquest,* ed. Carlos Cortes (New York: Arno Press, 1976), pp. 52–80; and Richard Griswold del Castillo, *The Los Angeles Barrio, 1850–1890: A Social History* (Berkeley and Los Angeles: University of California Press, 1979). For the earliest study that outlines major dynamics of property loss, see Pitt, *Decline of the Californios;* and Tomás Almaguer, "Class, Race, and Capitalist Development: The Social Transformation of a Southern California County, 1848–1903" (Ph.D. diss., University of California, Berkeley, 1979). On the transformation of San Jose in northern California, see George J. Sánchez, *Adaptation to Conquest: The Mexican Community of San José, 1845–1880,* Working Paper Series, no. 4 (Stanford: Stanford Center for Chicano Research, 1984). For an examination of this process, with its antecedents and consequences, see Monroy, *Thrown Among Strangers;* and Ríos-Bustamante and Castillo, *Illustrated History of Mexican Los Angeles.*

45. On this process elsewhere in the Southwest see Montejano, *Anglos and Mexicans,* pp. 27–28; Arnoldo De León, *The Tejano Community, 1836–1900* (Albuquerque: University of New Mexico Press, 1982); Deutsch, *No Separate Refuge;* William de Buys, "Fractions of Justice: A Legal and Social History of the Las Trampas Land Grant, New Mexico," *New Mexico Historical Review* 56 (January 1981): 71–97; Howard Lamar, *The Far Southwest, 1846–1912: A Territorial History* (New Haven: Yale University Press, 1966); Thomas Sheridan, *Los Tucsonenses: The Mexican Community in Tucson, 1854–1941* (Tucson: University of Arizona Press, 1986).

46. The immigrants were still primarily of German and Prussian background, but Poles and immigrants from Western Europe (primarily England and France) also contributed to expand this population during the 1860s and 1870s.

47. Robert Glass Cleland, *The Irvine Ranch* (San Marino: Huntington Library, 1962), p. 44. Teodocio Yorba filed claims for the rancho Lomas de Santiago in October 1852 (Land Grant Case 186 S.D.). The claim was confirmed by the land board in August 1854, and by the District Court on December 12, 1856. The patent was one of the first issued; it was issued after this sale in 1868 for over 47,000 acres of land. The validity of the grant was contested many times thereafter; the last appeal was rejected by the Supreme Court as late as October 1934.

48. Teodosio Yorba, "Yorba Family Papers, 1863–1873," Leming Collection, Bancroft Library, University of California, Berkeley.

49. Cleland, *Irvine Ranch,* pp. 41–43. José Sepúlveda placed a claim for Rancho San Joaquín in November 1852 (Land Grant Case 185 S.D.). The grant was confirmed by the land board in 1855. The appeal by the attorney general—which was virtually automatic—was dismissed in 1857. The patent was issued a comparatively short ten years thereafter, in 1867, for 48,803 acres.

50. The claim was filed by Bernardo Yorba et al. for the rancho Santiago de Santa Ana in November 1852 (Land Grant Case 346 S.D.). The grant was confirmed by the board in 1855. The appeal was dismissed in 1857. The patent was not issued until 1883. Four cases were brought to court in the 1880s to challenge the validity of the grant, in 1880, 1883, 1884, and 1887.

51. C. E. Roberts, *The Partition of the Rancho Santiago de Santa Ana,* Orange County Historical Research Project No. 3105 (Santa Ana: Federal Writers' Project, Work Projects Administration, 1936), pp. 20–22, 61.

52. Tax Assessment Records, 1875, Orange County Archives (microfilm).

53. I must qualify the idea of *marriage patterns* by noting that I refer to the oldest female in the household, who is not necessarily the wife. Only in 1880 is the legal relationship between household members and head of household listed; those data suggest that the oldest female usually was a wife, but especially among Californios, who often had female-headed households, she was sometimes instead the mother, daughter, or sister.

54. The average age of these heads of household in each respective census year is 38, 36, 42, 41, and 42. The parents were thus born roughly (again, using averages) between 1822 for the first census year to 1868 for the last, but the variation is relatively large and would incorporate many of the marriages that took place between 1860 and 1880.

55. Helena Modjeska, *Memories and Impressions of Helena Modjeska: An Autobiography* (New York: MacMillan, 1910), p. 295.

56. For a discussion of the meaning of ethnic diversity in the definition of American towns during this period, see Olivier Zunz, *The Changing Face of Inequality: Urbanization, Industrial Development, and Immigration in Detroit, 1880–1920* (Chicago: University of Chicago Press, 1982), pp. 15–88.

57. Camarillo, *Chicanos in California,* p. 26, and idem, *Chicanos in a Changing Society,* p. 53. The barrio is thus seen as a place of resistance to a dominant Anglo population.

58. C. Loyal, *The Squatter and the Don: A Novel Descriptive of Contemporary Occurrences in California* (San Francisco: C. Loyal, 1885), p. 123.

59. See Arnoldo de León, *They Called Them Greasers: Anglo Attitudes Toward Mexicans in Texas, 1821–1900* (Austin: University of Texas Press, 1983), for the origin and use of this term.

60. Kathleen Crawford, "María Amparo Ruiz Burton: The General's Lady," *Journal of San Diego History* 30, no. 3 (1984): 198–202.

61. Ibid., pp. 204–205.

62. Ibid., pp. 204, 207–209.

63. Loyal, *Squatter and the Don,* p. 222.

64. Women writers who develop gender, class, and race themes in a similar manner for Tejano society are discussed by Gloria L. Valásquez Treviño, in

"Cultural Ambivalence in Early Chicana Prose Fiction" (Ph.D. diss., Stanford University, 1985).

65. Lorenzano, "Memorias," p. 30. On one of these ranchos, the mission grew cotton that was combed, spun, and made into cloth and clothing at the mission (p. 7). On her purchase of the third rancho, see p. 28.

66. Ibid. On the narratives, see Genaro Padilla, "The Recovery of Chicano Nineteenth-Century Autobiography," *American Quarterly* 40, no. 3 (Fall 1988): 286–306; and idem, *My History, Not Yours: The Formation of Mexican American Autobiography* (Madison: University of Wisconsin Press, 1993). On Bancroft's work, see below, chapter 5.

67. Lorenzano, "Memorias," pp. 5, 6, 11, 14.

68. Ibid., pp. 28–30.

69. Silvia Marina Arrom, *The Women of Mexico City, 1790–1857* (Stanford: Stanford University Press, 1985), pp. 61–62.

70. Ibid., pp. 64–65.

71. Castañeda, "Sexual Violence," p. 26.

72. Guitérrez, *When Jesus Came*, p. 190.

73. Bowman, "Prominent Women," p. 154; Isabel Yorba, *Guadalasca*, Land Grant Case 177 S.D., 1852.

74. Bowman, "Prominent Women," p. 155; Vicenta Sepúlveda, *Sierra*, Land Grant Case 362 S.D., 1852; William Heath Davis, *Seventy-five Years in California* (San Francisco: John Howell Books, 1967).

75. Bowman, "Prominent Women," p. 161; María Juana de los Angeles, Land Grant Case 281 S.D., 1852.

76. Pérez, "Una vieja," p. 21.

77. Arrom, *Women of Mexico City*, pp. 65–68.

78. Padilla, *My History*, p. 113.

79. Harrington, "Will of Don Tomas Yorba," p. 26.

80. Stephenson, *Don Bernardo Yorba*, 68.

81. Padilla, *My History*, esp. pp. 117, 124–125, 133, 143, 147.

82. Marrón, "Recuerdos."

83. Joan Jensen, *Promise to the Land: Essays on Rural Women* (Albuquerque: University of New Mexico Press, 1991), p. 1; and Lee Virginia Chambers-Schiller, *Liberty, a Better Husband: Single Women in America, the Generations of 1780–1840* (New Haven: Yale University Press, 1984).

84. Griswold del Castillo, *La Familia*, p. 32. See Deena Gonzalez, "The Widowed Women of Santa Fe: Assessments of the Lives of an Unmarried Population, 1850–1880," in *Unequal Sisters: A Multicultural Reader in U.S. Women's History*, ed. Ellen Carol DuBois and Vicki L. Ruiz (New York: Routledge, 1990), pp. 34–50. From 1850 to 1880, women over fifteen without husbands made up at least 10 percent of the adult population of Spanish-surnamed women in Santa Fe (p. 38).

85. These and the following statistics are all derived from the Federal Manuscript Censuses of 1860, 1870, 1880, 1900, and 1910, but property values (in land and assets) were recorded only in 1860 and 1870.

Chapter 3

1. Tax Assessment Records, 1875, 1889, Orange County Archives (microfilm); Federal Manuscript Censuses, San Juan Village, 1880; San Juan Township, 1870.

2. Padilla, *My History*, p. 229.

3. Federal Manuscript Census, San Juan Village, 1880.

4. Among the suits not mentioned in the following pages was M. Mendelson v. Ramón Yorba, Civil Case No. 1062, Orange County Court, January 30, 1895. Mendelson sued for a debt of $553.34, to be paid in gold coins. Mendelson placed a writ of attachment on Yorba's property, but the case was dismissed when Yorba paid the debt. In Mendelson v. Gregorio Ríos et al., Civil Case No. 904, filed in February 1894 at the Orange County Court, Mendelson accused the Ríos family of being squatters on his land (evidently land he had somehow acquired from the family in the first place). The case was won by default, as the Ríos family was reportedly living in Baja California by that date.

5. Familia Aguilar, *Libro del Padre Mut*, 1866–1886, 73/108, vol. 2, pp. 62, 64, 75, 82, Bancroft Library, University of California, Berkeley.

6. Tax Assessment Records, 1886, 1889, Orange County Archives (microfilm).

7. Tax Assessment Records, 1889, Orange County Archives (microfilm).

8. Mendelson v. Rosa Pryor, Civil Case No. 94, Orange County Court, February 1890.

9. Ibid.

10. This and subsequent sketches of specific families are developed from the court transcripts and the federal manuscript census and tax assessment records for each respective year.

11. Mendelson and Oyharzabal v. María Espíritu Olivares et al., Civil Case No. 636, Orange County Court, December 9, 1892.

12. Delfina Olivares, Interview with Suzanne Jansen, August 3, 1971, Oral History Collection, California State University, Fullerton, O.H. 711, pp. 2–3.

13. Ibid., p. 18.

14. See the entire interview of Daisy Yorba Winterbourne, Interview with Karen Wilson Turnbull, July 24, 1975, Oral History Collection, California State University, Fullerton, O.H. 1463.

15. Mendelson v. A. G. Aguilar, Civil Case No. 1717, Orange County Court, December 13, 1898.

16. Josefa Serrano de Ríos v. Ricano Dominguez et al., Civil Case No. 325, Orange County Court, January 31, 1891.

17. Josefa Serrano de Ríos v. James Miller, George Hayford, and the Southern Pacific Railroad Co., Civil Case No. 506, Orange County Court, November 19, 1891.

18. For a comparative view, see Steven Hahn, *The Roots of Southern Populism: Yeoman Farmers and the Transformation of the Georgia Upcountry, 1850–1890* (New York: Oxford University Press, 1983).

19. *Santa Ana Weekly Blade*, February 13, 1890.

20. See Américo Paredes, "José Mosquada and the Folklorization of Actual Events," in *Folklore and Culture*, 177–214; and on representations of women in

corridos, see María Herrera-Sobek, *The Mexican Corrido: A Feminist Analysis* (Bloomington: Indiana University Press, 1990).

21. Josefa Serrano de Ríos v. James Miller et al.

22. Federal Manuscript Census, 1900.

23. D. Gonzalez, "Widowed Women of Santa Fe," p. 44.

24. Ibid., p. 39.

25. Don Doram, Interview with author, February 14, 1992.

26. Paul Arbiso, Interview with Karen Wilson Turnbull, December 30, 1975, Oral History Collection, California State University, Fullerton, O.H. 1464; David Belardes, Interview with author, February 14, 1992; Don Doram interview.

27. Deutsch, *No Separate Refuge,* p. 58.

28. On how women are made into pawns within the honor-status system, see Gutiérrez, *When Jesus Came,* esp. pp. 176–206.

29. D. Gonzalez, "Widowed Women of Santa Fe," pp. 44–45.

30. Federal manuscript censuses for 1860, 1870, 1880, 1900, and 1910.

31. Evelyn Villegas, Interview with author, February 16, 1992.

32. Don Doram, interview (cited above).

33. Harvey, "The Luiseno," pp. 10–11.

34. Shipek, *Pushed into the Rocks,* p. 54.

35. Clinton Hart Merriam, *Studies of California Indians* (Berkeley and Los Angeles: University of California Press, 1955), pp. 87, 89, 118.

36. Ibid., p. 91.

37. Ibid., pp. 87, 91–92.

38. Heizer, *Federal Concern,* p. 87; Familia Aguilar, Libro del Padre Mut.

39. Gladys Pryor Landell, Interview with Karen Wilson Turnbull, July 28, 1975, Oral History Collection, California State University, Fullerton, O.H. 146, pp. 15–16.

40. Evelyn Villegas and Don Doram interviews.

41. Joseph Yorba, Interview with Paul Clark, January 9, 1976, Oral History Collection, California State University, Fullerton, O.H. 1465, pp. 3–4.

42. Charles Saunders and Father St. John O'Sullivan, *Capistrano Nights: Tales of a California Mission Town* (New York: R. M. McBride & Co., 1930), pp. 129–137.

43. Ibid., p. 133. Naháchis journeyed to the reservations on map 1.

44. Ibid., pp. 134–135.

45. In San Juan between 1900 and 1910, the native-California parentage of California-born heads of household with Spanish surnames increased from 73 to 81 percent on the father's side, and from 85 to 91 percent on the mother's side. Elsewhere in Orange County, however, California-born heads of household tended increasingly to be the offspring of Mexican parents after 1900.

46. Saunders and O'Sullivan, *Capistrano Nights,* p. 51.

47. Paul Arbiso interview, pp. 16–17.

48. Alfonso Yorba, "San Juan Capistrano Mission Documents, 1866–1886," vol. 1, Bancroft Library.

49. Familia Aguilar, *Libro del Padre Mut.*

50. Saunders and O'Sullivan, *Capistrano Nights,* pp. 18–22.

51. Ibid., pp. 81–82.

52. Ibid., pp. 184–189.

53. Ibid, pp. 109–110.

54. The following discussion is based on Walter J. Ong, *Orality and Literacy: The Technologizing of the Word* (New York: Routledge, 1988), esp. pp. 20–57.

55. The federal manuscript censuses of 1860–1880, 1900, 1910.

56. Kathleen Crawford, "Maria Ampara Ruiz Burton," p. 200, and Lorenzano, "Memorias," pp. 4–5.

57. Paul Arbiso interview, pp. 9–10.

58. Joseph Yorba interview, p. 1.

59. See entire Paul Arbiso interview.

60. *Fifteenth Census of the United States, 1930: Agriculture* (Washington, D.C.: Government Printing Office, 1931), vol. 3, pt. 3, pp. 386–387.

61. Donald H. Pflueger, ed., *Charles C. Chapman: The Career of a Creative Californian, 1853–1944* (Los Angeles: Anderson, Richie & Simon, 1976), p. 110.

62. Clara Engle, "Orange County Citrus Strike, 1936: Historical Analysis and Social Conflict" (M.A. thesis, California State University, Fullerton, 1975), p. 107.

63. W. W. Cumberland, *Cooperative Marketing: Its Advantages as Exemplified in the California Fruit Growers Exchange* (London: Oxford University Press, 1917), p. 36.

64. Ibid., p. 187.

65. *Orange County Historical Series* 2 (1932): 26.

66. Charles C. Teague, *Fifty Years a Rancher: A Recollection of Half a Century Devoted to the Citrus and Walnut Industries of California and to Furthering the Cooperative Movement in Agriculture* (Los Angeles: Ward & Ritchie Press, 1944), pp. 97–102.

67. *Fifteenth Census of the United States, 1930: Agriculture*, vol. 3, pt. 3, County Table VII, p. 422.

68. In 1880, 55 percent of Anglo-Americans in Orange County farmed; by 1900 that percentage had declined to 49 percent, and ten years later it stood at only 39 percent (Federal manuscript censuses of 1880, 1900, 1910).

69. Santa Ana Chamber of Commerce, Minutes, 1899. The chamber of commerce sought subscriptions of land and capital to attract the large Cutting Fruit Packing Company. In addition, the canneries had a policy aimed at stimulating local planting of certain fruits; in 1920, canning was one of the largest industries in the county, and numerous small plants coexisted with the large corporate branch plants established in Orange County.

70. Federal Manuscript Census, San Juan Town, 1910. Californios and Indians headed 72 households that constituted 56 percent of the village and rural population in San Juan town and township (42 percent headed by Californios and 14 percent headed by Indians). Most of these 72 households were located within San Juan village. The Californio and Indian populations accounted for approximately 370 persons of an estimated 550 total population in San Juan township in 1910.

71. Paul Arbiso interview, p. 16.

72. Father St. John O'Sullivan, "Happenings at Mission San Juan Capistrano

from March 25, 1917, to March 1, 1921," MS A 3–900.0, San Juan Capistrano Mission Archives.

73. See Carey McWilliams, *Southern California: An Island on the Land* (1949; Santa Barbara: Peregrine Smith, 1973), pp. 70–83; and Monroy, *Thrown Among Strangers,* pp. 260–267.

74. See David Thelen's discussion of memory as group process and the meaning of memory for the interpretation of history in "Memory and American History," *Journal of American History* 75, no. 4 (March 1989): 1117–1129. For a discussion of contemporary ethnographic trends influenced by an interpretation of ethnicity as constructed through a dynamic process that involves the shaping of memory, see Michael Fischer, "Ethnicity and the Post-Modern Arts of Memory," in *Writing Culture: The Poetics and Politics of Ethnography,* ed. James Clifford and George Marcus (Berkeley and Los Angeles: University of California Press, 1986), pp. 194–233.

75. Petition of the Club Hispano Californio de San Juan Capistrano, September 5, 1935, Orange County Archives, Board of Supervisors file, "Roads," B75–1:13, 1987/26/228.

76. Resolution of the Board of Supervisors of Orange County, California, August 26, 1936, Orange County Archives, Board of Supervisors file, "Roads," B75–1:13, 1987/26/228.

77. "Mapa del Pueblo de San Juan de Arguello," drawn by Alfonso Yorba, 1934, San Juan Capistrano Mission Archives.

78. Alfonso Yorba, "Old San Juan: Last Stronghold of Spanish California," *Southern California Quarterly,* March 1935, pp. 7–13.

79. The Mission Indian Federation was formed in 1918 to contest the policies and power of the Bureau of Indian Affairs. The federation led the opposition to the privatization of reservation lands through division into individual allotments. It also fought for self-government on the reservations. Initially headed by a white reformer, the federation was composed mostly of Indians. A branch of the federation was founded in San Juan in 1924.

80. Don Doram interview.

81. According to the California Indians' Jurisdictional Act, May 18, 1928, sec. 1.

82. Copy of the Federal Roll approved in 1933, listing California Indians who qualified under section 1 of the act of May 18, 1928; copied and in the possession of Don Doram.

83. Paul Arbiso interview, p. 13; Delfina Olivares interview, p. 2; Gladys Landell interview, p. 9.

84. Delfina Olivares interview, p. 4.

85. Paul Arbiso interview, p. 11.

86. Gladys Landell interview, p. 3.

87. Ibid., p. 7.

88. Ibid., p. 23.

89. Evelyn Villegas, Don Doram, and David Belardes interviews.

90. Evelyn Villegas interview.

91. Ibid.

92. Saunders and O'Sullivan, *Capistrano Nights,* p. 55.

93. Russell Cook, Interview with Suzanne Jansen, Oral History Collection, California State University, Fullerton, O.H. 1027, p. 4.

94. Russell Cook interview, p. 5.

95. Ethel Rosenbaum Pease, Interview with Suzanne Jansen, August 3, 1971, Oral History Collection, California State University, Fullerton, O.H. 646b, p. 3. The question of terminology was of course more awkward by 1971 because of the civil rights movement. These difficulties are clear in other parts of the interview; for example, at one point she stated, "They call themselves 'Chicano' but I dislike the word. I call them Indian, Spanish, or Spanish-American people." Immediately following this, however, she said, "I guess you would call them Latin people."

96. Ibid., pp. 20–21.

97. Ibid., p. 2.

98. H. L. Remmers, Interview with Suzanne Jansen, August 3, 1971, Oral History Collection, California State University, Fullerton, O.H. 713, p. 12. By the 1930s and early 1940s, however, the younger workers, Remmers stated, were going to college to become professionals and teachers and were working during the summers in their high school and college years.

Chapter 4

1. Nicolás Kanellos, *History of Hispanic Theater*, p. xv; Ybarra-Frausto, "I Can Still Hear the Applause," p. 47.

2. Studies of this era of immigration and social change include Camarillo, *Chicanos in a Changing Society;* Deutsch, *No Separate Refuge;* Manuel Gamio, *Mexican Immigrants to the United States: A Study of Human Migration and Adjustment* (Chicago: University of Chicago Press, 1930); M. García, *Desert Immigrants;* Ricardo Romo, *East Los Angeles;* David Montejano, *Anglos and Mexicans in the Making of Texas, 1836–1986;* Rios-Bustamante and Castillo, *An Illustrated History,* and many of the essays in Del Castillo, *Between Borders.*

3. M. García, *Desert Immigrants,* pp. 14–16. See also Ira G. Clark, *Then Came the Railroads: The Century from Steam to Diesel in the Southwest* (Norman: University of Oklahoma Press, 1958).

4. Kanellos, *History of Hispanic Theatre,* p. 19.

5. See Mary Vaughan, "Education and Class in the Mexican Revolution," *Latin American Perspectives* 2 (Summer 1975): 17–33; and idem, "Women, Class, and Education in Mexico, 1880–1928," *Latin American Perspectives* 4, no. 1/2 (Winter/Spring 1977): 138.

6. Kanellos, *History of Hispanic Theatre,* pp. 3 and 15; and Camarillo, *Chicanos in a Changing Society,* pp. 60–65.

7. Lawrence Levine (*Highbrow/Lowbrow: The Emergence of Cultural Hierarchy in America* [Cambridge, Mass.: Harvard University Press, 1988], esp. pp. 13–81) explains why English-language theater ceased to attract all classes to a shared public space and culture. Shakespeare, opera, and classical music had been the common property of a broad English-speaking audience for the first two-thirds of the nineteenth century. Gradually, and unevenly, theatrical genres be-

came differentiated by social class, and economic groups became associated with particular theaters that offered either "serious" or popular culture. Levine further argues that the decline of the oratorical style that had made Shakespeare popular in nineteenth-century America (still an oral residual culture to a certain degree) changed the relationship between legitimate theater and its audience. The decline of oral culture among the middle and upper classes, and the subsequent creation of a "highbrow" national culture, reflected the efforts of an emerging elite for whom the accoutrements of status were increasingly to be found in cultural media that supposedly required selective knowledge, behavior, and location to appreciate. As this change occurred, vaudeville and the movie houses became ever more attractive as providing the egalitarian atmosphere that the theater and opera house had once bestowed.

8. For a general history see Luis Reyes de la Maza, *El teatro en Mexico durante el porfiriato* (Mexico City: Impr. Universitária, 1964).

9. Much of the information about ticket prices, play offerings, and so forth in what follows is taken from *The Carlos Villalongín Dramatic Company Collection, 1848–1954*, Benson Latin American Collection, General Libraries, University of Texas, Austin (hereafter cited as *CVDC*), oversize mss., folder 2.

10. William Slout, "Tent Rep: Broadway's Poor Relation," in *American Popular Entertainment: Papers and Proceedings of the Conference on the History of American Popular Entertainment,* ed. Myron Matlaw (Westport, Conn.: Greenwood Press, 1977), p. 152.

11. Robert Snyder, *The Voice of the City: Vaudeville and Popular Culture in New York* (New York: Oxford University Press, 1989), p. 52.

12. See Bill Smith, "Vaudeville: Entertainment of the Masses," in Matlaw, *American Popular Entertainment,* pp. 13–14.

13. See oversize mss., folder 2, *CVDC*. This broadside also announced the forthcoming plays *Las dos huérfanas, Los pobres de México, La mujer adúltera,* and *Almas rústicas.*

14. Broadside in oversize mss., folder 2, *CVDC*.

15. Oversize mss., folder 2, *CVDC*.

16. For a longer discussion of the California–El Teatro Digno de La Raza (which showed films in Spanish and Yiddish during 1931–1932), see Kanellos, *History of Hispanic Theatre,* pp. 36–38.

17. Broadside in oversize mss., folder 2, *CVDC*.

18. See E. J. Hobsbawm, *Nations and Nationalism Since 1780* (New York: Cambridge University Press, 1991), esp. pp. 101–130.

19. Juan Miguel de Losada, *El grito de Dolores* (Mexico City: Juan R. Navarro, 1850), *CVDC,* shelf 51, and handwritten promptcopy, shelf 52. The company also performed Lozada's *Los mártires de Tacubaya* (1869); see *CVDC,* shelf 53 (acquired 1911, a period when the patriotic genre was popular). Constancio Suarez's *El Cura Hidalgo, ó el glorioso grito de independencia* (Mexico City, 1901), *CVDC,* shelf 85.

20. Benedict Anderson, *Imagined Communities: Reflections on the Origin and Spread of Nationalism* (London: Verso, 1993), p. 6; and see Hobsbawm, *Nations and Nationalism,* pp. 67–73.

21. Luciano Frías y Soto, "El 5 de mayo," ms. dated 1889, *CVDC,* shelf 36.

The promptbook was copied by hand by Luis Hernández on May 27, 1889, for the collection of Antonia Hernández.

22. Anonymous, *Maximiliano I,* copied 1911, *CVDC,* shelf 6. This play was also copied by hand by Luis Hernández in 1911.

23. Jean Franco, *Plotting Women: Gender and Representation in Mexico* (New York: Columbia University Press, 1989), pp. 81–83. Also see María Herrera-Sobek, "The Discourse of Love and Despecho: Representations of Women in the Chicano Décima," *Aztlán* 18, no. 1 (1987): 69–82, for a discussion of the complexity of gender representation in the *décima.*

24. Kanellos, *History of Hispanic Theatre,* pp. 24–25.

25. Lalo Astol, "Mis memorias," MxAm/MSS/019, Lalo Astol Collection, Rare Books Room, Benson Latin American Library, University of Texas, Austin, pp. 1–7.

26. File locator of the Astol Collection, Rare Books Room, Benson Latin American Library, University of Texas, Austin.

27. Information contained in the "Mexican American Manuscripts Finding Aid" file, Rare Books Room, Benson Latin American Library, University of Texas, Austin.

28. See, for example, the promptbook for Jacinto Benavente's play *La malquerida* (Madrid, 1913), *CVDC,* shelf 17. This promptbook is inscribed with a stamp "Circuito de Teatros, Texas–California, Sept. 29, 1915." Other promptbooks define smaller routes, for example that for Juan Velásquez's *Mujer adúltera* (undated ms., *CVDC,* shelf 162), which shows the troupe going in 1916 to a number of places in Arizona and Sonora.

29. I am influenced here by the *histoire des mentalités,* and especially the work of Robert Darnton. For a brief description of the *histoire des mentalités,* see Darnton, *The Great Cat Massacre and Other Episodes in French Cultural History* (New York: Random House, 1985), pp. 3–7.

30. Antonio Cortijo y Valdés, *El cardinal y el ministro* (Madrid: D. A. Vicente, 1848), *CVDC,* shelf 163a. Within this genre see also Luis Mariano de Larra, *La oración de la tarde* (Mexico: Aguilar y Hijos, 1880), *CVDC,* shelf 25b; this was one of five of Larra's plays in the Villalongín repertoire.

31. Antonio Cortijo y Valdés, *El cardinal y el ministro, CVDC,* shelf 163a, p. 55. p. 55.

32. Mariano Asorno, *San Felipe de Jesús, Protomártir Mexicano* (1616), undated ms., *CVDC,* shelf 16.

33. José Zorrilla y Moral, *Don Juan Tenorio* (Mexico City, 1884), *CVDC,* shelf 104; also see Walter Owen, *Don Juan Tenorio* (Buenos Aires: Walter Owen, 1944). And see Lalo Astol, "Mis memorias," p. 6.

34. Anonymous, *Las cuatro apariciónes de la Virgen de Guadalupe* (n.d.), *CVDC.* The first basilica to the Virgin of Guadalupe was built in 1555, which caused a controversy and efforts to halt the spread of the cult until around 1648, when the first Guadalupe scholars began to discuss her appearance as a miracle. She was incorporated by the Creole elite as a national image during the eighteenth and nineteenth centuries. See Jacques Lafaye, *Quetzalcóatl y Guadalupe: The Formation of Mexcian National Consciousness, 1531–1812* (Chicago and London: University of Chicago Press, 1974).

35. The Teatro Campesino, founded during the Delano grape strike of 1965,

took up many of the plays from the era I am discussing, both because they remained meaningful to their audience and as vehicles for building on the historical basis of Spanish-language theater with miracle, mystery, and historical plays. They performed, for example, *La virgen del Tepeyac* (a version of *Las cuatro apariciones de la Virgen de Guadalupe*), *La pastorela,* and *Don Juan Tenorio.* For more information, see Jorge Huerta, *Chicano Theater: Themes and Forms* (Houston: Arte Público Press, 1982); and Judith Weiss, *Latin American Popular Theatre: The First Five Centuries* (Albuquerque: University of New Mexico Press, 1993); also see Yolanda Julia Broyles, "Women in El Teatro Campesino: ¿A poco estaba molacha la Virgen de Guadalupe?" in *Chicana Voices: Intersections of Class, Race, and Gender,* ed. Teresa Córdova et al. (Austin: Center for Mexican American Studies, 1968), pp. 162–187.

36. See José Joaquín Fernández de Lizardi, *La noche más venturosa, CVDC.*

37. María Herrera-Sobek presented a paper from her ongoing work and forthcoming book on the *pastorelas* at the Theater Conference, University of California, Irvine, in February 1992. See also Joel Romero Salinas, *La pastorela mexicana: origen y evolución* (Mexico City: Fondo Cultura Nacional, 1984).

38. On syncretization, see, for example, Arthur L. Campa, *Spanish Religious Folktheatre in the Southwest* (Albuquerque: University of New Mexico Press, 1934); Aurelio M. Espinosa, *The Folklore of Spain in the American Southwest* (Norman: University of Oklahoma Press, 1985); Joseph Marie, *The Role of the Church and the Folk in the Development of the Early Drama in New Mexico* (Philadelphia: University of Pennsylvania Press, 1945).

39. Helen Walker, "The Conflict of Cultures in First Generation Mexicans in Santa Ana, California" (Master's thesis, University of Southern California, 1928), pp. 74–75. Walker, a social worker, refers to them as "grotesque masks."

40. Gilbert G. Gonzalez, "Mexican Communities in Orange County," *Journal of Orange County Studies* 3/4 (Fall 1989/Spring 1990): 25.

41. José Limón, "La Llorona, The Third Legend of Greater Mexico: Cultural Symbols, Women, and the Political Unconscious," *Renato Rosaldo Lecture Series* 2 (1984–1985): 76.

42. Alfredo Torroella, *El mulato* (Mexico City: N. Chávez, 1870), *CVDC,* shelf 92. The promptbook contains an introduction to the audience by the author in traditional nineteenth-century style—very direct and personable, he esteems the audience and explains the purpose of the play. It was performed in Mexico City in 1870, when Torroella was director of the Teatro Nacional, and into the twentieth century in the Southwest.

43. Ramón Balladares y Saavedra, *La mancha de sangre,* undated ms., *CVDC,* shelves 94 and 95; *La Cabaña de Tom,* manuscript dated 1893, *CVDC,* shelf 93.

44. Félix González Llana and José Francos Rodríguez, *El pan del pobre* (Madrid: R. Velasco, 1894), *CVDC,* shelf 34a.

45. The book was in such demand that the 105 copies at the Los Angeles Public Library were always checked out; see McWilliams, *Southern California,* p. 74.

46. Kanellos, *History of Hispanic Theatre,* p. 46; also see George Hadley-

Garcia, *Hispanic Hollywood: The Latins in Motion Pictures* (New York: Citadel Press, 1990), p. 34. Adalberta Elías González's work was very important for placing Southwest and border history into the theater; González was also a novelist.

47. Juan B. Padilla, *Ramona: drama californiano, tomado de la película del mismo nombre y dividido en tres actos y en prosa, CVDC,* shelf 63a. Padilla typed this manuscript in Piedras Negras, Coahuila, Mexico, on November 22, 1930, and gave it as a present to Carlos Villalongín.

48. Helen Hunt Jackson, *Ramona: A Story* (New York: New American Library, 1988).

49. Museo Nacional de Culturas Populares, *El país de las tandas: teatro de revista, 1900–1940* (Mexico City: Secretaría de Educación Pública, 1984), p. 61.

50. For a sense of performers' versatility between (and the interrelationship of) genres, see Tomás Ybarra-Frausto, "La Chata Noloesca: figura del donaire," *Revista Chicano-Riqueña* 11, no. 1 (1983): 41–51; Lalo Astol, "Mis memorias," pp. 10, 16; and Kanellos, *History of Hispanic Theatre,* pp. 19–20.

51. Museo Nacional de Culturas Populares, *Ver para creer! El circo en México* (Mexico City: Secretaría de Educación Pública, 1986), p. 99.

52. This presentation of the *carpa* is drawn from Ybarra-Frausto's excellent article "I Can Still Hear the Applause," esp. pp. 47, 51–52.

53. On repatriation, see Abraham Hoffman, *Unwanted Mexican Americans in the Great Depression: Repatriation Pressures, 1929–1939* (Tucson: University of Arizona Press, 1974); and Marjorie Walker Saint, "Woven Within My Grandmother's Braid: The Biography of a Mexican Immigrant Woman" (Senior thesis in History, University of California, Santa Cruz, 1991).

54. Devra Weber, "The Struggle for Stability and Control in the Cotton Fields of California: Class Relations in Agriculture, 1919–1942" (Ph.D. diss., University of California, Los Angeles, 1986), p. 168.

55. In the tense climate produced by mass strikes in agriculture during 1935 and 1936, these committees applied to the Santa Ana City Council for permits to hold these shows; see Santa Ana City Council [hereafter cited as SACC], Minutes, May 6, 1935.

56. SACC, Minutes, August 5, 1935.

57. SACC, Minutes, May 18, 1935. The Alianza Hispano-Americana, formed in Tucson, Arizona, in 1894, became the most extensive Mexican organization in the nineteenth-century Southwest. Established as a mutual aid society, it also fought for civil rights and supported Mexican workers during strikes.

58. Luis Olivos and family, Interview with author, February 14, 1992.

59. Josefina Andrade, Interview with author, February 12, 1982.

60. One case, from 1932, was dismissed by the State Supreme Court; see mention of it in Louis Reccow, "The Orange County Citrus Strikes of 1935–1936" (Ph.D. diss., University of Southern California, 1971), p. 64. Segregation in Santa Ana's movie theaters lasted until 1946; see Walker, "Conflict of Cultures," p. 7; and Gloria Pérez, Interview with author, April 6, 1982.

61. Lary May, *Screening Out the Past: The Birth of Mass Culture and the Motion Picture Industry* (New York: Oxford University Press, 1980), pp. 165–166.

62. Cathy Peiss, *Cheap Amusements: Working Women and Leisure in Turn-of-the-Century New York* (Philadelphia: Temple University Press, 1986), pp. 139, 149–153. For further discussion on how film contributed to shape the culture of working women, see Elizabeth Ewen, *Immigrant Women in the Land of Dollars: Life and Culture on the Lower East Side, 1890–1925* (New York: Monthly Review Press, 1985), pp. 216, 222; May, *Screening Out*, pp. 209–230; and Vicki Ruiz's discussion in *Cannery Women, Cannery Lives: Mexican Women, Unionization, and the California Food Processing Industry, 1930–1950* (Albuquerque: University of New Mexico Press, 1987), p. 35.

63. See Hadley-Garcia, *Hispanic Hollywood*, pp. 38–39, 62.

64. Alex Saragoza, *Mexican Cinema in Cold War America, 1940–1958* (Berkeley: Chicano Studies Library Publ., 1983), p. 4; and Moises Gonzalez Navarro, *Población y Sociedad en Mexico, 1900–1970* (Mexico, UNAM: 1974), vol. 2, pp. 91–92.

65. Saragoza, *Mexican Cinema*, pp. 5, 9–11, 15.

66. The following is drawn from my interview with Luis Olivos and family, February 14, 1992.

Chapter 5

1. On violence, see David J. Weber, ed., *Foreigners in Their Native Land: Historical Roots of the Mexican Americans* (Albuquerque: University of New Mexico Press, 1973), pp. 139–202. For an excellent study that illustrates the ways in which economics and politics shape "race relations," see Montejano, *Anglos and Mexicans,* esp. pp. 157–254 for the period of time discussed here. For an excellent study that presents a complicated understanding of race in nineteenth-century California, see Almaguer, *Class, Race, and Capitalist Development.*

2. Reginald Horsman, *Race and Manifest Destiny: The Origins of American Racial Anglo-Saxonism* (Cambridge, Mass.: Harvard University Press, 1981), p. 1.

3. Ibid., pp. 208, 263; Joshua Giddings, in *Congressional Globe,* 29th Cong., 1st sess., app., p. 644 (May 12, 1846), quoted in Horsman, *Race and Manifest Destiny,* p. 263. Also see Thomas Gossett, *Race: The History of an Idea in America* (New York: Schocken Books, 1965).

4. For three examples of this mentality among scholars, see John R. Commons, *Races and Immigrants in America* (1907; reprinted New York: Augustus Kelly, 1967); Lothrop Stoddard, *The Rising Tide of Color Against White World-Supremacy* (New York: Scribner, 1920); and J. Oakesmith, *Race and Nationality: An Inquiry into the Origins and Growth of Patriotism* (London: Heinemann, 1919).

5. For a full account of the lynching, see Jean Riss, "The Lynching of Francisco Torres," *Journal of Mexican American History* 1, no. 2 (Spring 1971): 90–112; *Anaheim Gazette,* August 25, 1892.

6. *San Francisco Chronicle,* August 22, 1892.

7. *Santa Ana Standard,* August 1892.

8. *Santa Ana Weekly Blade,* August 18, 1892; *Santa Ana Standard,* August 27, September 10, 1892.

9. *Santa Ana Standard,* August 27, 1982.

10. *Santa Ana Weekly Blade,* August 11, 1892. The article also argues that Torres might try to travel the rail route of the Southern Pacific toward Yuma, where most of the section gang was Mexican and "nearly all of them are hard characters and have been known to shelter criminals on several occasions."

11. *Santa Ana Standard,* August 27, 1892. The Indians of Mesa Grande are, in fact, members of the Kuemuaay, or Diegeño, nation. Here, in an Executive Order in 1875, the federal government extended trusteeship to the village on land they had continuously inhabited. Further lands were reserved for the Kuemuaay in acts of 1883, 1925, and 1926. See Hirshen, Gammill, Trumbo, and Cook, *A Study of Existing Physical and Social Conditions and the Economic Potential of Selected Indian Rancherias and Reservations in California* (Sacramento: State of California, 1976).

12. *Santa Ana Weekly Blade,* August 25, 1892.

13. *Santa Ana Weekly Blade,* August 18, 1892. This solidarity was similar to that shown for bandits and folk heroes who fought against perceived injustice; see Pedro Castillo and Albert Camarillo, eds., *Furia y muerte: los bandidos chicanos,* Monograph No. 2 (Los Angeles: Chicano Studies Center, University of California, Los Angeles, 1973); and Camarillo, *Chicanos in California,* pp. 17–18. For a discussion of lynchings and racial violence, see McWilliams, *Southern California,* pp. 60–61.

14. *Santa Ana Weekly Blade,* August 25, 1892.

15. *Las dos repúblicas,* August 26, 1892.

16. National Association for the Advancement of Colored People, *Thirty Years of Lynching in the United States, 1889–1918* (New York: NAACP, 1919).

17. Paul S. Taylor, "Foundations of California Rural Society," *California Historical Quarterly* 24, no. 3 (1945): 204; Saxton, *Indispensable Enemy;* Lucie Cheng and Edna Bonachich, *Labor Immigration Under Capitalism: Asian Workers in the United States Before World War II* (Berkeley and Los Angeles: University of California Press, 1984).

18. See Suchen Chan, *This Bittersweet Soil. The Chinese in California Agriculture, 1860–1910* (Berkeley and Los Angeles: University of California Press, 1986), p. 58. For more on African-Americans in California, see Forbes, *Black Africans and Native Americans,* p. 65. For more on legislation against native Americans in California, see above, chapter 2.

19. Chan, *This Bittersweet Soil,* pp. 273–301. Also see Ronald Takaki, *Strangers from a Different Shore: A History of Asian Americans* (Boston: Little, Brown, 1989); Roger Daniels, *Asian America: Chinese and Japanese in the United States Since 1850* (Seattle: University of Washington Press, 1988); Valerie Matsumoto, *The Cortez Colony: Family and Community Among Japanese Americans, 1919–1982* (Ithaca, N.Y.: Cornell University Press, 1993); Cheng and Bonacich, *Labor Immigration Under Capitalism;* Evelyn Nakano Glenn, "Occupational Ghettoization: Japanese Women and Domestic Service, 1905–1940," *Feminist Studies* 6, no. 3 (Fall 1980): 352–386.

20. Cited in John Walton Caughey, *Herbert Howe Bancroft: Historian of the West* (Berkeley: University of California Press, 1946), p. 385; Bancroft, *California*

Pastoral, 1796–1848 (San Francisco: History Co., 1888); Bancroft, *History of California*.

21. Herbert Howe Bancroft, "Personal Observations During a Tour Through the Line of Missions of Upper California" (n.d.), MS C-E 113, pp. 32, 84, Bancroft Collection, Bancroft Library, University of California, Berkeley.

22. Ibid., pp. 85, 42, 55, 69–71, 87.

23. Padilla, "Recovery of Chicano Nineteenth-Century Autobiography," p. 300. Also see Padilla's analysis of these narratives in *My History*.

24. See Richard Wade, *The Urban Frontier: The Rise of Western Cities, 1790–1830* (Cambridge, Mass.: Harvard University Press, 1959); and John Reps, *Cities of the American West: A History of Frontier Urban Planning* (Princeton: Princeton University Press, 1979).

25. Charles Swanner, *Santa Ana, a Narrative of Yesterday* (Claremont, Calif.: Saunders Press, 1953), p. 141.

26. The following description of the late-nineteenth-century town was drawn from federal manuscript censuses and directories for the city of Santa Ana (1916, published in Santa Ana by the Santa Ana Directory Co.), Orange County (1923, 1933, 1941; Long Beach: Western Directory Co.), and southern Orange County (1947; Santa Ana: Western Directory Co.).

27. In 1902 the interurban railroad recruited four hundred Mexican laborers to work on the construction of track to extend the railway from central Los Angeles with two lines—one to Santa Ana and the other to Redondo Beach. See Romo, *East Los Angeles*, p. 69.

28. Kathleen Les, *Santa Ana's Architectural History* (Santa Ana: Santa Ana Historical Survey, 1980), p. 20.

29. Santa Ana Chamber of Commerce et al., "Orange County, Southern California" (1908), pp. 14–15 (originally published in the *Pacific Electric Magazine*, February 1908).

30. *Santa Ana Evening Blade*, April 2, 1906. For an analysis of the development of the idea of whiteness for the working class, see Roediger, *Wages of Whiteness*.

31. *Santa Ana Evening Blade*, May 25, 1906; federal manuscript censuses for 1900 and 1910; Swanner, *Santa Ana*, pp. 94–141; *Santa Ana Evening Blade*, May 24, 1906.

32. See Saxton, *Indispensable Enemy;* Kathy Paupst, "A Note on Anti-Chinese Sentiment in Toronto," *Ethnic Studies* 9, no. 1 (1977); Jules Alexander Karlin, "The Anti-Chinese Outbreak in Tacoma, 1885," *Pacific Historical Review* 23, no. 3 (1954); Roy Warton, "Denver's Anti-Chinese Riot, 1880," *Colorado Magazine* 42, no. 4 (1965).

33. *Santa Ana Evening Blade*, May 25, 26, 1906.

34. Federal manuscript censuses of 1900 and 1910; Joe O'Campo, Interview with author, July 25, 1982.

35. *Mexicans in California: Report of Governor C. C. Young's Mexican Fact-finding Committee* (San Francisco: California State Printing Office, 1930), pp. 51–55.

36. *Fact Book: Santa Ana of Orange County* (Santa Ana: Santa Ana Chamber of Commerce, 1937).

37. *City of Santa Ana* (Santa Ana: City Department of Surveyor, 1915).

38. SACC, Minutes, March 7, 1921.

39. SACC, Minutes, November 23, 1923.

40. Walker, "Conflict of Cultures," p. xviii.

41. Tax Assessment Roll, vol. 7, Orange County, 1920, Orange County Archives, Santa Ana.

42. Señor Camarillo, Interview, Mexican-American Project, Bowers Museum Archives, Santa Ana, 1982.

43. Trina Campos, Interview, Mexican-American Project, Bowers Museum Archives, Santa Ana, 1982.

44. María Holguín, Interview, Mexican-American Project, Bowers Museum Archives, Santa Ana, 1982.

45. Cecilio Reyes, Interview, Mexican-American Project, Bowers Museum Archives, Santa Ana, 1982.

46. See appendixes 1 and 4 for a discussion and tabulation of employment figures and appendix 5 for an analysis of city directories.

47. This was common elsewhere as well; see Pedro Castillo, "Mexicans in Los Angeles, 1890-1920" (Ph.D. diss., University of California, Santa Barbara, 1978), p. 80; and Camarillo, *Chicanos in a Changing Society*, p. 145.

48. Gilbert G. Gonzalez, "Labor and Community: The Camps of Mexican Citrus Pickers in Southern California," *Western Historical Quarterly* 22, no. 3 (August 1991): 291-296.

49. Ibid.

50. Jessie Mejía, Interview, Mexican-American Project, Bowers Museum Archives, Santa Ana, 1982.

51. SACC, Minutes, June 17, October 23, 1922; January 29, 1923; May 10, 1920.

52. R. Rangel, Interview with author, July 10, 1987.

53. This information comes from the city directories, 1916, 1923, 1933 (see note 26).

54. *Santa Ana Register* [hereafter cited as SAR], September 16, 1920.

55. SAR, September 16, 1931; 1933; September 16, 1935.

56. In 1936, public figures such as a councilman from the Santa Ana City Council, the chief of police, and a county supervisor were invited and presented short speeches; see SAR, September 16, 1936.

57. The following account is taken from the *Anaheim Gazette*, September 20, 1900.

58. Paul Chapman, *Schools as Sorters: Lewis M. Terman, Applied Psychology, and the Intelligence Testing Movement, 1890-1930* (New York: New York University Press, 1988), pp. 19-20.

59. R. S. Woodworth, "Comparative Psychology of Races," *Psychological Bulletin* 13 (1916): 388-396.

60. Proctor, "Educational and Vocational Guidance" (1925), cited in Chapman, *Schools as Sorters*, pp. 126-127.

61. Cited in Thomas R. Garth, "A Review of Racial Psychology," *Psychological Bulletin* 22 (1925): 344.

62. See, for example, Gilbert G. Gonzalez, *Chicano Education in the Era of*

Segregation (Philadelphia: Balch Institute Press, 1990); M. García, *Desert Immigrants,* pp. 110–126; Francisco Balderama, *In Defense of La Raza: The Los Angeles Mexican Consulate and the Mexican Community, 1926–1936* (Tucson: University of Arizona Press, 1982), pp. 55–72.

63. *Santa Ana Register,* July 8, 1913.

64. Santa Ana City Schools, Santa Ana Unified School District [hereafter cited as SACS], Minutes, November 12, 1918.

65. A request for two rooms at Roosevelt School for a Mexican night school was granted on November 8, 1915 (SACS, Minutes, November 22, 1915). On January 14, 1915, an elementary evening school was established in Santa Ana for the general public (SACS, Minutes, March 7, 1916).

66. SACS, Minutes, August 19, 1918.

67. SACS, Minutes, January 13, 1919.

68. Ibid.

69. Joe O'Campo interview.

70. SACS, Minutes, June 5, 1919.

71. SACS, Minutes, March 13, 1928.

72. SACS, Minutes, April 10, 1928.

73. SACS, Minutes June 8, 1921. Salary figures suggest that, at least to 1939, these wage differentials continued; SACS, Minutes, July 10, October 9, 1939.

74. SACS, Minutes, May 29, 1923. The policy not to hire "married lady teachers" had been approved in a Santa Ana City School Board meeting on May 27, 1919.

75. SACS, Minutes, April 26, 1929.

76. SACS, Minutes, January 25, 1929. A separate petition against removal was signed by "Mexican residents." The school board minutes did not record how many Mexicans signed the petition, and apparently the petitioners did not attend the meeting.

77. Letter to the Santa Ana Board of Education from the Chamber of Commerce Advisory Committee, May 8, 1928. At that date, the Chamber of Commerce expected the urban and industrial expansion of the 1920s to continue. That did not occur until World War II, however. After the war, the city began to rezone the residential property within the barrio, and by 1948 the barrio had lost many homes to the freeway; by 1960 it had lost even more homes to industry.

78. SACS, Minutes, January 29, 1929; Letter to the Santa Ana Board of Education from the Chamber of Commerce Advisory Committee, May 8, 1928.

79. SACS, Minutes, January 29, 1929.

80. Letter to the Santa Ana Board of Education from the Chamber of Commerce Advisory Committee, May 8, 1928.

81. SACS, Minutes, April 26, 1929.

82. Joe O'Campo interview.

83. SACS, Minutes, June 12, 1934.

84. Merton E. Hill, "The Development of an Americanization Program, Ontario, California, 1928," in *Aspects of the Mexican-American Experience* (New York: Arno Press, 1976), pp. 1–119.

85. Josefina Andrade interview.

86. Genevieve Humingston, "An Occupational Survey of Orange County, 1940" (Master's thesis, University of Southern California, 1944), pp. 74, 82. It is difficult to determine the percentage of graduates who were Mexican. Before 1940, only one to three Mexicans graduated from high school each year in Santa Ana, and in a good number of years there were no Spanish-surnamed graduates. From 1940 to 1946, owing to war production and a changing economy, Mexicans constituted 4–5 percent of high school graduates, a small but increasing percentage of junior college students, and a fairly large percentage of adult education students.

87. NA, RG 102, Letter Box 6–1–2–8, National Archives, Washington, D.C., refers to Child Bureau studies from 1923, 1925, and 1926 and cites Marion Hathway, *The Migratory Worker and Family Life* (Chicago: University of Chicago Press, 1934).

88. NA, RG 102, Letter Box 6–1–2–8, Letter of March 10, 1936, Valdosta, Georgia.

89. NA, RG 102, Letter Box 6–1–2–4, Letter of September 6, 1933.

90. See the 1919 study of oyster and shrimp canning communities on the Gulf Coast in Hathway, *Migratory Worker.*

91. The division of labor within the camps by "race" is also discussed in Gonzalez, "Labor and Community."

92. NA, RG 102, Letter Box 6–1–2–4, Letter received September 20, 1933.

93. Here I refer to the excellent study of Tamara K. Hareven, *Family Time and Industrial Time: The Relationship Between the Family and Work in a New England Industrial Community* (New York: Cambridge University Press, 1982); and Tamara K. Hareven and Randolph Langenbach, *Amoskeag: Life and Work in an American Factory-City* (New York: Pantheon Books, 1978).

94. SACS, Minutes, June 12, 1934. In 1927, the superintendent of schools was asked by Mexican parents to adopt a program for the walnut season that would allow children to make up lost school time; SACS, Minutes, September 6, 1927. Apparently, such a program was never instituted.

95. On deportations, see G. Sánchez, *Becoming Mexican American,* pp. 209–225; and Hoffman, *Unwanted Mexican Americans.*

96. SACS, Minutes, September 20, 1937.

97. For a study that examines one aspect of youth culture, see Joan W. Moore, *Homeboys: Gangs, Drugs, and Prison in the Barrios of Los Angeles* (Philadelphia: Temple University Press, 1978); also Arturo Madrid-Barela, "In Search of the Authentic Pachuco," *Aztlán* 4, no. 1 (1973). During race riots in Los Angeles in 1943, *pachuco* youth were reportedly the specific targets, but the riots constituted a "virtual state of siege" against the entire Mexican community (Camarillo, *Chicanos in California,* p. 67). On youth culture, see G. Sánchez, *Becoming Mexican American,* pp. 253–269.

98. On immigrant pathways, see G. Sánchez, *Becoming Mexican American,* pp. 219–240.

99. Josefina Ramírez, Interview with author, July 22, 1982.

100. For critiques of the idea that geographic mobility can measure consciousness and community, see Zunz, *The Changing Face of Inequality;* and Edward Davies II, "Regional Networks and Social Change: The Evolution of

Urban Leadership in the Northern Anthracite Coal Region, 1840–1880," *Journal of Social History* 16 (1982–1983): 47.

101. Josefina Andrade interview.

102. U.S. Census Bureau, *National Census, 1920* (Washington, D.C.: Government Printing Office, 1921), table 8: "Manufacturers—California," p. 88.

103. Douglas Monroy, "An Essay on Understanding the Work Experiences of Mexicans in Southern California, 1900–1939," *Aztlán* 12, no. 1 (1981): 63–65.

104. *Los Angeles Times,* June 26, 1977.

105. Donna R. Gabaccia, "Sicilians in Space: Environmental Change and Family Geography," *Journal of Social History* 16, no. 3 (1982–1983): 53.

106. Walker, "Conflict of Cultures," p. xx.

107. Ibid., p. xxi.

108. For example, SACC, Minutes, April 26, 1920, notes that a "committee of Mexican gentlemen" obtained a "permit to hold a Mexican celebration May 5, 1920 at Logan Street school grounds." On April 20, 1923, it was similarly noted that the grocer Mr. Ruíz was given a permit to build a platform on Logan Street "to use for dancing and other entertainment," to raise money for building a Mexican church.

109. SACC, Minutes, June 17, 1929; March 12, 1934.

110. See, for example, SACC, Minutes, August 7, 1933; November 20, 1933.

111. Walker, "Conflict of Cultures," pp. xxii, 74.

112. Jovita Hernández, Interview with author, January 5, 1985.

113. Lucas Lucio, quoted in U.S. Senate, *Hearings Before a Subcommittee of the Committee on Education and Labor,* 76th Cong., 3d sess., 1941, pt. 70, p. 25911.

114. Cumberland, *Cooperative Marketing,* p. 35.

115. Harry Schwartz, *Seasonal Farm Labor in the United States, with Special Reference to Hired Workers in Fruit and Vegetable and Sugar-Beet Production* (New York: Columbia University Press, 1945), p. 103.

116. Walker, "Conflict of Cultures," pp. xxiii, 35.

117. Thomas Douglas, "Living Standards of Orange County Mexican Families," Dept. of Social Welfare, Orange County, California, March 9, 1940, Orange County Archives, Santa Ana.

118. Ruiz, *Cannery Women, Cannery Lives,* pp. 37, 59; Paul S. Taylor, "Mexican Women in Los Angeles Industry in 1928," *Aztlán* 11, no. 1 (1980): 113.

119. Cumberland, *Cooperative Marketing,* p. 162; Teague, *Fifty Years a Rancher,* p. 97.

120. Humingston, "An Occupational Survey," p. 74.

121. See Ruiz, *Cannery Women, Cannery Lives,* esp. pp. 1–39; and Mario García, "The Chicana in American History. The Mexican Woman of El Paso, 1880–1920—A Case Study," *Pacific Historical Review* 49, no. 2 (1980): 325–327.

122. Taylor, "Mexican Women in Los Angeles Industry," p. 103.

123. Lucy Romero, Interview with author, March 31, 1982.

124. Vicki Ruiz, "Obreras y Madres: Labor Activism Among Mexican Women and Its Impact on the Family," *Renato Rosaldo Lecture Series* 1 (1985): 19–38. On this consciousness as it was expressed in strikes, also see Devra Weber, "Raiz Fuerte: Mexicana Farmworkers" (typescript), pp. 15–18, 21; idem, "Mex-

ican Women on Strike: Memory, History, and Oral Narrative," in *Between Borders: Essays on Mexicana/Chicana History,* ed. Adelaida R. Del Castillo (Encino, Calif.: Floricanto Press, 1990), pp. 161–174; and idem, "Struggle for Stability," p. 168.

125. *Los Angeles Times,* June 26, 1977.

126. Jovita Hernández interview.

127. Lucy Romero interview.

128. See *Mexicans in California,* pp. 125–129; Balderama, *Defense of La Raza,* pp. 9–10; and the Spanish-language newspaper *El espectador,* February 19, 1937 (Stanford University Library, Special Collections).

129. See Ronald Lopez, "The El Monte Berry Strike of 1933," *Aztlán* 1, no. 1 (1970): 101–114; Carey McWilliams's account in *Factories in the Fields: The Story of Migratory Farm Labor* (Boston: Little, Brown, 1939); and Devra Weber, "Struggle for Stability."

130. Juan Gómez-Quiñones, "The First Steps: Chicano Labor Conflict and Organizing, 1900–1920," *Aztlán* 3, no. 1 (1972): 12–39; Devra Weber, "The Organizing of Mexicano Agricultural Workers, Imperial Valley and Los Angeles, 1928–1934: An Oral History Approach," *Aztlán* 3, no. 2 (1973): 307–345; idem, "Mexican Women on Strike: Memory, History, and Oral Narrative," in Del Castillo, *Between Borders,* pp. 175–200; Emma Pérez, "A La Mujer: A Critique of the Partido Liberal Mexicano's Gender Ideology on Women," in ibid., pp. 459–482; Doug Monroy, "Anarquismo y Comunismo: Mexican Radicalism and the Communist Party in Los Angeles During the 1930s," *Labor History* 24, no. 1 (1983): 34–59.

131. Dorothy Healey, "Oral History," bound ms., Southern California Library for Social Studies and Research, Los Angeles.

132. U.S. Senate, *Hearings Before a Subcommittee of the Committee on Education and Labor,* 76th Cong., 3d sess., 1941, pt. 70, p. 25898.

133. See Clarke A. Chambers, *California Farm Organizations: A Historical Study of the Grange, the Farm Bureau, and the Associated Farmers, 1929–1941* (Berkeley and Los Angeles: University of California Press, 1952), pp. 37, 42–43. The Associated Farmers affiliated local packing houses, agricultural cooperatives, and individual growers into an anticommunist labor organization that had significant power with local sheriffs and as a state and federal lobby. It organized systematic arrests and surveillance of strikers. See U.S. Senate, *Hearings Before a Subcommittee of the Committee on Education and Labor,* 76th Cong., 3d sess., 1941, pt. 56, p. 25017.

134. See Louis Reccow, "The Orange County Citrus Strikers of 1935–1936" (Ph.D. diss., University of Southern California, 1971), p. 134; Clara Engle, "Orange County Citrus Strike, 1936" (Master's thesis, California State University Fullerton, 1975); *Santa Ana Journal,* June 12, 1936; *La Habra Star,* June 12, 1936; *Brea Progress,* June 12, 1936; *Yorba Linda Star,* June 12, 1936.

135. Lucy Romero interview; *Santa Ana Register,* July 7, 1936.

136. See the *Santa Ana Register,* July 7, 11, 15, 1936.

137. See Ruiz, *Cannery Women, Cannery Lives;* Mario García, *Mexican Americans: Leadership, Ideology, and Identity, 1930–1960* (New Haven: Yale University Press, 1989); Camarillo, *Chicanos in California;* Guadalupe San Miguel,

Jr., "Mexican American Organizers and the Changing Politics of School Desegregation in Texas, 1945 to 1980," *Social Science Quarterly* 63, no. 4 (1982): 703–704; Mendez et al. v. Westminster School District of Orange County et al., 64 Federal District Court 544 (1945).

Conclusion

1. Recall that Pablo Tac survived smallpox but died from another illness in Rome at the age of twenty. Modesta Avila died in prison in her mid-twenties; her obituary in a Santa Ana newspaper referred to her loosely as a prostitute, thus obliterating her own sense of rightful action and legitimate place in society. Luis Olivos suffered severe illness after he lost his theaters during the redevelopment of Santa Ana's downtown. To meet the new building standards and other expenses imposed in the redevelopment district required more expenditure of cash than he could gain from the theater business alone; but the unfavorable treatment he received from the city—treatment delivered, so it was rumored, because he had purchased a theater west of Main Street, thus crossing the long-established racial boundary of the city center—suggests the weight of Santa Ana's race history into the 1980s.

2. Louis Young, ed., *The Decade Show: Frameworks of Identity in the 1980s* (New York: Fleetwood Lithographic, 1990), esp. p. 402.

3. See Amalia Mesa-Bains, "The Real Multiculturalism: A Struggle for Authority and Power," in *Different Voices: A Social, Cultural, and Historical Framework for Change in the American Art Museum* (New York: Association of Art Museum Directors, 1992).

4. Mendez et al. v. Westminster School District of Orange County et al., 64 Federal District Court 544 (1945); and Westminster School District of Orange County et al. v. Mendez et al., 161 2d 755, 9th Circuit Court of Appeals, California (1947).

5. T. W. Adorno, Else Frenkel-Brunswik, Daniel Levinson, and R. Nevitt Sanford, *The Authoritarian Personality*, pt. 1 (New York: John Wiley, 1964), p. 103.

Selected Bibliography

Citations for unpublished archival material are to be found in the notes.

Adorno, Rolena. "New Perspectives in Colonial Spanish American Literary Studies." *Journal of the Southwest* 32, no. 2 (Summer 1990): 173–191.

Adorno, T. W., Else Frenkel-Brunswik, Daniel Levinson, and R. Nevitt Sanford. *The Authoritarian Personality*. New York: John Wiley, 1964.

Almaguer, Tomás. "Class, Race, and Capitalist Development: The Social Transformation of a Southern California County, 1848–1903." Ph.D. diss., University of California, Berkeley, 1979.

———. "Ideological Distortions in Recent Chicano Historiography: The Internal Model and Chicano Historical Interpretation." *Aztlán* 18, no. 1 (1987).

Anderson, Benedict. *Imagined Communities: Reflections on the Origin and Spread of Nationalism*. London: Verso, 1993.

Arrom, Silvia Marina. *The Women of Mexico City, 1790–1857*. Stanford: Stanford University Press, 1985.

Balderama, Francisco. *In Defense of La Raza: The Los Angeles Mexican Consulate and the Mexican Community, 1926–1936*. Tucson: University of Arizona Press, 1982.

Bancroft, Herbert Howe. *California Pastoral, 1769–1848*. San Francisco: History Co., 1888.

———. *History of California*. 7 vols. San Francisco: History Co., 1884–1889.

Bannon, John Francis. *The Spanish Borderlands Frontier, 1512–1821*. New York: Holt, Rinehart & Winston, 1970.

Bolton, Herbert. "The Mission as a Frontier Institution in the Spanish-American Colonies." *American Historical Review* 23 (1917): 42–61.

Bowman, J. N. "Prominent Women of Provincial California." *Southern California Quarterly* 39, no. 2 (1957): 149–166.

Camarillo, Albert M. *Chicanos in California: A History of Mexican Americans in California*. San Francisco: Boyd & Fraser, 1984.

————. *Chicanos in a Changing Society: From Mexican Pueblos to American Barrios in Santa Barbara and Southern California, 1848–1930*. Cambridge, Mass.: Harvard University Press, 1979.

Campa, Arthur L. *Spanish Religious Folktheatre in the Southwest*. Albuquerque: University of New Mexico Press, 1934.

Carp, Richard M., ed. *Saber es poder/Interventions Urban Revisions: Current Projects for the Public Realm*. Venice, Calif.: Gemini Graphics, 1994.

Castañeda, Antonia. "The Political Economy of Nineteenth-Century Stereotypes of Californianas." In *Between Borders: Essays on Mexicana/Chicana History*, ed. Adelaida R. Del Castillo. Encino, Calif.: Floricanto Press, 1990.

————. "Presidarias y pobladoras: Spanish-Mexican Women in Frontier Monterey, Alta California, 1770–1821." Ph.D. diss., Stanford University, 1990.

————. "Sexual Violence in the Politics and Policies of Conquest: Amerindian Women and the Spanish Conquest of Alta California." In *Building with Our Hands: New Directions in Chicana Studies*, ed. Adela de la Torre and Beatríz Pesquera. Berkeley and Los Angeles: University of California Press, 1993.

Castillo, Edward. "The Assassination of Padre Andres Quintana." *California History* 68, no. 3 (Fall 1989): 116–152.

————. "An Indian Account of the Decline and Collapse of Mexicanos' Hegemony over the Missionized Indians of California." *American Indian Quarterly* 13, no. 4 (Fall 1989): 391–408.

Castillo, Pedro, and Albert Camarillo, eds. *Furia y muerte: los bandidos chicanos*. Monograph No. 2. Los Angeles: Chicano Studies Center, University of California, Los Angeles, 1973.

Caughey, John Walton. *Herbert Howe Bancroft: Historian of the West*. Berkeley: University of California Press, 1946.

Chan, Sucheng. *This Bittersweet Soil: The Chinese in California Agriculture, 1860–1910*. Berkeley and Los Angeles: University of California Press, 1986.

Chapman, Paul. *Schools as Sorters: Lewis M. Terman, Applied Psychology, and the Intelligence Testing Movement, 1890–1930*. New York: New York University Press, 1988.

Cleland, Robert Glass. *The Cattle on a Thousand Hills: Southern California, 1850–1880*. 2d ed. San Marino, Calif.: Huntington Library, 1962.

Commons, John R. *Races and Immigrants in America*. 1907; reprinted New York: Augustus Kelly, 1967.

Conde, Bruce. "Santa Ana of the Yorbas." *Southern California Quarterly* 21, no. 1 (1939): 60–79.

Cook, Sherburne, ed. *The Conflict Between the California Indian and White Civilization*. Berkeley and Los Angeles: University of California Press, 1976.

Cumberland, W. W. *Cooperative Marketing: Its Advantages as Exemplified in the California Fruit Growers Exchange*. London: Oxford University Press, 1917.

Dana, Richard Henry. *Two Years Before the Mast and Twenty-four Years After*. New York: P. F. Collier & Son, 1909.

de la Torre, Adela, and Beatríz M. Pesquera, eds. *Building with Our Hands: New Directions in Chicana Studies*. Berkeley and Los Angeles: University of California Press, 1993.

Del Castillo, Adelaida R., ed. *Between Borders: Essays on Mexicana/Chicana History*. Encino, Calif.: Floricanto Press, 1990.

De Léon, Arnoldo. *They Called Them Greasers: Anglo Attitudes Toward Mexicans in Texas, 1821–1900*. Austin: University of Texas Press, 1983.

Deutsch, Sarah. *No Separate Refuge: Culture, Class, and Gender on an Anglo-Hispanic Frontier in the American Southwest, 1880–1940*. New York: Oxford University Press, 1987.

DuBois, Ellen Carol, and Vicki L. Ruiz, eds. *Unequal Sisters: A Multicultural Reader in U.S. Women's History*. New York: Routledge, 1990.

Engelhardt, Zephyrin, Fr., O.F.M. *The Missions and Missionaries of California*. Vol. 3. San Francisco: James Barry Co., 1912.

———. *San Juan Capistrano Mission*. Los Angeles: Standard Printing Co., 1922.

Engle, Clara. "Orange County Citrus Strike, 1934." Master's thesis, California State University Fullerton, 1975.

Fields, Barbara. "Ideology and Race in American History." In *Region, Race, and Reconstruction: Essays in Honor of C. Vann Woodward*, ed. J. Morgan Kousser and James M. McPherson. New York: Oxford University Press, 1982.

Fischer, Michael. "Ethnicity and the Post-Modern Arts of Memory." In *Writing Culture: The Poetics and Politics of Ethnography*, ed. James Clifford and George Marcus. Berkeley: University of California Press, 1986.

Foner, Eric. *Nothing but Freedom: Emancipation and Its Legacy*. Baton Rouge: Louisiana State University Press, 1983.

Forbes, Jack D. *Black Africans and Native Americans: Color, Race, and Caste in the Evolution of Red Black Peoples*. New York: Basil Blackwell, 1988.

———. "Black Pioneers: The Spanish-speaking Afroamericans of the Southwest." In *Minorities in California History*, ed. George E. Frakes and Curtis B. Solberg. New York: Random House, 1971.

Franco, Jean. *Plotting Women: Gender and Representation in Mexico*. New York: Columbia University Press, 1989.

Gabaccia, Donna R. "Sicilians in Space: Environmental Change and Family Geography." *Journal of Social History* 16, no. 3 (1982–1983): 53–66.

Gamio, Manuel. *Mexican Immigrants to the United States: A Study of Human Migration and Adjustment*. Chicago: University of Chicago Press, 1930.

García, Mario T. *Desert Immigrants: The Mexicans of El Paso, 1880–1920*. New Haven: Yale University Press, 1981.

———. "Merchants and Dons: San Diego's Attempt at Modernization, 1850–1860." In *Mexicans in California After the U.S. Conquest*, ed. Carlos Cortes. New York: Arno Press, 1976.

———. *Mexican Americans: Leadership, Ideology, and Identity, 1930–1960*. New Haven: Yale University Press, 1989.

García, Richard. *Rise of the Mexican American Middle Class: San Antonio, 1929–1941*. College Station: Texas A and M Press, 1991.

Garth, Thomas R. "A Review of Racial Psychology." *Psychological Bulletin* 22 (1925): 343–367.

Geiger, Maynard. "Mission San Gabriel in 1814." *Southern California Quarterly* 53, no. 3 (1971): 237–38.

Gentilcore, R. Louis. "Missions and Mission Lands of Alta California." *Annals of the Association of American Geographers* 51 (March 1961): 46–72.

Gómez-Quiñones, Juan. "The First Steps: Chicano Labor Conflict and Organizing, 1900–1920." *Aztlán* 3, no. 1 (1972): 12–39.

———. *Sembradores, Ricardo Flores Magón y el Partido Liberal Mexicano: A Eulogy and Critique.* Los Angeles: Chicano Studies Center, University of California, Los Angeles, 1977.

Gómez-Quiñones, Juan, and Luis Arroyo. "On the State of Chicano History: Observations on Its Development, Interpretations, and Theory, 1970–1974." *Western Historical Quarterly* 7 (1976): 155–185.

Gonzalez, Deena. "La Tules of Images and Reality: Euro-American Attitudes and Legend Formation on a Spanish-American Frontier." In *Building with Our Hands: New Directions in Chicana Studies,* ed. Adela de la Torre and Beatríz Pesquera. Berkeley and Los Angeles: University of California Press, 1993.

———. "The Widowed Women of Santa Fe: Assessments of the Lives of an Unmarried Population, 1850–1880." In *Unequal Sisters: A Multicultural Reader in U.S. Women's History,* ed. Ellen Carol DuBois and Vicki L. Ruiz. New York: Routledge, 1990.

Gonzalez, Gilbert G. *Chicano Education in the Era of Segregation.* Philadelphia: Balch Institute Press, 1990.

———. "Labor and Community: The Camps of Mexican Citrus Pickers in Southern California." *Western Historical Quarterly* 22, no. 3 (August 1991): 289–312.

———. "Mexican Communities in Orange County." *Journal of Orange County Studies* 3/4 (Fall 1989/Spring 1990): 19–27.

Griswold del Castillo, Richard. *La Familia: Chicano Families in the Urban Southwest, 1848 to the Present.* Notre Dame, Ind.: University of Notre Dame Press, 1984.

———. *The Los Angeles Barrio, 1850–1890: A Social History.* Berkeley and Los Angeles: University of California Press, 1979.

———. *The Treaty of Guadalupe Hidalgo: A Legacy of Conflict.* Norman: University of Oklahoma Press, 1990.

Gruzinski, Serge. *The Conquest of Mexico: The Incorporation of Indian Societies into the Western World, 16th–18th Centuries.* Trans. Eileen Corrigan. Cambridge: Polity Press, 1993.

Guest, Francis. "Cultural Perspectives on California Mission Life." *Southern California Quarterly* 61, no. 1 (1983): 1–77.

Gutiérrez, David. "The Third Generation: Recent Trends in Chicano/Mexican American Historiography." *Mexican Studies/Estudios Mexicanos* 5, no. 1 (Summer 1989).

Gutiérrez, Ramón. "Unraveling America's Hispanic Past: Internal Stratification and Class Boundaries." *Aztlán* 17, no. 1 (1986): 79–101.

———. *When Jesus Came, the Corn Mothers Went Away: Marriage, Sexuality, and Power in New Mexico, 1500–1846.* Stanford: Stanford University Press, 1991.

Hadley-Garcia, George. *Hispanic Hollywood: The Latins in Motion Pictures.* New York: Citadel Press, 1990.

Halbwachs, Maurice. *The Collective Memory.* Trans. Francis J. Ditter, Jr., and Vida Yazdi Ditter. New York: Harper & Row, 1980.

Hall, Stuart. "Cultural Identity and Diaspora." In *Identity: Community, Culture, Difference,* ed. Jonathan Rutherford. London: Lawrence & Wishart, 1990.

Harrington, M. R. *Chinigchinich.* Banning, Calif.: Malki Museum Press, 1978.

———, trans. "Will of Don Tomas Yorba Year of 1845." *Southern California Quarterly* 33, no. 1 (1951): 25–38.

Harvey, Herbert. "The Luiseno: An Analysis of Change in Patterns of Land Tenure and Social Structure." In *American Indian Ethnohistory: California Indians,* vol. 2. New York: Garland, 1974.

Heizer, Robert F. *The California Indians Versus the United States.* Socorro, N.M.: Ballena Press, 1978.

———, ed. *The Eighteen Unratified Treaties of 1851–1852 Between the California Indians and the United States Government.* Berkeley: Archaeological Research Faculty, 1972.

———, ed. *Federal Concern About the Conditions of California Indians, 1853 to 1913. Eight Documents.* Socorro, N.M.: Ballena Press, 1979.

———, ed. *Handbook of North American Indians,* vol. 8: *California.* Washington, D.C.: Smithsonian Institute Press, 1978.

———, ed. "Report of Special Agent John G. Ames on the Condition of the Mission Indians, 1873." In *Federal Concern About Conditions of California Indians, 1853 to 1913: Eight Documents.* Socorro, N.M.: Ballena Press, 1979.

Herrera-Sobek, María. "The Discourse of Love and Despecho: Representations of Women in the Chicano Décima." *Aztlán* 18, no. 1 (1987): 69–82.

———, ed. *Reconstructing a Chicano/a Literary Heritage: Hispanic Colonial Literature of the Southwest.* Tucson: University of Arizona Press, 1993.

Hewes, Minna, and Gordon Hewes. "Indian Life and Customs at Mission San Luis Rey: A Record of California Indian Life Written by Pablo Tac, an Indian Neophyte." *The Americas* 9 (1952). 87–106.

Hill, Merton E. "The Development of an Americanization Program, Ontario, California, 1928." In *Aspects of the Mexican-American Experience,* ed. Carlos E. Cortes. New York: Arno Press, 1976.

Hobsbawm, E. J. *Nations and Nationalism Since 1780.* New York: Cambridge University Press, 1991.

Hoffman, Abraham. *Unwanted Mexican Americans in the Great Depression: Repatriation Pressures, 1929–1939.* Tucson: University of Arizona Press, 1974.

Hornbeck, David. *California Patterns: A Geographical and Historical Atlas.* Palo Alto, Calif.: Mayfield, 1983.

Horsman, Reginald. *Race and Manifest Destiny: The Origins of American Racial Anglo-Saxonism.* Cambridge: Harvard University Press, 1981.

Huerta, Jorge. *Chicano Theater: Themes and Forms.* Houston: Arte Público Press, 1982.

Humingston, Genevieve. "An Occupational Survey of Orange County, 1940." Master's thesis, University of Southern California, 1944.

Hurtado, Albert. "Controlling California's Indian Labor Force: Federal Administration of California Indian Affairs During the Mexican War." *Southern California Quarterly* 61, no. 3 (1979): 217–238.

———. *Indian Survival on the California Frontier.* New Haven: Yale University Press, 1988.

Hutchinson, C. Alan. *Frontier Settlements in Mexican California: The Higar-Padres Colony and Its Origins, 1769–1835.* New Haven: Yale University Press, 1969.

———, ed. *A Manifesto to the Mexican Republic.* Berkeley and Los Angeles: University of California Press, 1978.

Jensen, Joan M. *Promise to the Land: Essays on Rural Women.* Albuquerque: University of New Mexico Press, 1991.

Kanellos, Nicolás. *A History of Hispanic Theatre in the United States: Origins to 1940.* Austin: University of Texas Press, 1990.

———. *Mexican American Theater: Legacy and Reality.* Pittsburgh: Latin American Literary Review Press, 1987.

———, ed. *Hispanic Theatre in the United States.* Houston: Arte Público Press, 1984.

Kroeber, A. L. *Ethnographic Interpretations.* Berkeley: University of California Press, 1957.

Lamar, Howard. "From Bondage to Contract: Ethnic Labor in the American West, 1600–1890." In *The Countryside in the Age of Capitalist Transformation: Essays in the Social History of Rural America,* ed. Steven Hahn and Jonathan Prude. Chapel Hill: University of North Carolina Press, 1985.

Layne, Gregg. "The First Census of the Los Angeles District: *Padron de la Ciudad de Los Angeles y su jurisdicción año 1836.*" *Southern California Quarterly* 18, no. 3 (1936): 81–99; orig. census pp. 1–63.

León-Portilla, Miguel. *Endangered Cultures.* Trans. Julie Goodson-Lawes. Dallas: Southern Methodist University Press, 1990.

Levine, Lawrence. *Highbrow/Lowbrow: The Emergence of Cultural Hierarchy in America.* Cambridge, Mass.: Harvard University Press, 1988.

Limerick, Patricia Nelson. *The Legacy of Conquest: The Unbroken Past of the American West.* New York: W. W. Norton, 1987.

Limón, José. "La Llorona, The Third Legend of Greater Mexico: Cultural Symbols, Women, and the Political Unconscious." *Renato Rosaldo Lecture Series* 2 (1984–1985): 59–93.

Locklear, William R. "The Anti-Chinese Movement in Los Angeles." In *Racism in California: A Reader in the History of Oppression,* ed. Roger Daniels and Spencer C. Olin, Jr. New York: Macmillan, 1972.

Lomelí, Francisco A. "Fray Gerónimo Boscana's 'Chinigchinich': An Early California Text in Search of a Context." In *Reconstructing a Chicano/a Literary Heritage: Hispanic Colonial Literature of the Southwest,* ed. María Herrera-Sobek. Tucson: University of Arizona Press, 1993.

Lopez, Ronald. "The El Monte Berry Strike of 1933." *Aztlán* 1, no. 1 (1970): 101–114.

Loyal, C. *The Squatter and the Don: A Novel Descriptive of Contemporary Occurrences in California.* San Francisco: C. Loyal, 1885.

McWilliams, Carey. *Southern California: An Island on the Land.* 1946; Santa Barbara: Peregrine Smith, 1973.

Martínez, Oscar J. *Troublesome Border.* Tucson: University of Arizona Press, 1988.

Matlaw, Myron, ed. *American Popular Entertainment: Papers and Proceedings of the Conference on the History of American Popular Entertainment.* Westport, Conn.: Greenwood Press, 1977.

Merriam, Clinton Hart, ed. *Studies of California Indians.* Berkeley and Los Angeles: University of California Press, 1955.

Mexicans in California: Report of Governor C. C. Young's Mexican Fact-Finding Committee. San Francisco: California State Printing Office, 1930.

Mintz, Sidney W. *Sweetness and Power: The Place of Sugar in Modern History.* New York: Viking, 1985.

Modjeska, Helena. *Memories and Impressions of Helena Modjeska: An Autobiography.* New York: Macmillan Co., 1910.

Monroy, Douglas. *Thrown Among Strangers: The Making of Mexican Culture in Frontier California.* Berkeley and Los Angeles: University of California Press, 1990.

Montejano, David. *Anglos and Mexicans in the Making of Texas, 1836–1986.* Austin: University of Texas Press, 1987.

Mörner, Magnus. *Race Mixture in the History of Latin America.* Boston: Little, Brown, 1967.

Museo Nacional de Culturas Populares. *El país de las tandas: teatro de revista, 1900–1940.* Mexico City: Secretaría de Educación Pública, 1984.

———. *Ver para creer! El circo en México.* Mexico City: Secretaría de Educación Pública, 1986.

Nicolás, León. *Las castas en México colonial.* Mexico City, 1924.

Nunis, Doyce, Jr. *The Drawings of Ignacio Tirsch: A Jesuit Missionary in Baja California.* Los Angeles: Dawson's Book Shop, 1972.

Oakesmith, J. *Race and Nationality: An Inquiry into the Origins and Growth of Patriotism.* London: Heinemann, 1919.

Padilla, Genaro. *My History, Not Yours: The Formation of Mexican American Autobiography.* Madison: University of Wisconsin Press, 1993.

———. "The Recovery of Chicano Nineteenth-Century Autobiography." *American Quarterly* 40, no. 3 (Fall 1988): 286–306.

Paredes, Américo. *Folklore and Culture on the Texas-Mexican Border.* Ed. Richard Bauman. Austin: Center for Mexican American Studies, University of Texas, 1993.

Pérez, Emma. "A La Mujer: A Critique of the Partido Liberal Mexicano's Gender Ideology on Women." In *Between Borders: Essays on Mexicana/Chicana History,* ed. Adelaida R. Del Castillo. Encino, Calif.: Floricanto Press, 1990.

Phillips, George Harwood. *Chiefs and Challengers: Indian Resistance and Cooperation in Southern California.* Berkeley and Los Angeles: University of California Press, 1975.

———. *Indians and Intruders in Central California, 1769–1849.* Norman: University of Oklahoma Press, 1993.

Pitt, Leonard. *The Decline of the Californios: A Social History of the Spanish-*

speaking Californians, 1846–1890. Berkeley and Los Angeles: University of California Press, 1966.

Reichlen, Henry, and Paule Reichlen. "Le Manuscrit Boscana de la Bibliothèque Nationale de Paris: Relation sur les Indiens Acâgchemem de la Mission de San Juan Capistrano, Californie." *Journal de la Société des Américanistes* 60 (1971): 233–273.

Reyes de la Maza, Luis. *El teatro en Mexico durante el porfiriato*. Mexico City: Impr. Universitária, 1964–68.

Ríos-Bustamante, Antonio, and Pedro Castillo. *An Illustrated History of Mexican Los Angeles, 1781–1985*. Los Angeles: Chicano Studies Research Center, University of California, Los Angeles, 1986.

Riss, Jean. "The Lynching of Francisco Torres." *Journal of Mexican American History* 1, no. 2 (Spring 1971): 90–112.

Roberts, C. E. *The Partition of the Rancho Santiago de Santa Ana*. Orange County Historical Research Project no. 3105. Santa Ana: Federal Writers' Project, Work Projects Administration, 1936.

Roediger, David. *The Wages of Whiteness: Race and the Making of the American Working Class*. New York: Verso, 1991.

Romo, Ricardo. *East Los Angeles: History of a Barrio*. Austin: University of Texas Press, 1983.

Ruiz, Vicki. *Cannery Women, Cannery Lives: Mexican Women, Unionization, and the California Food Processing Industry, 1930–1950*. Albuquerque: University of New Mexico Press, 1987.

———. "Obreras y Madres: Labor Activism Among Mexican Women and Its Impact on the Family." *Renato Rosaldo Lecture Series* 1 (1985): 19–38.

Ruiz de Burton, Maria Amparo. *The Squatter and the Don*. Ed. Rosaura Sánchez and Beatrice Pita. Houston: Arte Público Press, 1993.

Saint, Marjorie Walker. "Woven Within My Grandmother's Braid: The Biography of a Mexican Immigrant Woman." Senior thesis in History, University of California, Santa Cruz, 1991.

Sánchez, George J. *Adaptation to Conquest: The Mexican Community of San José, 1845–1880*. Working Paper Series, no. 4. Stanford: Stanford Center for Chicano Research, 1984.

———. *Becoming Mexican American: Ethnicity, Culture, and Identity in Chicano Los Angeles, 1900–1945*. New York: Oxford University Press, 1993.

Sánchez, Rosaura, and Rosa Martinez Cruz. *Essays on La Mujer*. Los Angeles: Chicano Studies Center, University of California, Los Angeles, 1977.

Saragoza, Alex. *Mexican Cinema in Cold War America, 1940–1958*. Berkeley: Chicano Studies Library Publ., 1983.

Saunders, Charles Francis, and Father St. John O'Sulllivan. *Capistrano Nights: Tales of a California Mission Town*. New York: R. M. McBride & Co., 1930.

Saxton, Alexander. *The Indispensable Enemy: Labor and the Anti-Chinese Movement in California*. Berkeley and Los Angeles: University of California Press, 1971.

Schwartz, Harry. *Seasonal Farm Labor in the United States, with Special Reference to Hired Workers in Fruit and Vegetable and Sugar-Beet Production*. New York: Columbia University Press, 1945.

Scott, Joan W. *Gender and the Politics of History.* New York: Columbia University Press, 1988.

Shipek, Florence Connolly. *Delfina Cuero: Her Autobiography and an Account of Her Last Years.* Menlo Park, Calif.: Ballena Press, 1991.

———. *Pushed into the Rocks: Southern California Indian Land Tenure, 1769–1986.* Lincoln: University of Nebraska Press, 1987.

Soja, Edward W. *Postmodern Geographies: The Reassertion of Space in Critical Social Theory.* London: Verso, 1989.

Spicer, Edward. *Cycles of Conquest: The Impact of Spain, Mexico, and the United States on the Indians of the Southwest, 1533–1960.* Tucson: University of Arizona Press, 1962.

Stansell, Christine. *City of Women: Sex and Class in New York, 1789–1860.* New York: Knopf, 1986.

Stephenson, Terry E. *Don Bernardo Yorba.* Los Angeles: Glen Dawson, 1941.

———. "Tomás Yorba, His Wife Vicenta, and His Account Book." *Southern California Quarterly* 23, nos. 3–4 (1941): 127–156.

Swanner, Charles. *Santa Ana, a Narrative of Yesterday.* Claremont, Calif.: Saunders Press, 1953.

Sweet, David G., and Gary B. Nash, eds. *Struggle and Survival in Colonial America.* Berkeley and Los Angeles: University of California Press, 1981.

Tagliavini, Carlo. "L'evangelizzazione e i costumi degli Indi Luiseños secondo la narrazione di un chierico indigeno." In *XXIII International Congress of Americanists,* pp. 633–648. Easton, Pa.: Eschenbach Printing Co., 1905.

Taylor, Paul S. "Foundations of California Rural Society." *California Historical Quarterly* 24, no. 3 (1945).

"Mexican Women in Los Angeles Industry in 1928." *Aztlán* 11, no. 1 (1980): 99–132.

Teague, Charles C. *Fifty Years a Rancher: A Recollection of Half a Century Devoted to the Citrus and Walnut Industries of California and to Furthering the Cooperative Movement in Agriculture.* Los Angeles: Ward & Ritchie Press, 1944.

Thelen, David. "Memory and American History." *Journal of American History* 75, no. 4 (March 1989): 1117–1129.

Treviño, Gloria L. Valásquez. "Cultural Ambivalence in Early Chicana Prose Fiction." Ph.D. diss., Stanford University, 1985.

Walker, Helen. "The Conflict of Cultures in First Generation Mexicans in Santa Ana, California." Master's thesis, University of Southern California, 1928.

Weber, David J. *The Mexican Frontier, 1821–1846: The American Southwest Under Mexico.* Albuquerque: University of New Mexico Press, 1982.

———, ed. *Foreigners in Their Native Land: Historical Roots of the Mexican Americans.* Albuquerque: University of New Mexico Press, 1973.

Weber, Devra. "Mexican Women on Strike: Memory, History, and Oral Narrative." In *Between Borders: Essays on Mexicana/Chicana History,* ed. Adelaida R. Del Castillo. Encino, Calif.: Floricanto Press, 1990.

———. "The Organizing of Mexicano Agricultural Workers, Imperial Valley and Los Angeles, 1928–1934: An Oral History Approach." *Aztlán* 3, no. 2 (1973): 307–345.

———. "The Struggle for Stability and Control in the Cotton Fields of California: Class Relations in Agriculture, 1919–1942." Ph.D. diss., University of California, Los Angeles, 1986.

Weiss, Judith. *Latin American Popular Theatre: The First Five Centuries.* Albuquerque: University of New Mexico Press, 1993.

White, Raymond. *Luiseño Social Organization.* University of California Publications in American Archaeology and Ethnology, vol. 48, no. 2. Berkeley: University of California Press, 1963.

———. "The Luiseño Theory of 'Knowledge.'" *American Anthropologist* 59 (1957): 1–19.

———. "Two Surviving Luiseño Indian Ceremonies." *American Anthropologist* 55 (1953): 569–578

Ybarra-Frausto, Tomás. "I Can Still Hear the Applause: La Farándula Chicana—Carpas y Tandas de Variedad." In *Hispanic Theatre in the United States,* ed. Nicolás Kanellos. Houston: Arte Público Press, 1984.

———. "La Chata Noloesca: figura del donaire." *Revista Chicano-Riqueña* 11, no. 1 (1983): 41–51.

Zunz, Olivier. *The Changing Face of Inequality: Urbanization, Industrial Development, and Immigration in Detroit, 1880–1920.* Chicago: University of Chicago Press, 1982.

Bancroft Narratives

The following manuscript accounts are all to be found in the Bancroft Collection, Bancroft Library, University of California, Berkeley.

César, Julio. "Cosas de indios de California" (1878). MS C-D 109.

de la Guerra de Hartnell, Doña Teresa. "Narrativa de la ditinguida matrona californiana" (March 12, 1875). MS C-E 67.

Lorenzano, Apolinaria. "Memorias de la Beata" (1878). MS C-D 116.

Marrón, Felipa Osuña de. "Recuerdos del pasado" (1878). MS C-D 120.

Pérez, Eulalia. "Una vieja y sus recuerdos" (1878). MS C-D 139.

Pico de Avila, María Inocenta. "Cosas de California" (1878). MS C-D 34.

Sepúlveda, Ignacio. "Historical Memoranda" (July 9, 1874). MS C-E 65:14.

Oral Histories

Andrade, Josefina. With Lisbeth Haas. February 12, 1982.

Arbiso, Paul. With Karen Wilson Turnbull. December 30, 1975. Oral History Collection, California State University, Fullerton, O.H. 1464.

Belardes, David. With Lisbeth Haas. February 14, 1992.

Camarillo, Señor. 1982. Mexican-American Project, Bowers Museum, Santa Ana.

Campos, Trina. 1982. Mexican-American Project, Bowers Museum, Santa Ana.

Cook, Russell. With Suzanne Jansen. June 15, 1971. Oral History Collection, California State University, Fullerton, O.H. 1027.

Doram, Don. With Lisbeth Haas. February 16, 1992.

Hernández, Jovita. With Lisbeth Haas. January 5, 1985.

Holguín, María. 1982. Mexican-American Project, Bowers Museum, Santa Ana.

Landell, Gladys Pryor. With Karen Wilson Turnbull. July 28, 1975. Oral History Collection, California State University, Fullerton, O.H. 146.

Mejía, Jessie. 1982. Mexican-American Project, Bowers Museum, Santa Ana.

O'Campo, Joe. With Lisbeth Haas. July 25, 1982.

Olivares, Delfina. With Suzanne Jansen. August 3, 1971. Oral History Collection, California State University, Fullerton, O.H. 711.

Olivos, Luis, and Family. With Lisbeth Haas. February 14, 1992.

Pease, Ethel Rosenbaum. With Beverly Gallagher. May 5, 1971. Oral History Collection, California State University, Fullerton, O.H. 646a.

———. With Suzanne Jansen. August 3, 1971. Oral History Collection, California State University, Fullerton, O.H. 646b.

Pérez, Gloria. With Lisbeth Haas. April 6, 1982.

Ramírez, Josefina. With Lisbeth Haas. July 22, 1982.

Rangel, R. With Lisbeth Haas. July 10, 1987.

Remmers, H. L. With Suzanne Jansen. August 3, 1971. Oral History Collection, California State University, Fullerton, O.H. 713.

Reyes, Cecilio. 1982. Mexican-American Project, Bowers Museum, Santa Ana.

Romero, Lucy. With Lisbeth Haas. March 31, 1982.

Villegas, Evelyn. With Lisbeth Haas. February 16, 1992.

Yorba, Joseph. With Paul Clark. January 9, 1976. Oral History Collection, California State University, Fullerton, O.H. 1465.

Index

La abadía de Castro, 143, 144
Abila, Juan, 45, 47, 72, 83
Abila de Sánchez, Concepción, 45, 47, 83
Acágchemem: cultural persistence, 26–27;
    demographic decline, 14, 22, 23; mod-
    ern reclaiming of name, 227n3; pre-
    conquest spacial ordering, 16, 17, 21–
    22; Spanish territory conquest, 2, 3
    (map), 13–14, 21–22. See also Juaneños;
    Mission Indians; Mission San Juan
    Capistrano; specific Indian headings
Act for the Relief of the Mission Indians,
    61, 63
African-descent people, 29–30, 38
Agricultural Industrial Workers Labor
    Union, 207
Agriculture. See Economic systems; Land
    politics; Rancho society
Aguilar, A. G., 101
Aguilar, Blas, 236n20
Alcaldes, 18, 24, 28, 231n14; and emancipa-
    tion, 39, 41
Alianza Hispano-Americana, 159, 249n57
Allá en el rancho grande (Fuentes), 161–62
Amamix, Agapito, 14–15
American national identity, 10, 11–12, 126,
    211
Ames, John G., 59–61
Los amores de Ramona (González), 156
Amparo Ruiz, María, 78–79
Anaheim, 68, 71; establishment of, 65, 73;

ethnic diversity in, 75, 76, 174; and
    1936 strike, 208
Anderson, Benedict, 147
Andrade, Josefa, 160
Andrade, Josefina, 195–96
Anglo-Americans: backgrounds of, 68,
    238n46; and economic system, 65–66,
    69, 243n68; marriage patterns, 74; oral
    histories, 134–36; population size, 4;
    racial prejudice, 85–86, 102–3; and ran-
    cho society, 56; in U.S. rural society,
    66, 68–69, 70, 71, 72, 74, 76; white
    racial identity, 10, 126, 166, 211. See also
    U.S. conquest
Annales school of social history, 8, 228n8
Apis, Pablo, 237n41
Arbiso, Paul, 110–11, 122, 125, 131
Argüello, Santiago, 47
Arrom, Sylvia, 82
Artesia barrio, 159, 180, 193, 194, 202. See
    also Barrios
"Artifact Piece, The" (Luna), 210
Artisans, 24, 39, 48, 49, 53, 70, 94, 120,
    121, 216
Asorno, Mariano, 152–53
Associated Farmers, 207, 257n133
Astol, Lalo, 149–50
Avila, Modesta, 1–2, 89–91, 92, 93, 101,
    102; death of, 209, 258n1; literacy of,
    89, 118, 119
Avila, Vicente, 90
Ayelkwi, 20, 27

Compositor: Impressions
Text: 10/13 Galliard
Display: Galliard
Printer and Binder: Edwards Bros.